DATE		
JUL 1 0 1987		

N · E · I · L
DIAMOND
SOLITARY
S · T · A · R

Also by RICH WISEMAN:
Jackson Browne: The Story of a Hold Out

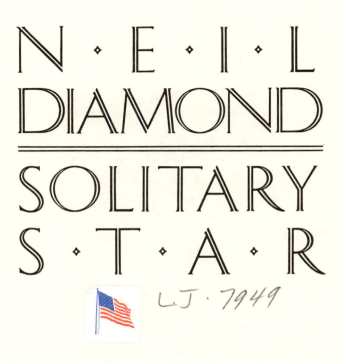

N · E · I · L
DIAMOND
SOLITARY
S · T · A · R

LJ · 7949

RICH WISEMAN

Dodd, Mead & Company
New York

No part of this book may be reproduced in any form
without permission in writing from the publisher.
Published by Dodd, Mead & Company, Inc.
71 Fifth Avenue, New York, New York 10003
Distributed in Canada by McClelland and Stewart Limited, Toronto
Manufactured in the United States of America
Designed by Alice Mauro
First Edition

1   2   3   4   5   6   7   8   9   10

Library of Congress Cataloging-in-Publication Data

Wiseman, Rich.
Neil Diamond, solitary star.

Discography: p.
Includes index.
1. Diamond, Neil.   2. Singers--United States--
Biography.   I. Title.
ML420.D54W6   1987   784.5′0092′4 [B]   86-32759

ISBN 0-396-08619-5

To Mom and Dad,
and Ginny

CONTENTS

PROLOGUE
POP KING

"My stomach is all butterflies," confessed Neil Diamond. "I'd much rather face an audience of 20,000 people."

Instead, Diamond and his wife, Marcia, were about to face eighty of the world's most notable people, including President and Mrs. Ronald Reagan. The event: a White House dinner in honor of Great Britain's Prince Charles and Princess Diana, in the midst of a three-day official visit to the United States.

It was no surprise that the Diamonds had graced the guest list along with the likes of Jacques Cousteau, Mikhail Baryshnikov, Leontyne Price, Peter Ueberroth, Peter Ustinov, William F. Buckley, Jr., Estée Lauder, Alan Shepard, Clint Eastwood, Tom Selleck, and Gloria Vanderbilt: Princess Di happened to be a staunch Diamond fan. Only the year before, she and Charles had attended Diamond's benefit performance for the Prince's Trust in Birmingham, England.

By the end of the dinner—lobster mousseline with Maryland crab, glazed chicken Capsicum, jicama salad—Neil had quelled his butterflies. He didn't even tense up when, after the White House orchestra began to play for the guests' dancing pleasure, Nancy Reagan approached him.

"It would be wonderful, and we all would love it, if you would sing a song for us," she said.

"Of course," he replied, his throat turning dry.

As Mrs. Reagan went to get him a glass of water, Neil strode over to orchestra leader Colonel John R. Bourgeois, who showed him a list of fifteen of his compositions that were included in the Marine Corps Band's repertoire. Diamond, whose knees had now begun to shake, selected "September Morn."

Gulping down the water, he took the stage as the Reagans and the other guests took their seats. Mustering as much surface calm as he could, he began to sing the love ballad. As he did, he found himself looking directly into the eyes of the Princess of Wales.

He saw that she was blushing.

Not wanting to embarrass her, he shifted his gaze to the left, to a broadly smiling President Reagan.

Singing "September Morn" to the President of the United States won't do, either, Neil thought. He moved his eyes again, past Prince Charles, past Jonas Salk . . .

"It was like being in a Fellini film," he would say later. "Unreal. At least it didn't feel real because every place I would turn, there was some extraordinary personality, one of the most famous faces in the world, watching me."

When Neil finished, he was rewarded with hearty applause and calls of "More!" His self-confidence surging, he suavely suggested that for his encore, "You Don't Bring Me Flowers," everyone rise and dance.

They did.

After Neil stepped off the stage, he found a familiar fan dressed in a midnight blue velvet gown approaching him. "Is it proper, in this country, for a lady to ask a gentleman to dance?" Princess Diana said. "Yes, it is," Neil replied, bidding farewell to Fellini and hello to Lerner and Loewe.

It was a long way from Brooklyn, where Neil Leslie Diamond was born, and where, by his own description, he was an "awkward," "gangly" kid who lacked self-esteem.

It was a long way from the years of dead ends in Tin Pan Alley.

And it was a long way from the writing of his gut-wrenching anthem "I Am . . . I Said" in 1971, in which—in a breathtaking display of chutzpah—he likened his own story to that of the frog who became a king.

But as he and Princess Diana glided on the White House dance floor that November night in 1985, not even his severest critics, including disillusioned former associates, could argue that Neil Diamond was anything but a king of pop. Butterflies and all.

·1·
BROOKLYN

"I've seen Neil really happy and funny and dancing and clowning—there are those moments. But there aren't a lot of them. He doesn't want to be happy. He doesn't like people to say he's happy.

"There's a thing in that. I think it all goes back to Brooklyn and his beginning. There are things that he did, like fencing—a strange thing for a boy from Brooklyn . . . He almost resents the fact that he wasn't born into royalty. He's just never special enough for him."
—a former key employee
of Diamond's

While he has paid lyrical lip service to an early life "filled to the brim" in his song "Brooklyn Roads," Neil Diamond has, in interviews, consistently taken a glass-is-half-empty view of his childhood. "I'd never want to go back to Brooklyn," he's said. "It's like a warm, old snapshot to me."

He was the "black sheep" in a family in which everyone else had a special talent. He always felt the outsider, the solitary boy, at school because his family moved around so much (he attended nine schools by the age of sixteen, he's asserted).

And he didn't think much of his father's work as the proprietor of various dry goods stores: "I spent most of my youth looking out of a shop window at the rest of the world. I learned very quickly the limitations of that."

On another occasion: "I used to dream of being rich."

What Neil has never seemed to grasp—or at least own up to publicly—is that he grew up rich in other ways.

The marriage certificate of Akeeba (Kieve) and Rose Diamond, wed December 18, 1938 in Brooklyn at the ages of twenty-one and twenty, respectively, confirms their middle-class lot. Kieve's address is listed as 2516 Mermaid Avenue, in the heart of Coney Island; Rose's is 1412 86th Street in nearby Bensonhurst.

The certificate also reveals information that hints at their mission in life; like many of their peers in this borough of unbroken dreams, they were the children of Jewish immigrants. Easygoing Kieve was the son of

Abram and Sadie Diamond from Poland; exuberant Rose was the daughter of Abraham and Molly Rapaport from the Soviet Union.

At family gatherings, Rose and Kieve's parents would tell the tales of their Atlantic crossings, their first sightings of the Statue of Liberty, and how they established a beachhead in the promised land from which their offspring could storm the American Dream.

Just over two years after they were married, Rose gave birth, on January 24, 1941, to Neil, a fresh troop. Almost two years later to the day, January 19, a second son, Harvey, was born.

Meanwhile, Kieve Diamond, whose laid-back, congenial demeanor belied his stubborn independence, established himself as a shopkeeper. First, there was A. Diamond, a stationery store in Bensonhurst. Then, after a stint in the Army in which he was stationed in Cheyenne, Wyoming (Rose and children accompanied him), there was Diamond's Haberdashery in the East New York section of Brooklyn. Then, five years later, in 1953, he opened Diamond's Dry Goods in teeming Flatbush.

They were good years, for the simple reason that Kieve and Rose Diamond loved life. Avid ballroom dancers, they would occasionally trek to the Palladium, the Latin dance mecca. They also danced regularly with their many friends in each others' homes. Meanwhile, their friends were often royally entertained by Kieve, who, deep down, was an unabashed ham.

He wasn't the first Diamond to regale others with his performing talent; his father was a doubletalk artist who performed in Yiddish and English around New York. But he was undoubtedly the first Diamond to prance around as Eartha Kitt, for example, lip-synching "C'est Si Bon," in costumes designed by Rose.

Recalling his dad's pantomimes, Neil has said: "I guess I got the bug [to perform] from that."

Certainly, Kieve had already given his elder son a grounding for whatever dream he chose to pursue—teaching him the value of self-reliance and hard work.

"Look, I was an introverted kid and it was easy to settle things with my hands . . . Before I discovered I could write, fighting was the only way I had of expressing myself."

—Diamond, from a
1969-era press bio

"Actually I was very much quicker to duck from a punch . . . I was the gofer."

—Diamond in 1976

While Neil has had trouble making up his mind just how involved he was in the Flatbush gang scene, he has been consistent in describing his teens in the same downbeat terms that he described his early youth. High school, he's said, was "four years in a coma."

That view, however, comes as news to Jim Gitter, a student at Erasmus Hall High School at the same time as Neil.

At Erasmus, Gitter was a member of one of the hippest cliques on campus. "We sort of made nonconformity conformity," he said. Another group that had the same kind of spirit, he added, was the handful of middle-class Jewish students who Diamond ran around with.

In describing the group, Gitter painted a picture of most-likely-to-succeed candidates: clean-cut, bright, studious, personable. He recalled a couple of Neil's pals being into basketball; a couple of others into Sinatra. All of them, he noted, seemed hep to rock 'n' roll.

Neil, actually, was the member of the clique he knew the least: "He was just a little distanced." Gitter did, however, hear about what a nice boy he was from a couple of cute Jewish girls whom both he and Neil dated.

Gitter, who was "into the piano" and writing songs at the time, added that he was surprised one day when one of the girls remarked that Diamond was a songwriter, too.

According to his legend, Neil was inspired to write his first song at camp, when he watched as a couple of kids played an original composition of theirs for guest performer Pete Seeger.

After learning the requisite three chords on his new guitar, the young teenager whipped out his first ditty, "Hear Them Bells." "I was so excited at finding a way of expressing myself," he has claimed, "that I didn't want to just talk. I started screaming at the top of my lungs."

Kieve and Rose Diamond had something to shout about themselves in 1956. Two years earlier, Kieve had relocated Diamond's Dry Goods to the middle of one of Brooklyn's most colorful, singular neighborhoods: Brighton Beach.

Sandwiched on the south side of Brooklyn between Coney Island, one of the seediest sections of the borough, and Manhattan Beach, one of the most exclusive, middle-class Brighton was the last stop on the BMT subway, and, come summer, a popular destination for beach buffs from around the city. Year-round, the Jewish community was a haven of another kind, with its residents' love of music and laughter—and of one another. Said Brighton Beach native Jack Packer, fated to become an important ally of Neil's: "[I remember] on 'Star Trek' where Spock says, 'Sacrifice the one for the many' and Kirk says, 'No, you have to have the many take care of one.' That's how it was in Brighton Beach. If somebody had a hardship in their life, we all shared in it."

Brighton Beach seemed the ideal Brooklyn neighborhood for the

Diamonds to sink their roots in. The success of Diamond's Dry Goods, 1055 Brighton Beach Avenue, made that move possible after Neil's sophomore year at Erasmus Hall.

As proof of their improving fortunes in life, Kieve and Rose, who worked as a saleslady, were able to afford a house, a status symbol in 1950s Brighton Beach. Their address, moreover, was just about as prestigious as Brighton got—90 West End Avenue, the demarcation line between Brighton Beach and Manhattan Beach. A short walk from their front door was the boardwalk that stretched to Coney Island; beyond, the beach, the Atlantic Ocean, and the endless horizon.

Socially, Kieve and Rose made themselves right at home. They joined the Shorefront YMWHA—the Young Men's and Women's Hebrew Association—as well as an autonomous offshoot, the Mr. and Mrs. Club. They also purchased memberships in the Brighton Beach Baths. They took to the dance floor weekly, and Kieve soon became known around Brighton for his hilarious pantomimes.

In short, Kieve and Rose found the good life. It was a fact that Neil, so expansive over the years about his family's struggles, has curiously neglected to bring up. Apparently he preferred that it not be known that, by the age of sixteen, he hailed from a family of some means as well as dreams.

Still, Neil couldn't have missed the moral of Kieve Diamond's success story, his ultimate lesson from dad: Persistence and hard work eventually do pay off.

"I'm much more emotionally reflective of my mother, who's more intense," Neil has commented. "I'm motivated, I'm pushed, I'm driven." While his drive didn't extend to his studies at Lincoln High School, where he was lucky to maintain a "C" average, his activities listing in the 1958 Lincoln annual spells purposefulness. He was General Organization councilman; he participated in the Sing, Class Nite and the Choral Group, and, most intriguingly, he was a member of Lincoln's fencing team.

According to Diamond, it was his "first hero," Cyrano de Bergerac, "a misfit . . . a great swordsman . . . a poet," who sold him on joining the fencing team after enrolling at Lincoln in the fall of 1956. In truth, he wanted a free eighth period, and the only way he could get it was to sign up for fencing. Herb Cohen, the team's captain, recalled seeking Diamond out in the cafeteria one day: "I told him, 'You're supposed to be on the fencing team.' He said, 'Well, all right.' 'We have practice, so come down.'

"And he did," Cohen continued. "And he was great! Very good coordination . . . very fast . . . very good spring in his legs for a thin guy

. . . very good lunge, and a good fighting spirit. And we said, 'That's it—you gotta be on the team!''

Diamond, it turned out, became an above-average fencer, and he helped the Lincoln High team make news. During his senior year, the squad, which didn't even have a coach, went on to win the New York City scholastic championships in a major upset. Herb Cohen: "Neil said that that was his first success in life . . . the first time he pursued a goal that was, in a certain way, out of his reach, and actually succeeded."

Neil had another rewarding experience at Lincoln: attending Ben Goldman's music appreciation class.

The middle-aged Goldman, who referred to himself as "the oldest teenager at Lincoln," happened to be a songwriter himself—of teen ballads, no less. At the time, he was actively hustling his tunes in Tin Pan Alley, Manhattan's legendary song emporium, and even getting some of them published. One of them, a ditty called "Wishing Well" that he cowrote with a student of his at the time named Neil Sedaka, had been recorded by a local artist named Jerry Dorn. In 1956 it hit the New York charts.

When Neil Diamond took his class, Goldman was scrambling to write another hit. He wasn't shy about utilizing his students—or "crumbs" as he affectionately called them—to help out, often taking class time to test his latest creation on them. "You don't have to tell me you like it," he'd say. "All I want to get is a reaction from you as a teenager."

Goldman claimed to have only a vague memory of Neil: "He was a quiet boy who sat next to Bobby Feldman," a rambunctious friend and neighbor of Neil's. However, Feldman, who later achieved a measure of songwriting glory himself as a cowriter of the Angels' "My Boyfriend's Back," recalled Goldman strong-arming Neil to collaborate with him on a couple of his tunes, as Bobby said he was wont to do with his more song-savvy "crumbs."

Neil, no doubt, was only too happy to oblige, if for no other reason than to be able to sit in class and listen to Ben Goldman brag about his latest song-plugging foray to Manhattan and his dealings with publishers and record company A&R (artist and repertoire) men. In Goldman's tales was a blueprint for making it as a songwriter.

After graduation in June of 1958, Neil could hear the siren call of a songwriting career in the form of a new pop confection from Connie Francis. The tune was "Stupid Cupid," and one of its two composers was Neil Sedaka.

Although Sedaka had graduated from Lincoln two years earlier, his legend had lived on to motivate Diamond: Sedaka's assembly performance of an original rocker, "Mr. Moon," which transformed him into a campus celebrity overnight, and his founding in 1956 of the pop group The Tokens, who had a modest local hit the next year, before Sedaka left to pursue his Tin Pan Alley dreams with writing partner Howard Greenfield, another Lincolnite. (The Tokens wound up scoring a number one hit with "The Lion Sleeps Tonight" several years later.) Now, "Stupid Cupid" was Top 20 evidence to Neil that Brighton Beach boys could hit pop's big time, too.

In the fall of 1958, Neil enrolled at New York University on a full fencing scholarship, a gift of sorts from his fencing mentor and fellow scholarship winner, Herb Cohen, who recommended him to the coach. Diamond's claimed scholastic goal: a premed degree. However, the laboratory he set up for himself in the finished basement of his parents' home, where he continued to live, was not for experiments of the biological kind. One only had to spy the old white player piano, the two guitars, the music stand, and the notebooks, to gather that Neil was seriously pursuing another course of study on his own.

Not exactly on his own. In 1959, he took on a partner who would help see to it that the songs he was creating would make it out of that room.

·2·
NEIL AND JACK

"You know my brother, Neil, plays a little guitar and he's written a bunch of tunes he'd like to have copywritten. But he really doesn't know how to commit them to paper. Would you be willing to come over and maybe jot these things down and do him a favor?"

It was with these words that Neil's brother, Harvey, approached fellow Lincoln High junior Jack Packer, an acquaintance of his, to come to the musical aid of Neil.

It is no surprise that Harvey would think of Jack. A musical star at Lincoln, the seventeen-year-old Packer had already displayed his booming, opera-trained voice in the all-city chorus, as well as in various school productions. Despite opposition from his father, a holiday cantor who had visions of a Broadway career for his son, Jack also had become enamored with contemporary pop, singing on a Ben Goldman demo, auditioning for an opening in The Tokens, and teaming up with various Lincoln students in musical allegiances that might span a performance in school or an evening of doo-wopping on a street corner. Imbued with what he called "the spirit of youth—you gotta understand, every kid was gonna make it," Jack Packer was game to collaborate with all musical comers.

And that included Neil Diamond. "Sure," Jack said when Harvey popped his question, "it would be my pleasure to help out."

Ironically, Neil was the only Diamond that Jack, who lived around the corner from Diamond's Dry Goods, didn't know.

What he'd seen of the Diamonds had impressed him. He was fond of Kieve for his "wonderful demeanor . . . [his] smile for everybody; he could have been a local politician." Rose, meanwhile, struck him as the personable type "who could mix and deal with the rich," which she did as a saleslady at the exclusive Harper's, on Kings Highway. And he regarded amiable Harvey as one of the boys.

Neil, he was surprised to discover as he sat down with him in his basement, was unlike the rest of his family. He was introverted, he didn't engage in small talk, and he was totally wrapped up in the business at hand: singing his songs with guitar accompaniment so Packer could commit the notes to paper.

Instead of being put off by Neil, however, Jack focused instead on the reason he'd come: Neil's music. He was rewarded.

"I recognized that he had a folk approach, an Americana approach," Packer said, a trace of wonder in his voice. "It was like folk-rock, but in 1959 there was no such thing as folk-rock.

"They were kind of strange, uneventful songs. But I was taken by the music; there was something about the sense of each song that got to me, that made me say to myself, 'This is something.' He was even using the minor mode. His songs had a little cry in them."

It took Packer several weeks to produce the lead sheets. During that time he and Diamond struck up what he called a "mutual admiration friendship," although Jack maintained it was an unusual friendship from the start: "Usually when I dealt with people on a one-to-one basis there was a personal feeling toward the relationship and the people. That never once was really prevalent with Neil. We didn't have any social bind whatsoever.

"Here I could talk, I was flamboyant, I could go on stage. And Neil was quiet, soft-spoken, introverted—you never knew what he was thinking about. He was happiest being in the basement playing on that guitar, practicing those four chords day and night."

Obviously, Neil's songs were all the bond they needed. By the time Jack finished his work for him, they were already talking about the next step—making demonstration records, which Neil could play for song publishers.

Jack approached this step with some foreboding. Despite Neil's membership in the mixed chorus at Erasmus Hall and the choral group at Lincoln, it was his emphatic opinion that Neil *"couldn't sing*—he like talked through the songs." Nor did Jack feel that Neil had any ambitions vocally: "All he was interested in was being a songwriter. I mean he never dreamed for one second of singing his songs when he wrote them."

Indeed, Diamond had another vocalist in mind for his demos: Jack Packer. Jack begged off. "Frankly, I couldn't sing his material because I had this Mario Lanza voice . . . it just wasn't in me to sing like Jerry Lee Lewis or the Everly Brothers and have a twang in my voice. And that's what his music needed; it had this earthiness about it."

So Neil and Jack decided that Neil should handle the vocals himself. To prepare him for his date in the studio, Packer gave him some vocal coaching. "I said, 'Neil, say this: [normal speaking voice] "My name is Neil Diamond,"' And he would say, 'My name is Neil Diamond.' I said, 'Now say this: "Myyyy nammmmme isss Neilll Diiiiammmmond."' And he'd repeat it. And then I'd say, 'Now do this: [sings] "Myyyy nammmmme issss Neillll Diiiiammmmond."' That's how I taught him to sing. He got to a certain point very quickly."

But not quickly enough for the sake of his first couple of demos.

"He came back and played them, and he could not cut it. I mean it was like Jule Styne singing his own material, or Marvin Hamlisch . . . Very unappetizing."

So what to do? Jack, who looked upon his fledgling association with Neil as a musical exercise, pondered that question by mulling over what he considered to be a basic truth about Neil's art: that he had a natural gift that maybe he didn't even understand . . . that the songs "would come out, and the exact form that they came out of him, that's where they stayed . . . in the raw . . . [that] he didn't have the capacity, or the penchant to elaborate on his themes."

Realizing that, he announced his conclusion to Neil: "'Listen,' I said, 'These songs need to be arranged. They need to have some sort of beginning, middle, climax.' And I said, 'I'd like to try and make vocal arrangements for you of these songs. Let me sing harmony to you.'"

Neil was instantly amenable. And so, Jack continued, "he started playing the songs and I started hitting the harmonies I heard in my head. And there was a ring to the voices. And all of a sudden the fact that I had this brilliant, muscular voice disappeared. And the fact that Neil had trouble with pitch, sustaining and phrasing—well now I was doing that for him, I was like holding him up by the bootstraps vocally.

"And we had a sound. I couldn't believe it."

The euphoria was mutual. "Neil reacted immediately—'Hey, we got something. Let's go make a demo.'"

Over the next few months Diamond and Packer journeyed to Tin Pan Alley to record a handful of Neil's tunes. They were the simplest demos, just their voices backed by Neil's rudimentary guitar playing. Yet they had their special touches, such as overdubbed vocal parts. Packer: "Our voices were placed kind of high . . . there was no bottom to our music. And we overdubbed Neil singing some baritone parts. And to get him to sing those harmonies—what an achievement!"

Listening to those recordings today, one can hear that "little cry" that Jack talked of in Neil's melancholy melodies and wistful lyrics. The titles alone are tip-offs of his brooding bent, even as a nineteen-year-old: "You Keep Me Wondering," "Gone Is My Love," "Don't Treat Me This Way," "Time Will Tell." While none of the tunes are grabbers—the often-trite lyrics read like typical adolescent laments—the simple, sad, folk-flavored music does have staying power. And when Jack's robust vocals don't overpower Neil's thinner, slightly countrified ones, they have a pleasing vocal blend—like a Brooklyn approximation of the Everly Brothers. Neil, an avid Everly Brothers fan at the time, even wore his hair high and walked around in cowboy boots.

Two people thrilled with the demos were Kieve and Rose Diamond; according to Jack, they were ecstatic that their elder son had designs on a songwriting career: "It was almost like they knew he was gonna succeed at it. It was amazing."

The better he got to know the Diamonds, the more convinced he was that Neil was a fortunate son. When asked if he recalled any one interesting feature of their home on West End Avenue, Packer didn't hesitate in responding, "Yes, l-o-v-e was in that house; Neil Diamond grew up in a house of love. The things around them didn't matter. They didn't put on a show, Kieve and Rose. Even their success they seemed to have taken in a gentlemanly, humane way."

By Jack's reckoning, Rose and Kieve's financial security played a role in their unqualified support of Neil's songwriting exploits. "I never saw their tax returns, but to my eye Neil was from the other side of the tracks, the better side. He was an advantaged young man. He had the financial backing of his parents to pursue his art at his own pace. I mean, other parents were telling their kids, 'You're a bum, go out and get a job.' I had no money. I had to work part time in supermarkets and drugstores. Being disadvantaged, I didn't have the clear head as a kid to pursue what I wanted, I always had to pursue in a mode that I thought would earn me money. Neil didn't have that problem. And if there was money to be invested in a demo, or gas pumped into the car, his parents took care of it."

Well, there was one time that Neil approached him to split the eighty-dollar cost of a demo. Jack had to tell him his parents couldn't afford to. The very idea that Neil would even ask rankled him. "He wasn't making me a partner in the songs, I wasn't getting remuneration for writing vocal arrangements, or creating the group," Jack explained. Kieve wound up footing the entire bill.

While Neil's parents were underwriting Neil's songwriting exploits, Mark Packer was doing his damndest to save his son from Diamond and rock 'n' roll in general. "I mean he was making my life miserable over the time I was spending with Neil," Jack sighed. "He used to say to me, 'If you don't get that no-talent out of this house, I'm going to break both of your legs and you'll never walk again.'"

But Jack had an important possession, a Webcor tape recorder, and since it was a pain to transport, he continued to risk his limbs by inviting Neil over to make practice recordings. In these face-to-face encounters between his dad and Neil, Jack said, "There was this quiet cold war going on, which I think put a strain on the relationship [between Neil and me]."

Yet, Neil and Jack rolled on as an unofficial duo. In early 1960 Kieve and Rose arranged for Neil to make his first public appearance, not in front of a group of Neil's peers, but rather a group of their *own* peers, at a dinner-dance at the Little Neck Country Club on Long Island. Jack agreed to sing with him.

Packer regarded the performance as just another gig. However, it was obvious to him that Neil approached the performance far differently, and totally unlike the spotlight-loving Kieve: "He was *very uptight,* to say the least. Somber. I realized that performing per se was not his forté whatsoever."

Jack gave this account of Neil Diamond's first live performance ever of his original pop songs:

"It might sound corny, but by the time we got through the first eight, sixteen bars, we were still alive, lightning didn't strike, the audience didn't leave, and we opened up and performed the music. But I think I have to rescind the word *perform.* Neil did not perform. He played the music. And I didn't gesticulate; if I would have *performed* it would have been out of place, for me it was just standing next to him. It was a very low-key production . . . home brewed.

"It all went pretty decently. We played the three or four songs, which were kind of alien for an adult audience in 1960. The harmonies were all right, and we finished together. And it was just a very plain, inauspicious performance of our material.

"But," Jack added, "I think it went a long way in giving Neil the confidence he might have needed to get up and perform."

Shy as he was about taking the stage himself, Neil had no qualms about journeying to Manhattan and plugging his demoed tunes to publishers. Jack, busy with school and the other musical irons he had in the fire at the time, left the legwork to Neil.

He did, however, introduce Neil to an agent friend of his father's, Murray Miller. It was Miller, he believes, who in 1960 made the connection for Neil at Allied Entertainment Corporation of America, a small, now defunct New York firm, with the music publishing company, Saxon Music.

It was at Allied that the demo-wielding Neil got his first break. The company agreed to publish several of his tunes; what's more, Allied offered Neil *and* Jack a recording contract with its novelty label, Duel Records. "They made us a group," Jack said.

Diamond and Packer were totally unprepared for such a turn of events. "We weren't pursuing it [being a recording duo]," he maintained. "I mean we sang together as a vehicle for him to promote his songwriting."

As they gazed at the contract, however, they found it easier and easier to picture themselves as a duo. Packer: "That contract was amazing. When I read it I thought I was made. So did Neil. This contract talked in the millions of dollars—that the company would take off *x* percentage if the record only grossed $750,000. I mean on and on!"

No matter that Allied didn't offer one penny's worth of an advance. With dollar signs dancing in their eyes, Neil Diamond and Jack Packer—Neil and Jack—signed on the dotted line.

Suddenly their trips into the city with Neil behind the wheel of the Diamonds' Valiant took on a new meaning. Packer: "When you have a contract that reads for millions of dollars and you're a young guy and you've always known that you have some calling in show business and you're going to make it one way or another, on these drives you almost felt that when you went over the Brooklyn Bridge into Manhattan that that entire island very shortly would be in your back pocket. And this euphoria would set in. Neil and I would giggle and kid each other and both be so high on life going into Manhattan to have a rehearsal, or to meet somebody. I mean, they were fun times, really fun times, those little trips together . . . We were in the *hub* of it, New York. Groups were making it by the *fistfuls*. And it was our time."

Jack's memory of his first Duel recording session with Neil is a vivid one—and totally pleasant, "like the first time you have sex . . . I can see Neil sitting on a stool, à la Perry Como, with his guitar, and I was standing next to him. And we were both singing into one mike. They had wanted to put us each on our own mikes, and when they did they just didn't get the ring they ultimately realized we had when we sang on the same mike." They cut Neil's "What Will I Do," a zippy Everly Brothers–flavored number, as well as his overwrought ballad "You Are My Love at Last," strongly reminiscent of the Jewish folk song "Ber Mir Bist Du Schein." "What Will I Do," they understood, would be the A side.

A funny thing happened on the way to the charts, however—"You Are My Love at Last" got played on the radio instead by New York deejays. Packer couldn't believe his ears: "The first time I heard it, I said, 'They're playing the *wrong song!*'" Compounding the trauma were the tacky violins that had been overdubbed on the track without Neil's or his knowledge, ethnicizing the tune even more. Jack dismissed the violins as a "gimmick—in those days the word was, 'You need a gimmick.'" But obviously the world was not ready for the first Jewish folk-rock song: "You Are My Love at Last" died a quick death, as did Neil and Jack's dream of instant riches.

Although Duel released one more Neil and Jack single, Jack has only a fuzzy memory of it, as well as of the parting after that with Duel. At the time, he explained, he had been forced to retreat into his senior studies and to begin contemplating college. His life reached its tumultuous peak the week before graduation when his father took seriously ill.

Still Jack was not ready to write *finis* to his association with Diamond. Both had reacted to their Duel debacle with resolve, and Jack claimed he and Neil had a fresh understanding: "I said [to him], 'Listen, buddy boy, I'm glad to participate with you. You call the shots, tell me where . . . and when . . . and I'll be there.'" Meanwhile, Packer decided to put off college until the spring, not only to give himself more time to prepare his entrance exam to the prestigious Manhattan School of Music, but also to give Neil and Jack, the duo, more time.

Demos in hand, Diamond took to the streets again with a vengeance. Reflecting on Neil's talent as a hustler, Jack said, "I've got to admit that Neil got us into an excellent position for success. He opened the doors that needed to be opened. He got to the people that if you had it you were going to make it."

One of those people was Morris Levy, founder of Roulette Records, one of the first independent rock 'n' roll labels. Packer: "After they heard our demos, and after they heard us sing live, he took us in the office and said, 'Listen, you got one problem: You both sing too good. Your pitch is too good. You gotta sing a little off key, man!'"

Persisting in singing as on key as they possibly could, Neil and Jack signed with 20th Century Fox Records soon afterward.

According to Packer, 20th Century Fox told Neil and him all the right things: "They were going to spend the money on the recording session and in promoting us that Duel didn't. We didn't even make any personal appearances when we were with Duel."

But that good news wasn't the half of it. They were to be produced by a rock 'n' roll songwriting great, Otis Blackwell, at the time a member of the label's A&R staff. Otis Blackwell's songs, among them "Don't Be Cruel," and "Great Balls of Fire," spoke for themselves.

Blackwell got right down to business. He wrote out charts to four Diamond tunes, brought Neil and Jack into the studio, hired a band, and produced demo recordings of the songs. "They sounded great," said Jack. Still undecided about which two he wanted to cut as Neil and Jack's first single, Blackwell set up a formal recording date anyway, figuring he could make up his mind in the studio.

The day of their session, Neil and Jack had one of their jubilant drives into Manhattan. Their exhilaration quickly gave way to anxiousness in the office, however. "We get in early in the morning, and Otis Blackwell isn't there," Packer recalled. "An hour goes by. Two hours go by. And still he doesn't show up. And the people there are really upset, here they had hired musicians."

Blackwell never made it. The only recording that Neil and Jack wound up doing that day were background vocals to a novelty tune comedian Buddy Hackett just happened to be recording, "Itsy Bitsy Teeny Weenie Yellow Polka Dot Bikini."

Figuring some sort of mixup, Neil and Jack waited to hear back from 20th Century Fox. They waited a day, a week, two weeks. Finally, they heard. Because of a "personal problem," Blackwell had left New

York for Europe the night before Neil and Jack's scheduled session. Just as soon as he decided to return to work, they were assured, the company would be in touch.

According to Jack, that was the last Neil and he heard from 20th Century Fox.

Not long after that, in January 1961, Jack Packer enrolled at Manhattan School of Music. His decision to pursue his studies was partly based, he said, on the "many disappointments in the recording industry," primarily Neil's and his.

He had girded himself for disappointments as well in college: "I had already been the star of the high school, so to speak, and everybody was warning me, 'You're going to be like a guppy in the sea now.'" Instead, he found himself singing solos with the glee club and snaring a part in an opera, the first freshman to do so. Meanwhile, he became immersed in his study of the classics.

In short, Jack said, "There was no room for rock 'n' roll and Neil Diamond in my life now."

But that was not the whole story behind his decision to cool it with Neil. He added that he was being subjected to mounting anti-Diamond rhetoric, not only from his father but also from "professional people in the recording industry, agents . . . They did not like Neil as a person," he claimed. "Neil was obnoxious. Most of the kids who came up to the record companies were bright-eyed and bushy-tailed, and Neil was a little terse [in] his retorts. He wasn't a tactician."

The continuing criticism of Neil, Packer implied, caused him to take another look at Diamond. What he saw, he confessed, "was a strange cat. Neil was not cut out of the same cloth as the other kids. Neil was a person unto himself." All the easier for Packer to remain cloistered at the Manhattan School of Music.

"So it just ended," Jack said. "Neil didn't call and I didn't pursue."

As it turned out, Neil had decided to do his future Manhattan pavement-pounding solitary man–style.

·3·
THRUST AND PARRY

"You've got to have the persistence and hard work to overcome all the early obstacles. People don't generally notice whether you're talented until after you've made it."

—Diamond

Now hooked on becoming a recording artist, Neil found himself playing a handful of his songs in 1962 for young Columbia Records staff producer Al Kasha.

Kasha was working in his office with another young singer/writer when Neil arrived for the audition with Columbia product manager Tom Catalano, who had been turned on to Diamond by Neil's original contact at the label, promotion man Sal Forlenza.

The artist, Bob Halley, in fact, was in the middle of singing a song of his at the piano when Catalano breezily announced, "This is Neil Diamond."

Kasha didn't appreciate the interruption. "Don't talk for a second; I want to hear the end of this tune," he admonished. So Catalano and the leather-jacketed Diamond stood quietly as Halley completed his country-rock song, which, like Bob Halley's recording career, was destined for obscurity. When he finished, Kasha turned to Neil and remarked after a pregnant pause: "If you can write something like this, you'll make it as a songwriter."

Kasha then proceeded to give a listen to Neil.

"My first impression of him was that I thought he was a better songwriter than a singer," he recalled. "I don't know if Neil felt that secure about himself as a singer." As for the songs, he thought they were "very good . . . I thought that he sounded like the Everly Brothers." Of the several tunes Neil performed, Kasha's favorite was "Clown Town," a peppy ditty with a she-done-me-wrong theme. After the audition, he suggested to Neil that they go into the studio in the next few months and record a couple of demos.

A few days later, Kasha met up with a music publisher friend, Frank Military, a professional manager at Sunbeam Music. At the time the Broadway-show publishing house, like many established Tin Pan Alley publishers, was changing its tune, literally and figuratively, about signing on teen-pop writers. Military wanted to know if Kasha could recommend any young tunesmiths.

"Yeah," Kasha said, "I have this guy, Neil Diamond, you should sign."

After auditioning Neil a few days later, that's what Military did.

By Neil's account, his decision to become a full-time staff writer at Sunbeam Music in the spring of 1962 had profound implications on his life. It meant dropping out of NYU a mere ten units short of getting his bachelor's degree. It meant formally scuttling his plans for becoming a doctor (which, according to him, he had lost an appetite for the previous year when a heart attack victim he encountered on the street died in his arms after "I gave him mouth-to-mouth resuscitation, heart massage and everything else I knew"). And, most importantly, it meant dedicating himself, in success-or-bust terms now, to a songwriting/recording career, without the safety net of a potential backup career. A scary situation. A brave undertaking by Neil. A PR man's dream scenario.

Records supplied by the registrar's office at NYU tell a different story, however.

Not only did Neil remain enrolled at the university when he went to work at Sunbeam Music, he remained enrolled there for another three years—for the entire time, in fact, that he was looking for the break in Tin Pan Alley that would launch his career.

Further, at the time he went to work for Sunbeam, he was no longer enrolled in the university's Washington Square College, the college NYU premed students attended. Instead, he had left the college in 1960 and enrolled the following year in NYU's School of Commerce, where he remained until he finally left NYU in 1965, "without completing the requirements for graduation."

These facts suggest two truths about Neil: that he was a very practical, realistic young man in 1962, and that, as a star years later, he was not above shading the facts of his past.

Neil's tale of his being fired from Sunbeam Music after a few months does square with the memory of Jay Morgenstern, then Sunbeam's vice-president and general manager. "There was no question in our minds that Neil was going to be an exceptional songwriter," he said. "He wasn't at the time."

Of the seventeen songs of Diamond's that the company published, Morgenstern only remembers being able to secure obscure "cover" recordings on two of them, even though the company launched a second campaign to place the songs in 1971, long after Neil had become a star.

A scan of the Diamond song folio Sunbeam published makes it clear why there were few takers. None of the tunes have the sparkle and originality, lyrically or musically, that spell hit. Also, most of them have a confessional country bent, not the most marketable of sounds in Tin

Pan Alley. But the unrelenting "woe-is-me" tone of these tunes—the majority of which feature a forsaken or jilted lover ruminating on his "Blue Destiny," to quote the title of one of the songs—would make them a hard sell in Nashville, too.

As it turned out, Sunbeam did Neil a favor by releasing him; he was now free to become involved in a new publishing situation that might offer him a greater opportunity to mix with and learn from songwriters who, like him, were aiming for the Top 40. Just such a situation arose for Diamond at Roosevelt Music in 1962.

Unlike Sunbeam, Roosevelt had its roots in rhythm and blues, and rock. The firm's president, Hal Fein, had put the publishing company on the map a few years earlier by assembling a great group of black writers: Otis Blackwell, Jesse Stone, Charley Singleton. But Fein wasn't one to sit on his copyrights; he also had the good sense in 1962 to take under his wing a young dynamo of a professional manager, Wes Farrell, who put out the word that Roosevelt was looking for fresh rock-writing talent.

Among the first young writers to find a home at Roosevelt was Diamond's Lincoln High friend Bobby Feldman, who had teamed up with Jerry Goldstein and Richard Gottehrer. Soon after that, Feldman brought Neil in to meet Farrell.

"Neil had a charisma about him," Farrell recalled of his live audition. "I didn't give a shit what he sang, he made it sound so good you thought it was the greatest song ever written." Neil was welcomed aboard at Roosevelt, at thirty-five dollars a week.

Compared to his productivity at Sunbeam, however, his output at Roosevelt in the few months he was there was curiously meager—a handful of tunes—an indication, perhaps, that he had other irons in the fire, or was temporarily tied up with NYU studies. "When I wouldn't see him for two, three days, I would get nervous," Farrell said. "I'd call, 'Neil, where the hell are you?'" Larry Weiss, another young Roosevelt writer at the time, confirmed his low profile: "Neil was very reclusive. He was like a shadow walking in and out of the office."

Diamond's shadow was present and accounted for at Roosevelt the day a little Tin Pan Alley magic was made, however.

"Hal was desperate to find a follow-up to 'Speedy Gonzales' for Pat Boone," Farrell recalled. "There were ten writers, including Neil and myself, sitting around the office . . . We knew we had about forty-eight hours to get the song out to the Coast to Boone.

"At eight everybody was exhausted, nobody had come up with an idea. And I said, 'We're a bunch of lonely guys sitting around here looking like a bunch of idiots. Let's write a song called "Ten Lonely Guys".'"

Larry Weiss: "We decided to write a song about a woman that had hurt all of us. Of course, the woman we were writing about was the music business."

Loosened up by a bottle of Scotch that Farrell had sprung for, the writers scribbled the lyrics in crayon on a wall in the music room. They then hustled downstairs to Alegro Studios, where they demoed the country-flavored tune; handling the lead vocals was Neil. (Explained fellow Roosevelt writer Stanley Kahan: "If you heard the rest of us sing— he had no competition whatsoever.")

The resulting recording, Farrell felt, was a hit—not for Pat Boone but for the Ten Lonely Guys featuring Neil Diamond.

An acetate of the tune made its way immediately to Phil Carle and Joe Kolski at Diamond Records. Recalled Bobby Feldman, another of the "Guys": "They wanted to put out the record . . . And they had full-page ads ready to go, pick hits, test pressings."

Immersed as they were in their imminent stardom, Farrell & Company neglected to put the horse before the cart and get the approval of their boss, Hal Fein, desperate to land that Pat Boone recording. To their dismay, Fein cut them off at the pass by withholding the tune from Diamond Records, which was his prerogative as its publisher. Without their signature song, the Ten Lonely Guys did one of the quicker fades in pop annals.

Within a few weeks, "Ten Lonely Guys," by Pat Boone, hit the airwaves. But now, minus 90 percent of the novelty factor, the song went no higher than number forty-five. Still, as his first tune to crack *Billboard*'s Hot 100, the record represented a minor milestone in Neil's fledgling career. It also merits an asterisk in the Diamond log of tunes: It seems to be the only chart record that he ever wrote or cowrote under a pseudonym—Mark Lewis.

Not long after the "Ten Lonely Guys" episode, Neil left Roosevelt Music. One day he paid a visit to another recent Roosevelt alumnus, Stanley Kahan, who had taken his own office in the 1650 Building on Broadway, which, like the Brill Building at 1619, was crammed with pop music publishers and songwriters. Kahan had begun to produce artists independently, and Neil had a proposition for him.

"Neil had written a Christmas song, and wanted me to produce it with some artist I was involved with," Kahan recalled. "I, frankly, was negative to the idea.

"Then he told me he had seen a group called the Rocky Fellers on 'The Ed Sullivan Show,' and they would be the perfect group to do this song. And I said, 'Hey, listen, if the Rocky Fellers are as good as you say, if you can get 'em, we'll do the song.' And really in my mind, I said, 'My God, this group has to be signed to fourteen different contracts.'"

A week later, the Rocky Fellers—a Filipino father and his four sons, ages nine to seventeen—walked into Kahan's office and proceeded to audition. "They were absolutely incredible," Kahan said. To his amazement, he found that they hadn't signed a record production deal—an oversight that he was happy to rectify. He also agreed with Neil—who had displayed his savvy in locating them in the first place—that he, Neil, should be involved percentage-wise as an associate producer.

Kahan secured $2,500 from a subsidiary label of United Artists Records to cut four "sides" with the Fellers. Included were Diamond's Latin-flavored Christmas song, "Santa Santa," and his "We Got Love." The cheery, commercial nature of the tunes suggested that Neil was finally getting some songwriting seasoning.

Kahan went to work with the group. "The problem," he said, "was that I kept working and working and Neil kept disappearing." Under the impression that Diamond was burdened by his college studies, Kahan took the lead in producing the Rocky Fellers. After UA passed on the tracks, it was also Kahan who shopped them to Scepter Records. Scepter released "Santa Santa" as a single, but the only place it was a hit was in the Fellers' native Philippines. However, the Fellers' second release, "Killer Joe," a tune that Kahan had cowritten with Bert Berns, fated to play a crucial role in Neil's eventual stardom, hit *Billboard*'s Top 20 in the spring of 1963.

A Rocky Fellers LP was the next logical step, but Neil's continuing absence from the scene told Kahan that he would have to go it alone. "Neil and I came to an agreement that we would separate," he said.

Amicable though the parting was, Diamond never bothered to explain to Stanley Kahan the real reason he performed his fast, curious fade with the Fellers. The fact was, Neil had scored an even bigger break in early 1963: a recording deal with Columbia Records.

Columbia staff producer Al Kasha had proceeded cautiously with Neil since their first meeting.

His first order of business was to go over Neil's lyrics with a fine-tooth comb, making constructive criticism. In the process, he bumped into Neil's "fragile" side. "I did feel a sense of protectiveness, of defensiveness," he remarked. "He couldn't take criticism well, and felt that he knew as well as I did, better than I did, what was a good song."

Still, they got on well enough for Kasha to record some demos with him, after which Kasha got the green light from Columbia's new A&R chief, Dave Kapralik, to do a full-fledged recording date. On January 24, 1963, his twenty-second birthday, Diamond stepped into Columbia's Studio B to record "Clown Town" and one of his Sunbeam tunes, "A Million Miles Away."

Kasha made a big production out of the session, bringing in not only a rhythm section, but also horn players and a female backup group called the Cookies (soon afterward, the group hit the Top 10 with "Don't Say Nothin' Bad About My Baby")."I think Neil was very nervous," Kasha said. "His voice was shaking a little bit."

Apparently, "A Million Miles Away" didn't go over with the Columbia brass. Shortly after the session, Kasha suggested to Neil that they write a tune together to go with "Clown Town." He told Diamond he had the title "At Night" in mind, and he began to lay out the upbeat love song to him. But Neil cut him short: "Well, let me finish it." Kasha: "He really didn't like to write with anyone else."

Neil did wind up completing the song, and, three months to the day after the January session, he returned to Studio B to record it, along with a dyed-in-the-wool country original, "I'll Never Be the Same."

It was then that Neil was officially welcomed into the Columbia family. In addition to landing a singles record deal, he was signed as a staff writer by Columbia's recently reactivated publishing company, April Blackwood Music. The company happened to be run by none other than Columbia's erstwhile product manager, Tom Catalano, Neil's original champion at the label. "Clown Town," in fact, was the first tune Catalano signed on in June of 1963.

"Neil was thrilled," Kasha said. "To him this was it." Kapralik and Kasha, however, viewed the Diamond project as no more than an experiment. Columbia, longtime haven for middle-of-the-road types like Ray Conniff and its former A&R director, Mitch Miller, had only recently begun signing contemporary pop acts, and, according to Kasha, "all of the promotion dollars were still going after the stars that Columbia was spending hundred of thousands of dollars on.

"So we said, 'Let's develop some young writers, do inexpensive dates, and then, if we hit, we're really going to look like heroes.'"

Diamond's "Clown Town," backed by "At Night," was released July 2. To commemorate the event, Neil had cocktail napkins printed up with his name and the name of the single, and he placed them inside the Ho-Ho, the Columbia building watering hole.

That seems to have been about the only promotion done for Columbia's newest artist. The single sank without a trace, postponing hero status for anyone involved with Neil at the label. Even given a promotional push, it is doubtful that either one of the sides would have dented the charts, however. The songs themselves were slight and the production gaudy, with the intrusive sounds of cheery horns, the Cookies and—in the case of "At Night"—a cornball repeating vocal figure serving to cover up Diamond's voice in spots. Given Al Kasha's concerns about Neil's vocal abilities, that might have been his aim.

Neil was not pleased with the sound himself. "He wanted a rougher kind of rock thing," said Carl D'Errico, a staff writer at April Blackwood at the time.

Neil was looking forward to getting another crack from Columbia. He was very unhappy when Kasha informed him that the Columbia brass had decided to ax him from the roster.

"One record," Neil muttered in disgust to Kasha. "They don't even give you a chance."

The news wasn't all bad in Diamond's life at the time. First, he remained a seventy-five-dollar-a-week staff writer at April Blackwood, and thus within striking distance of another record deal with Columbia.

Second, he had gotten married.

Her name was Jay Posner, of Long Island. Born June 22, 1941 in Manhattan, graduated from Hofstra University in June of 1963 with a B.S. in education, career goal: schoolteacher. (While her birth certificate reads "Jay," she preferred to sign her first name with an "e" on the end.)

Even though Diamond had dated in high school and college, he wasn't exactly a man of the world when he met Jay several years earlier, despite posing as an authority on romance matters to his friend Herb Cohen. (Once in high school, Neil tore up a photo of an ex-girlfriend Cohen was pining for, calmly telling his shocked friend, "You'll be much better off, Herb. Remember, she shits on the pot like everybody else.") Neil and Jay's meeting occurred in the Catskills, where Jay was vacationing at the time and where, at the Fun Crest Hotel, Diamond and Cohen were working as waiters for the summer. "Jay was a good swimmer," an acquaintance recalled. "But I think she pretended she didn't know how so he could teach her."

"She was very cute . . . intelligent," Cohen said of the brunette with the nice smile. "She was a very typical Jewish woman. Very conventional, very moral."

Although he never met Jay, Jack Packer figured she was quite a catch, "because, boy, did Neil run. I mean, to go from Brooklyn to Massapequa to see her, which in those days was an hour drive . . ."

As their relationship developed, Jay began accompanying Neil to the NYU Violet's meets. And, just as she rooted for him in his fencing matches, she began cheering him on in the other game he was playing, that of Tin Pan Alley musical chairs.

As it would turn out, Jay's work as a schoolteacher would help see to it that her husband had the freedom to continue to chase fame and fortune.

As his chase continued in mid-1963, Neil enjoyed the wholehearted support of at least one well-connected music biz type—Tom Catalano, the April Blackwood product manager. "I remember him turning to me and saying that one day Neil was going to be a superstar," recalled former Roosevelt Music writer Larry Weiss, who had also moved over to April Blackwood. He added that Catalano also predicted that he, Catalano, was going to play an important role in Neil's pop ascension.

Fellow April Blackwood writer Carl D'Errico thought Diamond was pretty special, too: "He had a feel for a simple kind of rock 'n' roll. And he had a certain amount of excitement when he played the guitar and sang his songs. It turned me on, just the rhythmic aspect."

One can hear proof of an emerging performance talent in a demo Diamond cut of a midtempo tune that he cowrote with D'Errico at the publishing company, "Farewell, Goodbye, So Long." The "little cry" that Jack Packer had heard in Neil's earliest tunes could now be heard in his voice, with pleasing results.

The tune was one of nine that Neil, obviously having reconsidered the wisdom of solo composing, collaborated on with the more pop-oriented D'Errico. One of the reasons they got along so well, D'Errico speculated, was that they were similar solitary souls who didn't "moan a lot" about their problems. Describing the same all-business Neil that Packer had described, the soft-spoken D'Errico added: "It was only through the songs that we'd express ourselves."

Neil and Carl were especially high on one of those songs, a rocker. The duo was hoping to get no less a star than Dion, then at the top of the pop heap with "Runaround Sue," "The Wanderer," and "Ruby Baby," to cut the tune.

Ever aggressive, Diamond managed to secure a meeting with Dion one day at his apartment on Fifty-seventh Street. As soon as the excited tunesmiths walked in his door, D'Errico said he could see that Dion was in a giddy mood.

"Neil got his guitar out, and he said, 'We've got this great song for you'—hyping him and everything," D'Errico recalled, chuckling. "And he started the tune. And he gave like one of the best performances I ever saw. Neil was selling the song—it was like unbelievable. And Dion's sitting there, going 'Yeaaahhhh! Yeaaahhhh!' Neil is singing harder. *'Yeaaaaahhhhh! Yeaaaaahhhhhh!'*

"So Neil finishes with a big chord, exhausted. And Dion looks at us, and he says, *'Nooooooooo!'* We looked at each other; we were in shock. All this 'Yeah!' through the song, and then he goes 'No!' at the end."

As it turned out, Dion's insincere "Yeahs!" were as close as they got to placing a song together. Neil had the same batting average for the dozen or so other songs he wrote or cowrote for April Blackwood: .000.

That abysmal record did not endear Neil to new April Blackwood president Dave Kapralik. In fact, one of the first things the former Columbia chief—who undoubtedly recalled Diamond's "Clown Town" folly—wanted Tom Catalano to do was to chop him from the roster.

Catalano vigorously protested: "Dave . . . he's getting ready to pop.

Let's go with him for another couple of months because it's a shame to drop him now. We're down $8,000 . . . so we go down $10,000 . . . it's no big deal."

Kapralik's decision stood, however, which meant that if Neil was going to achieve the success Catalano had been forecasting and if he, Catalano, was going to play an important role in that success, they were going to have to pick another time and place.

Catalano wound up taking it harder than Diamond, shedding tears as he broke the news to Neil. Neil walked around the desk and put his arm around him.

Doggedly determined as he was to become a star, Neil must have realized that he was at a crossroads in his life. By then, Neil Sedaka, the pride of Lincoln High, had scored thirteen Top 40 hits, and Bobby Feldman, his Brighton Beach friend and neighbor, had cowritten his number one smash for the Angels, "My Boyfriend's Back." By stark contrast, Neil had nothing to show for his five years of music hustle in the summer of 1964 except failed singles and a few obscure "cover" recordings.

And now, at twenty-three, he was unemployed, not even earning a minimal salary as a staff songwriter.

Neil had remained enrolled at NYU's School of Commerce for a reason, obviously, and a career in the straight world—perhaps in real estate, a subject Jack Packer vaguely recalled as Neil's "milieu" at NYU—must have loomed as an option.

Instead, Neil made his boldest move yet: He took an office on Broadway for thirty-five dollars a month and went into business for himself as a songwriter. He would continue to sell songs, and himself, thank you—not real estate.

It was the most modest of "offices" imaginable: a former storage room, eight feet square, located in the rear of a print shop above Birdland, the jazz club. But Neil was proud of it, hiring someone to paint the name of his new business in black on the smoked-glass portion of the door. The words that went up were a nod to his supportive wife: "Neil and Jay Enterprises."

Meanwhile, Neil squeezed in an old upright piano—and, in an unusual move, installed a pay phone.

There was a good reason for the pay phone, according to Carl D'Errico, who continued to write with him: "He'd put the dime in, call the operator, and say, 'Operator, I'm sorry, I was disconnected.' So she'd say, 'What number were you calling?' And he'd give her the number that he wanted, that he had never dialed. And she dialed it for him, and he got his dime back. So he never paid for his calls!"

Despite his later claim that he finally began "writing stuff that I wanted to write and not what some publisher demanded" in his new office, the fact was that Neil was even more willing than ever to dish up songs on demand. There was, after all, the matter of his rent, as well as the other expenses he was incurring as an independent contractor.

"In going around to various publishers, you'd get to know the types of songs *they* wanted," D'Errico explained. "So you'd kind of hedge your creativity by writing in that style. It would take maybe a couple of hours to write a song, and you'd get your seventy-five to hundred-dollar advance. And you'd be happy with that, although you'd be saying to yourself, 'Oh, I know they'll never record this thing.'"

One example of their mercenary tunesmithing was "That New Boy in Town," which they dutifully wrote in Neil Sedaka style, even down to the Sedaka-ish "dom-doobie-doo-dom-dom" vocal figure. To their surprise, however, the publisher, Suffolk Music, placed the tune with a young unknown named Jan Tanzy. The single, released in early 1965, however, caused nary a ripple.

While he was hustling his songwriting skills, Neil continued to search for another recording deal. He regarded Herb Rosen, an A&R man at Mercury Records, as one of his best bets.

Rosen had been encouraging Neil in his songwriting since he had been signed to Sunbeam Music. He felt that Diamond was "an inch away" from becoming a successful songwriter, held back only by his youth. He was also taken personally by the outwardly confident Diamond, who reminded him of Bobby Darin. "Bobby had an attitude at the time which I called a superstar attitude," Rosen explained. "It was nothing nasty . . . just an attitude like, 'There's nothing going to stop me from being a superstar.' And I saw the same thing with Neil. He was so aggressive and positive of himself."

Rosen confessed that Diamond's attitude occasionally irritated him. Like Al Kasha, he found Neil to be very sensitive to criticism: "He wouldn't accept my negatives about his works. When I would say, 'Well, I don't know about this song,' he would say, 'Well, maybe you don't know, but *I* know it's good.'"

Rosen's biggest gripe with Diamond, however, was nervy Neil's penchant for auditioning the same songs Rosen had turned down in previous meetings!

Finally, weary and exasperated by all the not-quite-there songs Diamond had foisted on him for three years, Rosen lost his cool with him one day.

"Neil, Neil—until you bring me some good material, I don't want to see your ass again!" he stormed.

"Do you really mean that?" Diamond said, momentarily taken aback.

Rosen said he really meant it.

On his songwriting rounds one day in February of 1965, some six months after he'd gone into business for himself, Diamond dropped into the offices of veteran music publishers George and Irwin Pincus. They cottoned to a couple of his tunes, and offered to cover the cost of demos. A call went out to a certain bubbly blonde known around New York as the Demo Queen.

But singing on demos wasn't Ellie Greenwich's sole forte. She and her husband, Jeff Barry, also happened to be one of the hottest songwriting teams in pop, cowriters, with Phil Spector, of such girl-group classics as "Be My Baby," "Then He Kissed Me," "Da Doo Ron Ron," and "Chapel of Love," and more recently—as staff writers for Jerry Leiber and Mike Stoller's Trio Music—coauthors, with George Morton, of the Shangri-Las' number one hit, "Leader of the Pack." If that wasn't enough, they were also beginning to make their names as producers, having produced a Top 20 hit, "The Kind of Boy You Can't Forget," by the Raindrops—actually themselves and Greenwich's sister Laura.

Ellie Greenwich didn't have any great expectations when she strolled into the Pincus offices to meet Diamond. "At the time," she said, "no one had ever heard of Neil Diamond. He was just a guy who wrote some songs.

"He was very, very soft spoken," she continued. "I mean firm in what he wanted, but very friendly and very warm. And he played me a couple of songs; one was called 'Call Me His' . . . And I thought he sang nicely, but I *loved* his writing."

Two days later, Ellie stepped into Associated Recording and recorded the demos with Neil. He was still on her mind when she returned to Leiber and Stoller's office later that afternoon: "I remember saying to Jeff that I had just done a demo for a guy named Neil Diamond. I said that I thought he really was very talented writing-wise, and that he sang pretty good. And I thought that maybe Jeff could meet him . . . that maybe we could work something out with him."

·4·
TOUCHÉ

When Ellie Greenwich first broached the subject of Diamond, Jeff Barry cut her short: "Nah, we don't have time." But Ellie was firm: "I think you really should listen to him."

Barry finally agreed to meet Neil several weeks later, and was glad he did. "After Neil left, he and I had a talk," Ellie recalled. "Jeff said he liked the way Neil wrote, but *loved* the way he sang. And as I had loved the way Neil wrote and liked the way he sang, I said, 'Wellll, with those kind of feelings, if we could put the two together maybe we could like do something with Neil Diamond.'"

The couple met together with Diamond, and then introduced him to Jerry Leiber and Mike Stoller. Shortly thereafter, the legendary writing/producing team, whose credits included "Hound Dog," "Jailhouse Rock," "Kansas City," "Stand By Me," and "Charlie Brown," signed Diamond to a three-month publishing deal at Trio Music at $150 a week with the understanding that Greenwich and Barry would produce Neil Diamond tracks for release on their label, Red Bird Records.

It wasn't quite the arrangement Jeff and Ellie had in mind. Having discovered Diamond, Ellie claimed that they had pursued "joint ownership" of Diamond with Leiber and Stoller. (In response, Mike Stoller said: "I can only tell you that they wanted to produce him for the label. And we signed him on the understanding that they were to be his producers.")

Greenwich said she and Barry didn't want to make waves with Leiber and Stoller over the ownership issue, opting for a "let's see what happens" approach. As it turned out, hardly anything did.

Just why Neil's stint at Trio Music was so uneventful seems to be a matter of debate. According to Jerry Leiber, he and his partner were tied up with other projects at the time and probably didn't move fast enough to satisfy Diamond: "I do remember there was some talk [with Barry and Greenwich], 'If you're not going to record Neil, give him a release.'"

Yet, Mike Stoller claimed that Barry and Greenwich were the reason a Neil Diamond record never wound up on the Red Bird label: "Jeff and Ellie told us that they had lost interest in Neil as a recording artist and no longer wished to produce him."

"Those were very hectic days," Jeff Barry said. "At the time Mike said, 'Hey, look, are you going to cut that Neil guy?' we might have been on our way to the Coast to work with Phil Spector, and had to cut a new Shangri-Las record . . . and we might have said, 'I don't know, Mike, we've got so much to do right now.' So Mike might have walked away feeling we're bored in general with him, or nothing's going to happen. And then we could have talked to Jerry a week later. Neil might have said, 'Look, why don't you guys record us,' and we could have . . . been back from the Coast and said OK. He might have said, 'I want to be out of Jerry and Mike, they haven't done anything,' so I might have said to Jerry at the time [give Neil his release]."

However it came about, the fact is after Neil's three months at Trio Music was up, he was on the streets again.

But not for long. Jeff and Ellie, who just so happened to have plenty of time on their hands now, huddled with him about going into business together. On June 25, 1965, they did just that, forming Tallyrand Music, Inc., as the exclusive publisher of his songs as well as the exclusive producer/exploiter of his recordings.

Under the terms of the contract, Diamond was installed as president of the firm, and made a 50 percent owner. He also was to draw a $150-a-week advance against writing royalties. As there was no money in the Tallyrand kitty, Barry and Greenwich agreed to loan enough money to the firm to cover those payments for at least six months.

All in all, it was an almost-unheard-of deal for a writer who hadn't yet scored his first chart hit, and an indication of Neil's business acumen. "I would have killed for ownership!" Greenwich exclaimed, reflecting on all the hit tunes she and Jeff had written without securing a portion of the publisher's share of the royalties.

But getting such a great deal from his Tallyrand partners was only the icing on the cake. To Neil, the idea that fellow Brooklynite Barry and Long Island–born Greenwich, with their track record, would commit themselves to his career like they had was the cake itself.

And yet Neil acted almost nonchalant about his association with them, at least in their company. His attitude took Greenwich by surprise. "He didn't go 'Oh wow, terrific!' like other people had done with us," she recalled. "He was kinda cool, like [matter-of-fact voice] 'Hey, that'll be great. I really respect you guys for what you've done.'"

Diamond's actions at the time, however, spoke of the new lease on life he was feeling. After eight years of almost continuous enrollment at New York University, he left the School of Commerce, and he and Jay, who was now pregnant, moved into their first house. Greenwich visited them, and found their wood-paneled cottage in Massapequa, Long Island, to be "really adorable . . . like a cute, little young-married-couple-who's-got-it-together-but-still-living-within-their-means" kind of place.

That fall, as Jeff, Ellie, and he began casting around for a record deal, Diamond's career received an unexpected boost: a hit song. What had happened is that Leiber and Stoller had gone into the studio with Jay and the Americans to record "Sunday and Me," an upbeat love song that Neil had written while under contract to Trio Music. The tune—which Neil heard for the first time on the radio the day that Jay gave birth to their daughter Marjorie—went on to crack *Billboard*'s Top 20.

It seemed the best of omens.

Among the record biz movers and shakers that Neil auditioned for in late 1965 was Atlantic Records vice-president Jerry Wexler. A specialist in soul and R&B (rhythm and blues)—he had produced such classics as Ray Charles' "I Got a Woman" and, only recently, Wilson Pickett's "In the Midnight Hour"—Wexler might not have seemed the type to get excited about Diamond and his country- and folk-flavored pop songs. But he claimed he was "knocked out" when Diamond played for him live in his office.

"Great songs—and a terrific voice," he recalled. "What I saw was the big commercial bucks, a long-running thing. It transcended rock noise. It wasn't a quickie because it was MOR [middle of the road], it was ballads, it had durability. And I was looking down the line, rather than at a spectacular, exploitive hit."

Atlantic seemed a sensible place for Neil to go. By then a powerhouse in the R&B field, the label, founded in 1948, had gradually expanded its roster to include R&B-flavored rock acts like the Coasters, as well as a straight-ahead rocker by the name of Bobby "Splish Splash" Darin. It was Darin, in fact, who had scored Atlantic's biggest hit to that point with "Mack the Knife." That cabaret-style tune transformed him from teen hero into a pop superstar. Among his fans was Neil, who was considering pitching Darin on recording a tune that he had recently written called "Solitary Man."

Enthused about the prospect of another Darin-style artist on the roster, Wexler wasted no time talking contract. By the end of the meeting, he had informally agreed to the terms of a recording deal with the trio from Tallyrand.

The next day, however, Wexler got a call from a former staff producer of his who had just started his own Atlantic-affiliated label. Bert Berns had also laid his ears on Diamond and he had a pitch of his own: "Listen, Jeff's a good friend of mine, and I love Neil. How about putting him on Bang Records instead of Atlantic?"

"Of course the intelligent thing for me to have done was to keep him on Atlantic, especially if hindsight were to prevail," Wexler said. "but I wanted to nurture this little, fledgling company that we had." So Wexler made another of his snap decisions, telling Berns that, yes, he would hand Diamond over to him.

Obviously, Neil approved of the Wexler-Berns juggling act; on January 6, 1966, Tallyrand Music entered into a contract for Neil's recording services with WEB IV, Bang Records' parent firm. Over the next twelve months, Tallyrand agreed to supply four Diamond singles to Bang; also, WEB IV was granted four one-year options to extend the deal. For signing, Tallyrand received a nominal advance of $2,500.

Why would Neil, Jeff, and Ellie choose to chance a one-man operation when they could have signed with Atlantic Records? One need only review the career of Bertram R. Berns, one of rock 'n' roll's unsung greats, to understand.

Only several years earlier, Berns had been a struggling songwriter. That's when Jerry Wexler, his first important patron, took him under his wing. "He was a very rudimentary musician, but everything he played had a great touch to it, very idiosyncratic," Wexler recalled. The funk-type songs themselves struck him as fresh and vital, in no small part because Berns had flavored many of them with his beloved Latin rhythms. "That's something that he picked up in Cuba," Wexler said, adding that Berns often referred to his stint as a Havana club owner during the Batista regime.

One of the first songs Wexler took from Bert was an earthy rocker with a hooky Latin chord progression that he had written with Wes Farrell. Wexler recalled that he and Phil Spector recorded a lousy version of the tune with Derek and Howard, "while Bert was sitting in the control room biting his nails—we didn't allow him to say anything." The record went nowhere, so it was up to Bert to produce "Twist and Shout" with the Isley Brothers in 1962. The song, later covered by the Beatles, put Berns on the songwriting/producing map. Meanwhile, that distinctive chord progression in "Twist and Shout," which came to be known as the "'La Bamba' bass line," became a Berns trademark.

Realizing he had a real talent on his hands, Jerry Wexler invited Bert into the studio with him to produce a song with Solomon Burke that Bert had written, "Cry to Me." The tune was a hit on the R&B charts, and it led to other Wexler-Burns coproductions at Atlantic. "And then," said Wexler, "I turned him loose as a producer on his own . . . At the end of the first year I think we figured out that Bert had graduated from $50 a week to $60,000 a year."

Relentlessly energetic and ambitious, Berns didn't limit himself to Atlantic projects, however. By 1965, in fact, he was poised to leave Atlantic for United Artists, where he had been offered a production deal and his own record label. "Well, you don't leave here—this is home," Wexler told him. "We'll do the same thing for you."

And that's how WEB IV and its subsidiary, Bang Records, came into being. To demonstrate his fellowship with his Atlantic sponsors/partners, Berns spelled out the names of both WEB and Bang by utilizing his own initials along with those of Atlantic cofounder Ahmet Ertegun; Ertegun's brother, Neshui Ertegun, an Atlantic executive; and Gerald Wexler.

When WEB IV was founded, Wexler said, it was agreed that the company's main focus would be on publishing Berns' and other writers' tunes, with record production taking a back seat. It wasn't fated to be: Bang Records had two hits right out of the box. The first was with none other than Neil's Lincoln High friend, Bobby Feldman, and his song-writing partners, Jerry Goldstein and Richard Gottehrer, who had resurfaced as the "Australian" gag group, the Strangeloves. The song: "I Want Candy." A couple of months after that, a discovery of Feldman-Goldstein-Gottehrer, the McCoys, gave Bang its first number one hit—"Hang On Sloopy," a version of the Berns-Wes Farrell collaboration "My Girl Sloopy."

"Bert was totally alive, very enthusiastic, and very energetic, and he *loved* hits . . . that great line, that great hook, that great chorus, that great rhyme, that thing you just *know* will make people happy," Jeff Barry said of the budding record mogul. But in truth, every day of the year was a celebration of sorts for the chain-smoking man with the tou-pée that just about fit. His excitement spilled over to whatever was con-suming him at the moment, be it motorcycle riding, sailing his boat (which he called "A Little Bit of Soap," after the hit he wrote for the Jarmels), or pool playing. "He would loan you a hundred dollars and totally forget about it," recalled Barry, "but if you owed him a quarter at the end of the game, he would make you get change if you didn't have it."

Bert was so active, so alive it was hard to believe he was in poor health. But the fact was he had a bad heart. "I remember Bert as always taking pills and always being afraid of getting sick," recalled Bobby Feldman.

Many people in Bert's position would have adopted a more mea-sured pace in life. But Berns wasn't programmed to cool it. How could he when people like Jeff Barry kept laying potential hitmakers like Neil Diamond on him?

At a preproduction meeting for Neil, recording engineer Brooks Arthur saw what the fuss was about: "Jeff played a couple of figures on the piano and Neil whipped out his guitar and started singing. I was hit right between the eyes. Distinctive voice, a real baritone! And his feel—it was sort of like a blend of the Brill Building and the New York Pal-ladium . . . that Latin feel. Great energy."

There was no need for Berns to preach to the converted, but he gave Arthur one of his frenetic pitches anyway: "I know you're a very busy man now, but this is what we got to do, man, we got to really dig in, get this thing going, hang in with Neil, we gotta break him. It's a real important project to me, and we can all have a long and serious run if we put the pieces together."

At that same meeting, Arthur added, Berns shared his magnificent "vision" for Diamond: "He wanted him to be *Elvis.* He wanted him to be the biggest pop star the world has known."

The first time she heard "Solitary Man," Ellie Greenwich said she thought it was an absolute hit: "It was different, it was very melodic, the idea of the Solitary Man was real interesting." She added that she didn't even consider that the lyric might be a reflection of its author: "Neil was married—why would he be a Solitary Man?"

However, another of his potential singles at the time, the rocking "Money, Money," needed work. Jeff Barry related the saga of its rewrite in a 1971 interview with *Melody Maker*: "D'you want to know some of the songs I wrote that people don't know I wrote? Well, I kinda helped Neil Diamond out an awful lot . . . He wrote a song called 'Money, Money' . . . and I said let's play it for Bert Berns. Bert being Bert, he wanted to hear songs about boy/girl and all that, which to me is the best way to go, too.

"He said, 'Ah, what's all this "Money, Money" stuff? It should be "Baby Baby, Cherie, Cherie."' I said yea, Cherry, Cherry, and on the spot I came up with . . . the chorus."

After "Money, Money" had been rewritten, Berns gave Barry and Greenwich $5,000 and told them to go in the studio. On Valentine's Day, Neil stepped into Dick Charles, a small studio on Seventh Avenue, and recorded "Solitary Man" and "Cherry, Cherry."

Jeff and Ellie demonstrated their inventiveness as producers by hiring a trio of trombonists to play on the tracks. "When the guys walked in with their cases, it looked like the Salvation Army—we're making a rock 'n' roll record with trombones!" exclaimed Artie Butler, the arranger/piano player on the session.

Ellie thought she had heard just the place for trombones on "Solitary Man": "No one could figure out what to do with the middle section. And I always loved what they call fugues . . . So Jeff and Artie said, 'If you know what you want, why don't you take a shot?'" The only problem was that Ellie wasn't an arranger and could write out music with all the speed of a stone carver. Still, she persevered with the aid of some music books, and after seventeen hours of tortuous work, she managed to commit her ideas to paper.

Barry worked in his own little bit of trombone magic on the cut, employing them to shadow Neil's vocals. Of the twenty-plus Diamond tunes he produced, "Solitary Man" is his favorite for that touch. "I

40

think it is a good example of not overproducing, letting the song come through," he noted.

Ironically, "Cherry, Cherry," which was also recorded with horns that day, did sound overproduced, at least to Bert Berns. A week later, Barry, Greenwich, and Diamond entered A&R Recording Studios and recorded the track again. This time there were no horns, just Neil on acoustic guitar, Herb Lavelle on drums, Dick Romoff on upright bass, and Artie Butler on acoustic piano, and a few riffs on organ, the only plugged-in instrument on the date. As with "Solitary Man," Jeff and Ellie sang background vocals, and contributed hand claps.

This version Berns loved.

Still, Bert made the decision to release "Solitary Man" first, which made sense, as the tune, with its inherent mystique, could serve as Neil's musical calling card. But before anything could be released under his name, Diamond had to decide what his stage name should be.

According to him, he had grown unsure about "Neil Diamond": "I thought . . . 'It's too normal. It's boring . . . And "Diamond" sounds like somebody made it up.'"

"I think he didn't realize that 'Neil Diamond' was quite a nice name and suited him fine," said Barry, who argued against "Eice Cherry," which Neil was considering. At the last minute, Neil saw it Jeff's way.

"Solitary Man" was released April 4. Touting Diamond's arrival on the scene was a two-thirds-page ad that Berns took out in *Billboard*. The ad featured a black-and-white side shot of a reflective Neil sitting with his guitar, and the words, "Bang Records proudly announces the birth of a great new artist, Neil Diamond . . . "

"Solitary Man" hit the airwaves at a time when folk-rock was still in full flower . . . when the Byrds were flying "Eight Miles High," the Mamas and Papas were getting bummed out on "Monday, Monday," and Nancy Sinatra's boots were walking all over the charts.

While rooted in the current sound, "Solitary Man" was no run-of-the-mill folk-rock record, however. It featured a vocalist who sounded like nobody on Top 40 radio at the time: of deeper voice, with a unique accent—a mix of East Coast and Everly Brothers. Then there were those trombones.

To top it off, the brooding lyric—this tale of a jilted, defeated loner retreating into his solitariness—was original and striking, definitely the stuff from which an image could be forged.

Los Angeles took "Solitary Man" in from the cold; it cracked the Top 10 there. It scored well in a few other markets, too. However, it only spent a brief time on the national charts, peaking at number fifty-five.

According to Bang's general manager, Julie Rifkind, who was in the trenches selling "Solitary Man," just getting it that high was an accomplishment. "It wasn't a hit at all," he recalled. "And if I'm patting myself on the back, it's only because it's the truth—we did a wonderful job as far as radio was concerned in getting it exposed. And we did an unbelievable job of moving it up the charts. 'Cause the theory was we believed in Neil Diamond as an artist, and that if this wasn't a hit, the next one was going to be a hit."

To help create interest in Neil on the record store level, Rifkind said that Bang gave thousands of his records away, starting with "Solitary Man": "If the distributor ordered 600 records and was sitting with them, I'd say, 'Look, I'm going to have to eat these records anyway. Take them to the stores, give them out for nothing.' At that time not many companies were doing that. Being a small, independent label we were able to do anything we wanted." (Regarding Bang's "independent" status, Bert Berns and Atlantic Records never did go into business together. According to Jerry Wexler, "We got into some rather heavy disagreements.")

Having been a one-and-done artist at Columbia, Neil could thank his lucky stars for Bang's commitment. Fortunately for him, Berns and Rifkind never were forced to reconsider their position. The reason was "Cherry, Cherry," his second Bang single.

Released in July, the rocker with Bert Berns' lucky Latin riff bomped onto the *Billboard* charts. It continued its climb in August and September. By October, it had peaked at glorious number six.

·5·
MAKING BELIEVERS

Bert Berns captured the excitement of the cheery "Cherry" period in his wacky liner notes for Diamond's first Bang LP, "The Feel of Neil": "The phones in our offices are ringing like mad. Distributors all over the country are screaming for a Neil Diamond LP . . . We book a gang of studio time and pray we can get Neil off the road."

The album was a rush job: Five of the twelve tunes were covers, "Red Rubber Ball," "La Bamba," "New Orleans," "Monday, Monday," and Barry-Greenwich's own "Hanky Panky." The banter at the beginning of that track—Diamond balks at singing the song as Jeff and Ellie chant "Do it!"—epitomized the freewheeling, high-spirited feeling of the album as a whole.

Lest "Feel of Neil" record buyers get the idea that the Solitary Man was having *too much* fun, he posed for the album cover photograph in black jacket, pants, and boots, fixing the camera with a convincingly sullen expression.

Meanwhile, out of the camera's range, Neil could be found shaking his head in disbelief that he had *finally* arrived as a pop artist. "He would almost like laugh every time he talked to you," mused engineer Brooks Arthur, "as if to say, 'I can't believe this is happening to me.'"

As selling LPs was not Bert Berns' and Bang's highest priority, "Feel of Neil" was left to fend for itself in the marketplace, peaking at a lowly number 130 in *Billboard*.

The single hits kept coming, however. The ballady "I Got the Feeling (Oh No No)" crested at number sixteen in October, and the infectious rocker "You Got to Me," Diamond's fourth release of 1966, peaked only two slots lower.

By then, Brooks Arthur said, the Diamond-Barry-Greenwich-Berns team had become a finely honed hit-making machine: "Neil would walk in and people would come to attention without him having to say, 'Let's go, guys.' And, laced together with the energy of Bert, the energy of Jeff, and the energy of Ellie—watch out, you had to fasten your safety belt, because things moved like a bullet!

"We'd cut three to four tracks in an afternoon. I'm talking about tracks—overdubs, background vocals, percussion, maybe horns, maybe strings, then Neil's vocal and a rough mix. And the next day Bert and I would come back and mix again. And Neil would be there with his guitar slung over his shoulder, or at his side, using it as a leaning post. And his body language was imposing, absolutely imposing. The guy was big time—big time in the way he was delivering the hits, big time in the way he was growing as a songwriter."

However, in some areas—his vocal performance, for example— Neil still had a few things to learn.

While Jeff Barry, who had had dreams of becoming a solo recording artist himself, downplayed his contributions to Neil's improvement as a singer, others saw his influence on Diamond. Said one of them, Artie Kaplan, a musician contractor who was an acquaintance of both Barry and Diamond: "I believe the inflections, the mannerisms, the phrasing on all those records was really Jeff. If the name wasn't Neil Diamond [on the labels], it might have been Jeff Barry."

But, of course, it *was* Neil Diamond's voice, and it was Neil who was getting famous. And now that he had a name, he found himself suddenly confronted with a new, crucially important challenge: becoming a face. The best way for him to do that was to perform.

"Once I got onstage, it was, for some reason, very natural for me. I took to it immediately."

—Diamond

Those were curious words considering Jack Packer's words-eye picture of an uptight, solemn, and totally uncharismatic Diamond at their first performance a half dozen years earlier.

Yet Neil speaks publicly about his first performances as a Bang recording artist with a breezy upbeatness. On his first series of dates, several three-song one-nighters in Florida and a performance at the Hollywood Bowl as part of a multiact rock extravaganza: "It was fantastic."

The truth was, Neil was just as terrible onstage in 1966 as he had been in 1960.

Musician contractor Artie Kaplan witnessed one of Neil's earliest onstage debacles, his performance at a marathon Philadelphia benefit for the wives and children of Pennsylvania prison inmates. "He stood in front of the audience and he sang and played his beat-up old acoustic guitar," Kaplan recalled. "And he was really awkward city. As he came off stage, they were half-booing and half not paying attention to the poor guy, only because they were waiting for the Four Seasons . . . somebody big.

"And I remember walking over to him and saying, 'Don't worry about it, Neil; it's gonna be OK.' And he was really down, probably quite frustrated about the fact that he wasn't getting the reception he thought he deserved. And maybe a little confused about not even knowing how to perform.''

It was obvious to Diamond that he needed seasoning. One place that he decided to get it was at disc jockey Jack Spector's weekend hops.

By 1966, Spector, one of the WMCA ''Good Guys,'' had created a niche for himself in the New York rock world with his weekend dance shows, which he staged at churches and high schools around the city. Each hop featured a handful of acts whose only pay for a four- to six-song set was the exposure and the experience in working a crowd. Commented ''Strangelove'' Bobby Feldman of the Spector hop: ''It was our Catch a Rising Star.''

The disc jockey was happy to welcome Neil aboard his bandwagon, not only because of his hit credentials, but also because he remembered him from Brooklyn as a nine-year-old. ''Him and a lot of kids would hang around and watch us big kids,'' Spector mused. ''And they'd be sent on little errands, for a Coke or an egg cream. The thing you'd do is let them keep the deposit for the bottle.''

The first time Spector put his former gofer on stage, he knew that Diamond had a lot of work in store. ''The way he performed at first— the word that instantly jumps to my mind is *tentative,*'' the deejay recalled. ''He didn't quite know what to do. He didn't have an act.'' Yet Spector added that he could sense a performer in Neil bursting to get out: ''You *noticed* Neil, you just *noticed* him. It was the way he carried himself. It was as though, 'I'm not there yet, but in my mind *I* know I'm a star.'''

At the same time Neil was spending his weekend nights singing for high school teens, he was gaining onstage seasoning in a totally different world at the Bitter End.

He had a special entrée into the Greenwich Village club, a red-hot haven of folk-flavored music and comedy at the time, for he had taken on Fred Weintraub, the club's owner, as his manager.

On the surface, it seemed an odd matchup. The burly, bearded Weintraub, a onetime piano player in a Havana brothel, effected an old beatnik image—despite the fact that he was a graduate of the Wharton School of Business. Diamond, meanwhile, was as square as they came, and a purveyor of infectious pop music that wasn't exactly from the cutting edge.

Yet each had something the other was interested in. Diamond's utter commerciality appealed to the bottom-line businessman in Weintraub (''Freddy always knew a way to make money,'' recalled Bitter End manager Bill DeSeta. ''I mean the guy had the Midas Touch''), and Weintraub's hip standing appealed to the career plotter in Diamond, who knew that if he was to have any staying power he would have to transcend the hop scene.

Of course it was one thing for Neil to enter the Bitter End world and another for him to actually be accepted, at least by the cliquey group of performers who hung out at the club. "In a sense we looked down our noses at him," said then singer-songwriter Jake Holmes. "There was a certain snobbery . . . he was not one of us folkies."

Neil was probably relieved to be the odd man out after he discovered just how flaky many of the denizens of the Bitter End actually were. Laughed Holmes: "Here he was the straightest guy in the world supposedly kicking off all these traces of this terrible Tin Pan Alley pop image of his . . . and he was thrust into a world of total insanity! Most of the people were so completely freaked out, drugged out, and spaced out."

Yet Neil, imbued with his usual sense of purpose, tenaciously stood his Bitter End ground. "We used to call him Hamlet because he was always walking around with the weight of the world on his shoulders," chuckled then-comic Mike Mislove, one of the Bitter End regulars. "You would never know that he was involved in a thing that was supposed to be fun, because he was so serious all the time."

(There was, in fairness to Neil, one Bitter End personality who claimed to have actually seen Diamond let his hair down. His name was George Memmoli, a comic who ran the club's late-night Drop-In improv sessions. Neil, he recalled, would often attend the sessions, presumably after putting his solitary striver persona to bed for the night, even taking it upon himself to call out bits from his seat in the last row. "They were great suggestions," Memmoli said, "Because they were right of the moment . . . what was happening as far as the [Vietnam] War was concerned, what was happening with the telephone company." The improv group's efforts, the comedian added, were often rewarded by one of Neil's "huge guffaws. He had a wonderful laugh . . . 'HAH HAH HAHHHH!' ")

Neil's first performances at the Bitter End were the same sorry affairs as his early hop appearances. "He was just *there*," Jake Holmes recalled. "He blended into the background . . . He just didn't have any sense of reaching out to the audience."

Weintraub, however, was a believer. According to Mike Mislove, the manager saw him as "much bigger than anybody else did at the time." He began to work extensively with Diamond in an effort to develop his onstage presence. He instructed him to put his guitar down for a song or two during his sets and really sell a song to an audience. He instructed him not to be so garrulous between songs because his nervous patter was putting people off. And he dressed him up, both physically—in blousy shirts, and tighter slacks, à la Tom Jones—and repertoire-wise, getting him to croon middle-of-the-road ballads such as "What Now, My Love."

Weintraub also put him to work. "Fred's theory was get 'em up on the stage, have 'em work every night, and let 'em develop," explained Jake Holmes. "He taught Neil that it can be a work in progress . . . that you can go on the road and flail around."

For that, Neil needed a band. Freddy helped him put his first one together by recruiting a few Village musicians at $125 a week.

Then it was off to Los Angeles, where, in December, Neil performed for a week at Dave Hull's Hullabaloo on Sunset, a dance club.

Neil, who wasn't yet getting rich off his Bang royalties, didn't exactly travel in style. He and band flew economy, and he took neither a roadie nor his own PA system. Stage clothes for the band were out of the question, too, so the scuffling musicians had to go onstage in their street clothes, which, guitarist Dick Frank, nineteen at the time, admitted were "less than gorgeous."

In Los Angeles, the band was put up at a West Hollywood motel miles away from the Hullabaloo. So Diamond rented a car for the band. One car. "There were three or four of us in that car," Frank groused. "We had to do everything together." To heap an indignity upon an indignity, penny-pinching Neil billed the band members for half the cost of the rental at the end of the week. "I protested bitterly," Frank said.

Diamond's Hullabaloo show was similarly cut-rate. "It was very shabby by today's standards, not well prepared," the guitarist commented.

Frank's account, however, was positively glowing in comparison to the devastating, though hilarious, review that appeared in the *Los Angeles Times*. In it, Digby Diehl captured Neil in all his flailing ingloriousness:

NEIL DIAMOND LOST IN
WORLD OF PERCUSSION

BY DIGBY DIEHL

Dave Hull's Hullabaloo is probably one of the cruelest places in the world to toss a songwriter. Yet there stands Neil ("I'm a Believer") Diamond hopelessly wafting his lyrics into that gigantic echo chamber over a writhing sea of teen-age flesh which is blandly unreceptive to anything but the thud and crash of percussion.

Diamond's opening night appearance at the club this weekend put nary a dent in the bobbing mass of hair spray and chewing gum, despite a dutiful attempt at enthusiastic vocalizing. "I Wrote the Book" [sic], his uptempo starter, sent the teenies bopping for all they were worth, apparently unaware that Diamond's guitar twanged impossibly flat.

Then, while a rusty tangerine spotlight bathed the dance floor, Diamond crooned an electronic organ-backed ballad, the words of which were indistinguishable.

"We have some of the most beautiful women in the world and some of the most beautiful problems in the world," said Neil suavely introducing "I Got the Feeling." After a travesty of this tune, during which he shifted tempos four times, he turned to the hard-hitting sounds of "La Bamba" and "Rock 'n' Roll Music."

The relative success of his Presley imitation was erased, however, in Diamond's outrageous rendition of "What Now, My Love." He sang a full minor second out of key while the drummer floundered miserably in search of the beat.

Crippled by an incompetent band and plagued by acoustical troubles, Diamond wandered through a dragging version of "I'm a Believer" before making a strategic retreat from the stage.

As a songwriter, his success has been assured with such hits as "Sunday and Me," "Solitary Man," "Cherry, Cherry," "I Got the Feeling," and "I'm a Believer." And as a recording artist, Neil has hit the Top 40; but his personal appearance at the Hullabaloo is sadly lacking in the evident talent that sparks his songs and records.*

Diamond and band then traveled to Bermuda, of all places, where Fred Weintraub had booked a two-week engagement for him at a Hamilton nightclub.

The first night, six people showed up. "I'll never forget the faces of the waiters who were not getting their usual tips," Neil later recalled. Several days later, he found himself taking an early plane back to New York.

As he returned to the performance drawing board, Diamond did have one happy diversion: monitoring the progress of a new tune of his that the Monkees had recorded, and which Diehl had mentioned in his review. In January 1967, "I'm a Believer" finally found a resting place on the *Billboard* charts . . . at number one.

Neil liked "I'm a Believer" immediately, but his original goal was to get the song cut by a country artist. "I remember him once kidding around with an acoustic guitar singing it in a deep drawl," said Bill Wexler, his keyboards player at the time, adding that Neil even had a singer in mind: Eddy Arnold, of "Make the World Go Away" fame.

Publisher Don Kirshner made that notion of Neil's go away. The cofounder of the Brill Building's legendary Aldon Music, home to such

*Copyright, 1966, *Los Angeles Times*

great teen-pop writing teams as Goffin-King and Mann-Weil, had gone on to head Columbia Screen Gems Music on the Coast. Now he was hustling hits for those teenybopper faves, the Monkees, a.k.a. "America's Answer to the Beatles." He called Neil one day to see if he had another "Cherry, Cherry" laying around that could serve as a follow-up to the group's initial smash, "Last Train to Clarksville." Neil: "I told him I didn't, but there was a song I had just completed that I liked very much, called 'I'm a Believer.' I went over and played it for him."

Kirshner was hot to make a deal, but only if Diamond forked over the publishing rights to Screen Gems. Under the special circumstances—the superbly hyped Monkees, after all, were only the hottest U.S. group going with their number-one-rated TV series—Neil said OK.

The next step was to get a track for the Monkees to overdub their vocals on. Turning the "Believer" project into a family affair, Kirshner hired Jeff Barry to produce the song.

Barry cut the track in New York using the same studio musicians who regularly played on Diamond's dates. Neil attended the session and laid down a reference lead vocal.

Barry then took the tape to Los Angeles, where he met the Monkees. He got on with all of them, save Michael Nesmith. "He was kind of slouched down on the couch," Barry recalled. "And I played the song, and everybody thought it was good. He said, *'That ain't no hit.'* And it got real embarrassing. He said, 'I'm a songwriter, too, and that's no hit. And I'm a producer, and that's no hit.'

"I didn't know what to say. Just kidding around, I said, 'You got to realize it's going to have strings on it.' Everybody knew I was kidding—you don't put strings on that record. But in his pomposity he said, 'Yeah, well, maybe OK with strings.' And everybody broke up . . . And he became furious."

Barry got ticked off himself; he banished Nesmith from the studio when Mickey Dolenz went in to cut the lead vocal.

The result was a hit, all right, *the* hit of 1967—commandeering the number one spot on *Billboard*'s Hot 100 chart for seven weeks straight. In the process it sold a reported five million copies in the United States alone.

Not only was Neil's Monkees connection destined to put some change in his pocket (his "A Little Bit Me, a Little Bit You" was fated to be the group's next release, eventually peaking at number two), it made him more visible to the press. Getting press, like performing, of course, was a crucially important way for him to heighten his profile.

Richard Goldstein was one of the first reporters to come knocking at his door. His sympathetic profile, which captured Neil in all his feeling-his-oats glory, appeared in the March 5, 1967 edition of the New York *World Journal Tribune.*

"If they know your name they use it," Neil said in reference to manager, agents, and record company executives. Then he exulted: "Nobody calls me 'baby' anymore."

The surprise of the interview came when Neil trashed "I'm a Believer," dismissing it as a "plain, happy, dumb" tune. In the process he served notice that teenybopper idol status for him was not an end, but a means to a more grandiose end: "After five or six more songs like 'I'm a Believer,' I should be able to write lasting songs, my way."

Diamond's ambivalent attitude toward his status as a teen fave in early 1967 was evident to the man Jeff Barry had hired to handle Neil's PR, Joe Cal Cagno, the father of Jeff's third wife (Barry and Greenwich were divorced in late 1965, although, of course, they continued to work together). "I thought he was a hunk that the girls would like, but his manner was not stardom," said Cal Cagno, a former gossip columnist for a passel of entertainment magazines. "Most talent that you groom for stardom, they're willing to work with you: 'Do you want me to change my hairdo? Do you want me to have my nose done?'" Neil, he said, didn't seem to be "pliable."

Indeed, Cal Cagno wound up having some trouble with Diamond. He would set up interviews for Neil, invariably with teenybopper publications—which had taken a keen interest in him—and then would have to persuade him to show. A few times, Neil didn't. Cal Cagno: "He'd call and say, 'Look, call 'em up and tell 'em something came up and I can't make it.' He was embarrassed."

The irony is that in the "fanzine" interviews that Neil did deign to give, the reticence he brought into the sessions—nothing like the braggart pose he had done with the New York *World Journal Tribune*—actually worked for him, enhancing his "Solitary Man" image. "The first thing you should know about Neil Diamond," an article in the March 1967 issue of *Flip* began, "is that he IS a 'Solitary Man'!" Accompanying the piece was a photo of a glum Diamond standing in the doorway of one of the magazine's offices, looking positively solitary and/or depressed at the prospect of appearing in the magazine.

At heart, however, Neil was also pragmatic. Thus, in the relative privacy of Jack Spector's Good Guy hops, he wasn't above playing teen idol to the hilt. He had the perfect musical vehicle to do just that with his first hit of 1967, the female prepubescent anthem, "Girl, You'll Be a Woman Soon."

Spector recalled Neil's performance of the song:

"He'd go down on his knees and work the girls at the edge of the stage . . . and touch hands, fingers. And he'd single one girl out, and maybe he would help lift her to the edge of the stage, and he'd work to her. He'd sing the entire song to that one girl, who at first would be giggly and nervous, but after a while would be looking at him in rapt attention."

Lest Diamond's facile manipulation of his female fans give the impression that he'd suddenly become a crack performer since his Hullabaloo and Bermuda disasters, band member Bill Wexler recalled an embarrassing Bitter End show of his at the time in front of no less a talent scout than Johnny Carson, who was considering Neil for an appearance on the "Tonight Show."

Diamond had insisted on singing the Tony Bennett ballad "If I Ruled the World" in the show, apparently to demonstrate his versatility. The problem, the keyboards player explained, was that "it was very difficult for him to sing in tune on songs other than three-chord songs"— in other words, songs Neil didn't write himself.

Sure enough, Wexler added, Neil botched the tune at the Bitter End, and the rest of his show wasn't very good either. He never did appear on the "Tonight Show," although Spanky and Our Gang, the act that shared the bill, did.

Less pressure-packed performances of Diamond's at the club, however, did reveal some progress. Part of his improvement, Jake Holmes theorized, was tied to the fact that the audiences "began to pick up on him. And it was then OK—feedback!"

In the spring of 1967, Neil began replacing members in his band. His first new hiree was drummer Tom Cerone.

It was the unlikeliest gig Cerone could have imagined the previous summer, when, in a car with some people, he heard "Cherry, Cherry" come blaring out over the radio. "And I hear it's by a guy named Neil Diamond," the self-described "acerbic cat" recalled. "And I'm laughing. 'Neil Diamond—what a name! It's probably some Puerto Rican kid from New York, and this is the last we're ever going to hear from this guy.'"

Soon after he joined forces with Neil, Cerone had a priceless story to tell on his boss, courtesy of Neil's bass player, Max Sandler:

"They were someplace in Texas, I think, where they were doing two shows. Neil had gotten paid so much before the show, and the rest between shows. And he had no place to put the money—the dressing room couldn't be locked—so he puts the money in his boot. And he goes out to do the second show.

"Now, all night long, the light man has missed Neil. Neil goes stage right, the light man is on stage left. It's a real fiasco. Until Neil's been dancing around on 'La Bamba,' the closing tune. Now the money has *worked its way out of the boot*. The money is now *falling out on the stage!* And Neil is trying to discreetly pick up the money. All of a sudden, the light man becomes an ace with the light! No matter where Neil goes the light is on him!"

Cerone recalled awkward moments in his first outings with Diamond as well. He also noted, shortly into a monthlong Dick Clark Caravan of Stars bus tour, that Neil wasn't exactly born to the breed of rock 'n' roll gypsy. "The bus lasted about three days," he recalled, laughing. "Then Neil said, '*The hell with this,*' and he sent Max back to New York to get a limo."

Still, Cerone was able to glimpse Neil's lurking sense of humor in an off-the-wall prank he pulled on one of his Caravan costars, Keith of "98.6" fame. During Keith's set one night, he came onstage uninvited with his guitar, cowboy hat, and sunglasses and casually strolled in front of Keith and band with a "What are we doing here?" look on his face.

Back in New York, Tom Cerone hired Artie Richards as Diamond's new guitarist. As with the drummer, there was an irony involved in Richards' arrival on the scene—a jazz buff who'd last been seen in a tuxedo backing a supper-club crooner in Atlanta, he had no idea that Diamond was engaged in rock. "Neil Diamond, he's a slick lounge singer—that's what's in my mind," he said.

When he left his audition with Cerone, of course, he knew better. Listening to the Diamond records he had been given back at his apartment, he became convinced the gig would be a cakewalk: "I didn't like what I heard on the records, and I said to myself, 'I can really make it sound better than this.'" For Richards, that meant jazzing up the guitar parts, literally.

Neil, on his first promotional trip to London at the time, wasn't around to pass judgment on Richards' handiwork. The first time Neil heard Richards play, in fact, was onstage at a dingy Brooklyn club called the Action House, where he was improbably billed with the psychedelic-flavored Vanilla Fudge.

Richards made an immediate impression—the wrong one. "Neil almost froze," Richards recalled. "He turned around and looked at me, and then around at the band, in stark terror. Like, 'What the hell is going on here?'"

It was then that Neil spoke his first words to Richards, other than his preshow hi-how-are-you: "Can I play your guitar?" Abashed, Richards surrendered it; in return, he received a tambourine. For the rest of the set he tapped on it. "It was extremely embarrassing," he said.

Richards extracted an obvious insight into Diamond from that rocky musical introduction: "Came to find that Neil is so *finicky* about what he wants to hear from a guitar player." He vowed to Neil after the show to stick to the feel of Neil in the future.

The gigs began to fly by, as Neil became ever more committed to putting his act together, literally and figuratively.

Some of the bills were every bit as off-the-wall as Diamond–Vanilla

Fudge. There was, for example, the night in Connecticut where he shared the stage with Junior Walker and the All Stars and King Curtis, and the audience, according to Tom Cerone, was "102 percent black." Afterward, he recalled, one young black woman ran up to Diamond and band, and exclaimed, *"I didn't know white people had any soul!"*

Then there was the Chattanooga, Tennessee, bill that promised a little something for every teen: the guitar-and-amp-bashing Who, Herman's Hermits, the psychedelic Blues Magoos, the countryish Billy Joe Royal . . . and Neil.

For those multiact extravaganzas, said Cerone, "You cleared your throat and you got off." Included in their small repertoire were his Bang hits to date, "I'm a Believer," and Neil's show-closer, "La Bamba." The one problem with spotlighting the Ritchie Valens hit like that was that Neil never got the Spanish lyrics quite right. "I remember one night some Spanish kid coming backstage and saying, 'Great show, great show—*what were you singing?*'"

As Neil gradually gained in popularity in 1967, the bills got smaller, and his shows got longer, allowing him the luxury of pacing his set. He liked starting out easy, especially when he was headlining, and the show was, in effect, presold. "It would be dark onstage," Cerone said. "All you'd hear would be the chords to 'Solitary Man.' Then he'd start singing the first verse, with just a pin spot on him. By the chorus, the band would build, and that's when we'd bring up the lights and start cooking." From "Solitary Man," the typical set would build a little, come back down, and finally, in Cerone's words, "kick ass."

By the summer, Neil had a new hit to perform at the end of his show: the gospel-flavored rocker "Thank the Lord for the Night Time." In the fall, he had more fodder for his more laid-back moments onstage: the countryish "Kentucky Woman."

Cerone and the rest of the band happened to be with Neil when he wrote 90 percent of "Kentucky Woman"—in the back seat of a car outside of Paducah, Kentucky. Tom was impressed with other aspects of Neil, such as his magnetism ("If he was in a room full of people you'd be drawn to him for some reason"), but it was Neil's ability to whip out tunes like "Kentucky Woman" that really knocked him out. "If you said to Neil, 'Give me a song about oranges named Billy,' he would come up with a viable song about oranges named Billy."

One day in the midst of musing on his boss, Cerone came up with what was, to him at least, the last word on Neil Diamond.

"You know what you are, man?" he blurted out in his razzy voice.

"What?" Neil replied suspiciously.

"You're a lucky Jew from Brooklyn who writes a nice ditty and thinks he's a country singer."

Neil smiled. "You may be right."

55

·6·
BAD BLOOD

People are looking for what they ain't got
Runnin' and pushin' for I don't know what
But I'm gonna stake out my own piece of shade
Count all the money I ain't never made
No, no, no, I ain't got a single plan . . .

Those lines, amusingly ironic considering Diamond's breakneck pace in 1967, serve as proof that he could write about almost anything he set his mind to—even solitary moments spent with a soft drink. The next two lines read:

Wind in my face and a Coke in my hand
*No, no, no, I'm happy right where I am.**

Aiming to cash in on his newfound celebrity, Neil wrote and sang another radio ditty for Coke that year, as well as performing spots for Thom McAn Shoes, Buick, and H.I.S. slacks. Bill Backer, the McCann-Erickson advertising executive who hired Neil for the Coca-Cola assignment, described Neil as a musical pitchman:

"Mostly, we worked with the writers, cowriting the songs. But Neil was more of a loner writer. After we sat and talked for two or three hours about the kinds of subjects [we were open to], the feeling of Coke . . . he went off and wrote himself. And what he wrote needed almost no changing at all—only a line here or there . . . He understood this project and hit it quicker than anyone that I have ever worked with."

The former School of Commerce student displayed his bottom-line fiscal orientation one day when his wife Jay was said to have remarked to him, "Tell me, what *was* your inspiration?" Expecting Neil to wax poetic on the reasons why he had chosen the lot of the singer-songwriter—as, in fact, he would do in interview after interview in the years to come—she was caught off guard, an acquaintance claimed, when he sardonically replied: "Paying the rent."

Thanks to his income from several sources now, Diamond was managing the rent on his and Jay's new Manhattan apartment just fine.

*Copyright 1967, the Coca-Cola Co.

But Neil was not content. When he wasn't tied up performing, recording, or working on jingles, he was scheming in 1967 on a superstar future minus Bang Records.

He had a good, artistic reason to sour on Bert Berns and his small label, he would claim: Berns' refusal to release "Shilo," a new song of his, as a single. Declaring his special attachment to this Son of "Solitary Man," a tale of a youngster who creates a fantasy friend to ease the pain of his loneliness ("It was me, it was the story of my life as a child"), he would contend that he pleaded with Berns to change his mind. But Berns, who didn't deem the song commercial enough, wouldn't budge. Denied a "part of my development" as an artist, Diamond would maintain that he had no choice but to contemplate a recording arrangement elsewhere.

In truth, Neil did seem to be boxed in at Bang. His second album, "Just for You," released in August, only climbed to number eighty in *Billboard*, additional proof of the label's lack of muscle and/or interest in selling LPs. In addition, Berns demonstrated a less-than-enlightened approach toward album packaging by placing "Solitary Man" and "Cherry, Cherry," the two hits from the "Feel of Neil" album, on "Just for You" as well!

At the same time he watched his second album sputter on the charts, Diamond had to be noting the phenomenal success that summer of the Beatles' "Sgt. Pepper's Lonely Hearts Club Band." The breakthrough "concept" rock album instantly broadened the recording horizons of rock and pop artists everywhere.

Still, the pragmatic businessman in Neil probably could have tolerated the situation at Bang Records a while longer if he had been getting rich there. Figures later released by WEB IV, however, confirmed that Neil wasn't.

According to the report, Diamond's biggest Bang payday was the period ending September 30 of that year, when Tallyrand Music was credited with royalties of $40,869.02. The figure is more than twice Tallyrand's next-biggest payday to that point, for the period ending June 30, 1967: $19,043.86. The total sum reportedly paid out by WEB IV through September 1967 was $120,583.21. Even by late-'60s standards, the amount—which was less "sessions costs" of more than $20,000—seemed like small potatoes considering that Neil had then totaled two Top 10 and three Top 20 hits.

The payments raised the question of just how many records Bert Berns had been giving away in Bang's freewheeling campaign to establish Diamond. Neil later supplied his own estimate: three for every seven sold. Perhaps the giveaways were crucial to his acceptance at the record store level, but Neil, after the fact of his stardom, was less than understanding, contending that Bang's "radical" policy on freebies had deprived Tallyrand of substantial royalties.

In short, leaving Bang had also become a matter of dollars and cents to Neil.

Joe Cal Cagno was the first member of Diamond's team to get a fix on his restlessness.

At the time, the initially unimpressed PR man had already changed his mind on Neil, after reading through a slew of his fan mail. Along with the expected love notes from teen female fans, he noted with surprise that there were many letters from adult women, some of whom were old enough to be mothers of teenyboppers. It was Diamond's "sad-eyed puppy" look, Cal Cagno theorized, that was at the root of his appeal to the older fans. "And [these women were going] 'Hey, you poor baby, you need stroking; let me take you home.'

"That's when I realized this guy can make it," he continued. The next time he talked to Jeff Barry, he made a prediction: "Neil's gonna make it not as a teenybopper; he's gonna be like Presley. Because the older people, the mothers, have a physical attraction to him."

Using samples of his fan mail as a lure, Cal Cagno pitched Neil to a journalist acquaintance of his, Mike McGrady of *Newsday*. After perusing the mail, McGrady agreed to do a feature on Diamond, and proceeded to tape an in-depth interview with him at Cal Cagno's home. When it came time to write the piece, however, McGrady decided to scrap the interview and focus, instead, on the fan mail.

The resulting offbeat piece, published in April, makes entertaining reading. The letters zig from giddy pledges of eternal affection ("You're a lethal kind of wonderful") to somber praise ("I admire you like I admire Thomas Jefferson") to motherly admonitions ("Your image as a Solitary Man deepens the emotional impact of your songs . . . [but] I think you should know that solitude can shut you off from common or personal understanding"). And the letters aren't all from women; one young man beseeched Diamond to help him become a pop "Idle" himself.

Neil was elated with the article, Cal Cagno recalled. And so was the PR man, although he had a gnawing concern over the unpublished interview he had heard Neil give to McGrady.

"Neil had plans," he said. "He wanted to be a big man. He wanted to strike out on his own. Definitely he had a scheme—boy, I felt it . . . '*My* plans are . . . *I'm* gonna do this . . . *I* wanna record . . .' He wanted to get into top-quality stuff, and you can't blame the man for that. But my gut feeling was he was going to go it alone, that none of the people who were involved at the moment—Jeff, Bert Berns, me—were included in his plans."

Cal Cagno voiced his concerns to his son-in-law. "I told Jeff, 'Jeff, are you sure you have an agreement that's pretty solid with this guy?'

He said, 'Sure.' So I said. 'Well, let me see the contract.' And he brought me the [Tallyrand] deal . . . and I read it. And I said, 'Make sure he picks up that option, otherwise you have nothing.' He said, 'You mean to tell me it's his own company and he's not going to pick up the option?' I said, 'I don't think he's gonna pick it up . . . From the way he talked—Jeff, I've been in this business too long, and he feels muscle.'"

But Barry, Cal Cagno maintained, was disbelieving: "No, no, what are you talking about? Neil? We're friends."

Six months later, Jeff Barry, and Ellie Greenwich, could believe it. "I was sitting up at the UA office [United Artists Publishing, where, at the time, she and Barry were signed as staff writers], and I remember Neil coming in," Greenwich recalled. "He said he had to talk to Jeff and I, he wanted to leave the label. And I remember going, *'Oh my god, you can't do that.'* And he says, 'Oh yes I can.'

"And I remember he said he would like Jeff and I to continue with him as his producers. And we just felt that that wouldn't be ethical. We couldn't walk out of a contract. And he claimed that he had gone to see some attorneys and felt he could."

What his counsel had discovered, Diamond briefed his shocked producers and partners, was the fact that Tallyrand Music's contract with WEB IV was devoid of the standard new artist clause granting WEB IV the *exclusive* right to manufacture and market his records. The absence of this clause, he maintained, left him free to sign with whichever label he wanted.

But, Barry and Greenwich wanted to know, what about *their* deal with him, which stated very clearly that Tallyrand had the exclusive right to contract with a record company for his services. According to Greenwich, Diamond "claimed that there was probably something in the contract that would let him go from Tallyrand." Greenwich professed to being stunned: "I mean, he was still the *president* of Tallyrand."

Soon afterward, WEB IV, as a matter of course, notified Tallyrand by registered mail that it intended to exercise its second option to extend its agreement with Neil Diamond/Tallyrand Music for another year. Keeping true to his declaration of independence from Bang, Neil refused to cash or deposit the $2,500 advance that accompanied the letter.

A profile on Diamond in the December 2, 1967 issue of *Billboard* didn't make mention of Neil's intentions vis à vis Bang Records, but it did provide a revealing portrait of the artist as a young boat rocker. On the subject of his songwriting, for example, he vowed not to play it safe in the future: "If a writer takes himself seriously, he will constantly experiment with not necessarily avant-garde material but with relatively untried musical and lyrical material." The headline of the piece was prophetic: DIAMOND GOING AFTER NEW VISTAS.

It didn't take long for word of Diamond's intentions to waft up to

Brooks Arthur at 20th Century Sound Studios, which he co-owned with Jeff Barry: "Bert and Neil are going to be breaking up: Neil wants out. That's the word on the street."

About that time, Arthur recalled getting a call from the Coast from a couple of friends of his, Al Gorgoni, a studio guitarist who had played on some of Diamond's sessions, and songwriter Chip Taylor ("Angel of the Morning," "Wild Thing"). Lately the two had become a producing/songwriting team and, Arthur was told, they wanted to book a "mystery" date at Century Sound two weeks hence.

"Time rolls on, and nobody really knows what the session is," Arthur recalled. "Then the call comes in telling me what the rhythm section is gonna be, how many mikes, what kind of mikes, how many vocals, how many backgrounds. And the buzz around town is that it's Frank Sinatra. Frank Sinatra coming to our little studio? What a joy!

"It's a 10 A.M. call, and we get there at 8 and get that room spanking clean. We have the A team there, and the musicians wander in, Chip Taylor walks in, Al Gorgoni walks in and starts to work out with the band.

"And then we know the artist is walking up the steps. We hear him. And who is it but Neil D.! Neil! Black pants, black shirt—he looked like he was ready to do a show. 'Hey, Brooks, how ya doin'? How's Marilyn, how's the kids? What do you think of this?'"

As Neil began recording a new song, "Brooklyn Roads," Brooks Arthur was thinking of a couple of things simultaneously: "I realized what was happening—there was no Bert Berns, no Jeff and Ellie . . . it was the end of an era. And I was sitting at the console and crying because the song touched me . . . a Brooklyn boy . . . so much."

Several days later, Arthur heard from an animated Bert Berns. "Hey, man—ha ha—I hear you cut Neil. Well, now it's out—we're not on terms."

Despite his outward show of joviality, Berns, bad heart and all, was having a fit and a half over the prospect of his star artist taking a hike. In his mind, Berns felt he had *made* Neil Diamond. He could hear his trademark Latin bomp in Neil's "Cherry, Cherry," and he could point to his no-holds-barred singles marketing campaign—yes, including giving away those thousands of records—as the reason why Diamond had shot up onto the charts. He had always been there in the trenches, eagerly participating in skull sessions, attending Diamond's recording sessions—literally jumping up and down with joy when he thought he heard a hit—and selling, selling, selling Neil Diamond. He knew that as a new artist, Neil never could have hoped to have received this sort of attention from the president of a major label.

And now Diamond, his name made, was showing his thanks by splitting for greener pastures, leaving Berns high and dry at precisely the time he felt Diamond was near to fulfilling his promise as the next Presley. It wasn't right, he felt, and, besides, he couldn't *afford* to let Neil go. He knew all too well that of the 2,182,454 records that Bang had sold from April 1, 1966 through September 30, 1967, 1,160,575—slightly more than half—had embodied the performances of Neil Diamond.

So Bert Berns fought back with all the street savvy he had.

Demonstrating to the music world as well as to Diamond that Bang Records still considered itself in the business of releasing Neil Diamond products, he dug into Bang's vaults and pulled out Diamond's rendition of the 1961 Gary U.S. Bonds hit, "New Orleans," which had appeared on the "Feel of Neil" LP. On December 13, he released it as Neil's eighth Bang single.

Five days later, he had his attorney send the following telegram to CBS Records, MGM Records, A&M Records, and Warner Brothers Records, companies, he believed, that Diamond and manager Fred Weintraub were talking to:

PLEASE BE ADVISED WEB IV MUSIC HAS EXCLUSIVE RIGHTS [TO] RECORDINGS OF NEIL DIAMOND FOR PHONOGRAPHIC RECORD PURPOSES AND OTHER RIGHTS. ANY INTERFERENCE WITH WEB IV'S RIGHTS AND ADVANTAGEOUS RELATIONS [WILL BE] IMMEDIATELY AND SUBSTANTIALLY DAMAGING.

Meanwhile, according to Diamond, "Bert started threatening me."

Asked for his perspective on the ugly turn in the Diamond-Berns feud, drummer Tom Cerone remarked: "I would advise you to go look at the logo for Bang Records . . . the smoking gun!"

A couple of scary things did happen at the time, although there was no proof that Berns was responsible. A performance of Diamond's at the Bitter End was abruptly halted when a stink bomb was tossed into the club. And Fred Weintraub claimed in a *Rolling Stone* interview that he was beaten up outside the Bitter End.

"It was hard. It was tough. Could be one of the toughest things Neil ever went through," said guitarist Artie Richards of that time.

Diamond sent his wife and daughter back to Long Island, but he hung tough himself. He packed a .38 and, two days after receiving Berns' telegram, he had his attorney, David Braun, fire off a letter in response. It read in part: "You are hereby advised that the notices served by your attorney constitute an attempt to damage our client's professional career. You will be held strictly accountable for any and all damages sustained by Mr. Diamond by reason of the untruthful statements."

A week later, Neil stopped accepting his weekly check from Tally-rand. That's when the second of Tallyrand's three one-year options on him expired, and—he would later claim—the third option was never formally picked up by a two-thirds vote of the Tallyrand board of directors. "Accordingly," he would assert, "I no longer regarded myself as under contract to Tallyrand," and thus, no longer associated with Jeff Barry and Ellie Greenwich.

While all this bad blood was being pumped, the year-end issue of the music trade weekly *Cash Box* hit the stands with a piece of pricelessly timed news: Neil had tied with Frank Sinatra for "Top Male Vocalist" of 1967. In an ad placed by his manager in that issue, Diamond added his own surreal touch to the feud by referring to the last two years of his career as "unbelievable."

Friday, December 29, sticks in Stephen Prince's mind as the day when relations between Diamond and Berns went from awful to potentially catastrophic. As assistant to Fred Weintraub at the time, Prince was behind the wheel of the manager's black Cadillac Fleetwood as Diamond and Weintraub hashed over a face-to-face meeting they had just had with Bert Berns. "They were not happy, and very upset," Prince remembered. "I am sure that Neil felt threatened. I felt threatened being in the car with him." Among the addled words he remembered being spoken: "We will get the bodyguards."

"I think they went to the district attorney," Prince added, "and they were going to give him bodyguards on Monday."

But Neil never did get his protection. The next day, Bert Berns died of a heart attack in his penthouse apartment on Seventy-second Street.

He was thirty-eight years old.

"I was sleeping, and Jeff called me and said that Bert had had a heart attack, and it was fatal," Ellie Greenwich recalled. "And I said, 'Well, how is he?' I mean, it didn't even connect. 'Ellie—he's *dead.*' And I just said, 'I can't even talk now' . . . I was like hysterical."

Tom Cerone heard the talk on the street: "The people [said], 'Neil caused that.'" But the drummer didn't buy it. "How could Neil cause that? He was doing business, you know what I mean?"

It could be said that Berns' widow, Ilene Berns, was doing business herself when on January 18, WEB IV Music, which she had taken over, filed suit against Tallyrand Music and Diamond in the Supreme Court, County of New York. In its action, WEB IV asked for a temporary injunction restraining Neil from recording for another label, as well as a declaratory judgment to the effect that the WEB IV–Tallyrand agreement was a binding one in which WEB IV had the exclusive right to

Diamond's recordings. Supporting the action were none other than Ellie Greenwich and Jeff Barry, who, as Tallyrand copartners, were "defendants" with Diamond in name only. "The omission [in the WEB IV–Tallyrand contract], if any, in specifically referring to 'exclusivity' is obviously inadvertent and should not be interpreted as even implying that the agreement of the parties was anything but exclusive," Greenwich wrote in her affidavit.

Diamond saw it differently in his answering affidavit, claiming that he noted the "non-exclusive" sales arrangement before he even signed the contract. He then took to the offensive himself, asserting that WEB IV had breached its contract with Tallyrand. Among the alleged breaches—later denied by WEB IV—were the company's failure to pay royalties on time, as well as recording costs in the sum of $11,000.

"There came a time in mid-1967 when the accumulating breaches by plaintiff produced a distinct souring of the relationship," Diamond wrote. "It was at that time that Tallyrand and I began to resist Bang's demands that we produce more master recordings—that is, recordings beyond our contractual requirements. When I informed Bang of this, in the person of Mr. Berns . . . Mr. Berns began to threaten me . . . He told me that he had the power to ruin my career . . . He said that he . . . 'owned' an interest in a new recording artist named Van Morrison and that it would be a simple matter for Bang to advance Morrison's career and stagnate mine by promotion, advertising and selection and timing of recordings to be released. I did not intend to permit this to happen."

As he engaged in the war of words with WEB IV, Neil demonstrated his confidence in his legal position by continuing his negotiations with other record companies, as well as granting an interview to *Newsweek* in which he sounded a bullish tone on both his short-term and long-term future.

Among his statements was his declaration that the new songs he was writing "are the toughest things I've done since being a busboy in the mountains . . . I can't settle for easy lyrics anymore. I don't just want hits, I want to write important songs."

On March 12, Supreme Court Judge J. Streit issued his ruling: "Plaintiff has failed to show a clear right to the relief demanded or that it will suffer irreparable injury . . . In weighing the equities, it would appear more harm would be suffered by Diamond in granting the [temporary] injunction than would the denial upon plaintiff . . .

"The motion is denied."

Six days later, Neil signed a five-year recording deal with a dark-horse candidate for his services, fledgling Uni Records, located in Hollywood, a very attractive 3,000 miles away.

·7·
PRACTICALLY NEWBORN

> *"They gave me total creative freedom."*
> —Diamond, on why he
> selected Uni Records

While Diamond's pact with Uni came as a surprise to many, it came as a shock to Columbia Records. According to the account in his auto-biography, company president Clive Davis had already shaken hands with Fred Weintraub on a deal that would have returned Neil to the Columbia fold. In a demonstration of the closeness between the two camps, Columbia's Walter Dean had filed an affidavit on Diamond's behalf in the WEB IV suit, in which he stated his own "consistent prac-tice" in inserting exclusivity clauses in recording contracts when exclu-sivity was intended.

While Davis fumed—he wrote that he was so upset by Diamond's action that he threatened to prohibit Columbia artists from appearing at the Bitter End—the upstart Uni team celebrated. The signing was the best thing to happen to the year-old label since it scored its first, and only, number-one hit the previous fall—the Strawberry Alarm Clock's psychedelic-tinged "Incense and Peppermints."

A subsidiary of MCA, the one-time agency giant that had moved into TV and film production exclusively a few years earlier, Uni Records was the brainchild of a then-MCA vice-president, Ned Tanen. Tanen, who would later assume the presidency of Universal Pictures, another MCA offshoot, learned firsthand about the burgeoning teen music mar-ket via the "Lloyd Thaxton Hop," a Los Angeles teen dance program that he was in charge of syndicating around the country. After selling the Thaxton show to 150 markets, an almost-unheard-of feat at the time for a teen program, he prevailed upon MCA chairman Lew Wasserman to let him found Uni Records to further cash in on rock music.

It was slow going the first year; even with "Incense and Pepper-mints," the company lost $500,000. Then some staff changes were made: Former Los Angeles promotion legend Russ Regan, who had started with the label as national promotion manager, was made presi-dent of the label; Pat Pipolo and Rick Frio, former Liberty Records executives, were hired as national promotion manager and national sales manager, respectively; and Hosia Wilson was hired to manage Uni's R&B department.

In early 1968, Tanen called a meeting of Uni's braintrust in Russ Regan's office. At the meeting, Regan handed out paper and pens to everyone and asked them to list the three artists they would most like to see Uni sign. The only name appearing on each of the secret ballots, Pipolo said, was Neil Diamond's.

Pat Pipolo recalled the ensuing discussion: "Neil had some limited success with Bang Records . . . But we all felt that he had been on the verge with those couple of records and he had never reached his full selling potential."

The longer they talked about Diamond, Pipolo continued, the more enthused they got. Not long afterward, Tanen was on a plane to New York.

Even without dangling the carrot of "creative freedom" in front of Neil, Tanen could make a persuasive case for Uni. If Neil dove into the Columbia pond, he would be just one more moderate to large fish among many other large fish; at Uni, however, he would be treated like the catch of the year, and thus be extended all promotional courtesies.

Also, MCA, as the owner of Universal Pictures, could offer Neil a possible future in television and films. In his earliest interviews, Neil had evinced an interest in an acting career, having been pushed in that direction by both Bert Berns and Fred Weintraub. (Weintraub would shortly demonstrate his own filmic bent by staking out a career as a Hollywood movie producer.)

On March 18, Diamond and Uni made it official. The five-year deal, Diamond would later claim, was worth $250,000—more than Clive Davis reported he offered. According to someone familiar with the deal, however, Neil signed for substantially less. Further, he was said to have been required to use his publishing company as collateral in the deal, just in case WEB IV eventually prevailed in its court action against him.

Neil put Uni Records' pledge of artistic freedom to the test immediately by requesting that "Brooklyn Roads," the song that he recorded several months earlier at Century Sound, be released as his first Uni single.

In his interview with *Newsweek,* Neil served notice that he regarded the three-minute "autobiography" of his adolescence as crucial to his development: "It will be everything a kid in Brooklyn was thinking, believing and seeing . . . And if only 10,000 people buy it and feel what I feel, I'll know I've really said something at last."

"Brooklyn Roads," however, promised to be a hard sell for Uni. Evocative and haunting as it was, it didn't seem to have the lyrical or melodic "hooks" that spelled hit.

Still, on April 8, "Brooklyn Roads" was released by Uni Records.

"In my heart I feel like I gave it every shot I could possibly give it," said Pat Pipolo. He recalled the feedback from radio station music directors: "'Call me a week from Tuesday' . . . 'It sounds interesting' . . . 'It's different' . . . 'Neil Diamond, he had a couple of hits last year.' All the things that say they don't like it."

In the end, the song went no higher than number fifty-eight on the *Billboard* chart.

The disappointing show of "Brooklyn Roads" wasn't the only disturbing news for Neil at the time. In March, Bang released his countryish ballad "Red Red Wine," off the "Just for You" LP, as a single. Like Bang's last Diamond release, "New Orleans," the tune failed to crack the Top 40. Suddenly, it appeared to the casual chart observer that Neil, with three straight flops, had lost his momentum as a recording artist.

It was an impression that Diamond was determined to put to rest. In April he returned to the studio in New York to record a batch of new tunes.

The sessions were noteworthy in a couple of respects. First, in a demonstration of his desire to run his own show, Diamond went in as coproducer, at a time when few artists were twirling knobs on their own sessions. (Neil had had some previous experience "behind the glass," having produced two of his compositions, "My Babe" and "Back From Baltimore," for pop singer Ronnie Dove in 1967.) Second, he invited a flash from his past, Tom Catalano, to coproduce.

On the basis of producing credits alone, Catalano seemed a surprising choice. The only producing outside of demo work the former April Blackwood product manager had done had been at Kapp Records, where he scored several regional hits with Lenny Welch. In the music publishing field, meanwhile, he had displayed his restlessness by short stints at Shapiro-Bernstein and Bob Crewe's Saturday Music, as well as at SESAC, the performing-rights society.

But as a singer of Neil Diamond's praises dating back to the day in 1962 that he introduced Diamond to Columbia's Al Kasha, he had been number one with a bullet. And that, obviously, was good enough for Neil.

In at least one or two of those first sessions, however, it was clear to one participant, arranger Joe Renzetti, that Neil was calling the shots.

Renzetti got a taste of Neil's domineering style at a prerecording meeting: "His directions were pretty clear and pretty definite . . . Basically at that point I was just a copyist . . . orchestrate whatever he had in mind. He didn't take advantage of my creative talents."

Later, in the studio, Renzetti observed a taskmaster whose style of producing reminded him, not surprisingly, of Jeff Barry's. "It's the repetition school," Renzetti commented. "'Let's do this, let's do it again, let's keep on doing this . . .'" The arranger wasn't a devotee of the style: "It's frustrating for the musicians. 'What do you want different?' 'Just do it again' or 'I don't know, it's just not quite right.' More jaded musicians begin to say, 'Hey, what's the point of this?'"

Renzetti recalled one nerve-racking instance where Diamond put several of New York's top session guitarists through their paces again and again. The song was Neil's Latinish rocker "Two-Bit Manchild," featuring an acoustic guitar figure that repeated throughout the tune. "At first he had three guitarists playing it," he said. "Then he would try one fellow, then the new guy—same figure. And he would listen to it for *minutes,* time after time after time. I thought it was excessive. I mean, I have a pretty good ear and I couldn't hear the difference."

The capper came when Neil ultimately scrapped all of the studio guitarists' takes and had Artie Richards, from his band, play the part.

"Two-Bit Manchild" was released in June as Neil's second Uni single. Pat Pipolo saw it as another difficult sell. "Neil was putting his personal agonies in song," he said, referring to the lyric, which cast the Solitary Man as a hard-bitten rambler.

Perfect guitar part and all, "Two Bit Manchild" went no further than number sixty-six.

While Neil was slumping on the charts in 1968, he was dutifully keeping his name in lights, literally, by touring—usually in weekend bursts, so as not to disturb the flow of his weekday songwriting and recording work.

By then, he had made his ambivalent attitude toward the road well known to his band. "He was pretty much of a loner, basically," recalled Artie Richards. "He loved to perform, but I don't think he liked all the stuff that went with it—the hoopla, the parties, and lots of people around. More times than not he was real withdrawn. We did a lot of dressing room routines in locker rooms in colleges, and on any given night he could wander off in a corner someplace in between sets, or before a set, and just be kind of sulky, quiet."

Tom Cerone recalled some crazy moments from the road, but they were mainly of the onstage variety. Once, the sound went out during a concert at a Baptist college down South, only to return at precisely the moment Neil snarled into the mike, "Jesus Christ, where's the fucking sound!" Another time, a girl in the front row at some long-forgotten auditorium latched onto one of Neil's legs and nearly pulled him off the stage (Cerone: "And Neil is still singing, a trouper to the end").

Offstage, however, the band took their cue from the boss and left nary a trashed hotel room in their wake. "This was not a party outfit at all," Richards said. Neil helped see to that, according to the guitar player: "There came a point when something was said: There will be no dope traveling with us, none in the hotel rooms, no smoking, nothing like that going on."

Needless to say, Richards presumed Diamond at the time to be the straightest of straights. "I don't think that he had ever smoked a joint in his life . . . I don't remember ever seeing him drink any booze."

Neil had not yet become a heavy smoker of unfiltered cigarettes, either—unlike his chain-smoking drummer. Cerone: "He offered to pay me I forget how much money if I could stop smoking. 'You're going to kill yourself, man!'"

Cerone did not take Neil up on his offer. And the band as a whole drew the line when he asked them to back him up at a benefit he said he wanted to stage for a new organization he was founding: Performers Against Drugs. Recalled Cerone, laughing: "We said to him, 'Your band can't play behind that show without being total hypocrites!'"

Neil had gone public with his would-be anti-drug campaign in early 1968. At that time, he said his organization would be called Musicians Against Drugs (MAD).

MAD, he told one New York reporter at the time, "will be made up of musicians who give their time and efforts to help young people addicted to drugs, and to dissuade and advise against drugs for young people considering them.

"I decided to do something about the problem because I've become upset with situations [with young people taking drugs] on my travels around the country. I also think the Beatles did a great disservice by their attitude towards drugs at one time . . .

"People see alcoholism as a form of illness among adults, and just so should these 'new' drugs be regarded among young people."

By the summer of 1968, Neil had changed the name of his would-be organization to Performers Against Drugs, yielding the more benign acronym PAD. But his anti-drug talk, as quoted in the July issue of *Song Hits*, was still blunt: "Drugs really don't turn you on. They just turn your life off and shake up your head a lot."

Asked by the *Song Hits* reporter why he would undertake such an enterprise as PAD, Neil replied, "I think it's like the poet, John Donne, said. 'No man is an island' and the Bible tells us, 'Do unto others as you would have them do unto you.'"

Someone who knew him better than most at the time, however, suspected that his motives for launching his anti-drug campaign were crasser ones—that he lusted for the "notoriety" that was sure to accrue to him for standing tall with his beliefs at a time when turning on had become a national pastime for young people.

As a matter of fact, Neil wound up displaying little of the ferocious stick-to-itiveness with his anti-drug group that he had in pursuing his career goals. In the end, no benefit concerts were held for PAD, no other artists spoke out on PAD's behalf, and, apparently, PAD never actually became a formal entity.

Moreover, in an interview published the month after the *Song Hits* piece, Neil talked a notably milder line in discussing pot with a *Los Angeles Times* reporter, even while revealing that he had recently penned the anti-marijuana "Pot Smoker's Song" and declaring himself opposed to legalization. In the interview he made no mention of his campaign, and he refrained from attacking hippies or Beatles. To top it off, he even portrayed *himself* as having used grass! "It has no more effect on me than a good screwdriver," he stated.

Diamond's suave declaration, as well as his subsequent dropping of PAD, appeared motivated at least in part by his sudden desire at the time to shake his un-hip image. "What am I, one of the Monkees?" he complained to Tom Cerone one day, bemoaning the fact that he was consistently identified in the press as the writer of the lightweight group's biggest hits.

Defensive as he was about his Monkees connection, he couldn't have been thrilled with the headline that appeared atop the *Los Angeles Times* piece: THE 'FIFTH MONKEE' SWINGS OUT ON HIS OWN. The piece itself, written by Digby Diehl, the reporter who had authored the unforgettable review of Neil's Hullabaloo show in 1966, was a positive one, however, in which Neil came on as the self-anointed spokesman for pop and rock.

"Rock will be the folk music of the future," Neil predicted. "The fact is that pop musicians are the torch bearers of the new American culture."

Given the opportunity to explain the role he and his music were playing in all of this, he launched into a description of his soon-to-be-released first LP for Uni Records. "I've got everything in it from rock to comedy—more Copland than country, though . . . None of these are just commercial songs like I've written before."

Two days after the article appeared, "Sunday Sun" was released, becoming Neil's third Uni single. More country than Copland in this instance, "Sunday Sun," in fact, sounded like Monkees material with its sugary melody and simple lyric about finding a little weekend peace in the park.

It flopped, too.

Having struck out in three attempts to grease the way for Diamond's album with a hit single, the powers that be at Uni went ahead and released the LP anyway in mid-October.

Mysteriously titled "Velvet Gloves and Spit," the album came with expensive packaging: a fold-out cover featuring a larger-than-life-size color photo of Neil's slightly menacing mug, as well as a strange inside shot of an unsmiling, shirtless Neil in brown leather jacket leaning on an armless mannikin.

As non sequiturs the title and mannikin photo were representative of the collection of disparate tunes. Apparently conceived by Diamond as a tour de force, the album wound up sounding, instead, simply forced. There's Neil the Brooklyn country singer on "Honey Drippin' Times," Neil the soulful balladeer on "Brooklyn Roads," Neil the glib rocker on "Holiday Inn Blues," Neil the spoofer of cabaret singers on "Knackelflerg," and Neil the social commentator on "The Pot Smoker's Song" (in which grass is linked, in the spoken ex-addict testimonies, to suicide and heroin). As such, "Velvet Gloves and Spit" is little more than a curiosity.

The problem for Neil was that very few record buyers were curious at the time. Not enough even to get "Velvet Gloves and Spit" on *Billboard's* Top 200 album chart.

As it turned out, his sudden inability to sell records wasn't the only thing on his mind at the end of 1968. In the early fall, he walked out on his wife—only a matter of weeks, according to acquaintances, before Jay gave birth to their second daughter, Elyn, on November 6.

The times he saw Neil and Jay Diamond together, PR man Joe Cal Cagno said they seemed "the *happiest* couple . . . She was in awe of what was happening to him, and she used to talk a lot like, [excited tone] *'Now, we're doing this and doing that.'* She didn't know he was going to make it, he didn't know he was going to make it . . . I think she gave him tremendous support."

Occasionally Jay would read some of her husband's fan letters to Cal Cagno over the phone. He recalled teasing her on one occasion about all the gushy sentiments. "I said, 'Wow, you better watch out.' 'Oh no, Neil is not that kind of guy—he's amused by it.' She thought it was a big joke."

Another acquaintance at the time explained that Diamond was a devoted dad, noting that he would see to Marjorie's 6 A.M. feeding when they were still living in their Long Island cottage. (Once or twice, groggy Neil inadvertently invited the police over for the morning ritual by opening a window without first turning off the alarm system.) As for Jay, the friend said: "She was a dynamite lady—really a very nice, sweet, kind, *hamish* girl. Unfortunately, it's the 'modus operandi' of a lot of women who get left."

Ellie Greenwich, who remembered Jay vaguely from Hofstra University, had her doubts, however, about her and Neil as a couple. "[When] I met her with Neil . . . I said, *'My god.'* A lot of people found them very mismatched. Sometimes she seemed more outgoing than Neil, and other times it would be reversed. It never seemed like they were both [in sync]."

"It was almost as though our destiny was preordained," Diamond would later say himself, in one of his rare comments on his relationship with Jay. "We were to be married, have children; the best we could hope for was a little house on Long Island . . . I didn't really begin to think about myself and my life until I began to travel and remove myself from that peer group. And I realized that that wasn't what I wanted at all."

Evidently helping the deterioration process along was Marcia Kay Murphey.

According to Neil, he met Murphey, two months older than he, on the set of the "Clay Cole Show," a local TV dance program, where she was working as a production assistant. He got to see more of her when, in 1967, Fred Weintraub hired her as a production assistant on his new syndicated television series, "Live From the Bitter End."

"I'm not sure what it was that attracted me to Marcia," he would say. "Maybe it was the sadness in her eyes . . . I saw this girl and she evidently understood great pain." A compatibly brooding companion, in other words, for the Solitary Man.

That poignant view, however, doesn't square with "Judy Disney," the David Steinberg monologue character that Neil would later claim to one of his musicians had been inspired by the Ohio-born, once-divorced Murphey. "Judy Disney" was blond, tall, a cheerleader, and, above all, *very* social. (A spokesman for Steinberg claimed that the comedian first met Marcia after he had invented "Judy Disney," and that the character had not been patterned after her.)

Nor does Diamond's description of Marcia square with the upbeat accounts of various Bitter End–era acquaintances.

"Marcia was fabulous," recalled Roy Silver, a former partner of Fred Weintraub's who later employed Marcia at his management-production company in Hollywood. "She was pretty and bright and super witty. She was a Gentile chick who could make it on an intellectual level with Jewish guys."

"She was a happy-natured person," recalled comedian Mike Mislove, who confessed to having had a crush on her.

"She was a gorgeous woman . . . delicious," recalled singer-songwriter Jake Holmes, who dated her briefly. "And she was very nice, very sweet, and very helpful to everybody."

Beneath that effervescent exterior, however, guitarist Artie Richards sensed a tenacious type, a woman who "would claw her way to the top somehow. A striver."

Marcia demonstrated her savvy and drive in her work. Roy Silver: "If you were in a production, you could just stand there and say, 'The extras,' and Marcia would say, 'Here's a list of all the people.' And

'What time is the screening?' And she would say, 'The film will be here at 4:30, I'll set up the screening room at 9:22. You have seat No. 14A, and the car will be there.'"

"Marcia was a pretty individual person, pretty liberated," said Bitter End manager Stephen Prince. "I think Neil liked the fact that she was pretty strong and independent."

Diamond also seemed proud of her pedigree. In contrast to his own ancestors, who he had claimed had come to the United States "in steerage," Marcia's ancestors, he proclaimed, sailed over on the *Mayflower*. Abraham Lincoln had been married in her great-granduncle's home, he said.

Needless to say, Marcia Murphey didn't have a trace of Brooklyn Roads in her past. "The complete antithesis of what I am," Diamond would declare.

As such, she represented a fresh start, new tomorrows, while Jay represented the past, a past that Neil seemed to be fleeing.

The fascination was mutual.

"I was trying to get Marcia to date me," said Mike Mislove, "and I was told by the other girl in the office that she had her sights fixed on Neil."

Fellow comedian and hootenanny host George Memmoli did not have to be informed of Marcia's crush: "When someone twitches every time someone passes her by, and she can't keep her eyes off him, it's kind of obvious."

Memmoli spoke of Marcia's hovering presence whenever Neil was slated to perform at the Bitter End. "She would come downstairs and say, 'George, what time is Neil going on? Is everything going to be OK? Is there anything you need?'"

Artie Richards noted Marcia's presence as well at shows, backstage, and so on. It was clear to him that she and Neil were an item, even though Diamond never said as much. "It's funny, men try to keep those things quiet," he commented. "Everybody knows that something's going on, but [he] never talks about it. It's like from his standpoint it's not happening . . . And this kind of stuff is hard on a person. It's hard on anybody who's around.

"This is when the real inaccessibility came into play . . . There was really no contact [between Diamond and the band] any more. There was little or nothing of him left."

Tom Cerone, however, has a vivid memory of a brief discussion he and Neil had at the time about Neil's personal plans: "I remember driving in the car. He had a Lincoln. And we were on Grand Central Parkway . . . coming in from the Island. We were talking about he was going to divorce Jay. And Jay had just become pregnant again. And I can remember saying to him, 'Listen, I'm not going to dip into your personal business, man, it's your life—but your timing stinks.'"

Neil, however, stuck with his decision to leave his wife. As Marcia was said to have told a friend years later: "He went out to get a package of cigarettes [one day] and never went back."

With a new woman by his side, as well as a new address—Hollywood, California—Neil seemed to be living, more than ever, the title of one of his "Velvet Gloves and Spit" songs, "Practically Newborn," as he began 1969. It was fated to be a year of bold moves as he sought to reinvent himself as a major recording artist.

·8·
MEMPHIS MAGIC

The first thing Diamond did in 1969 was make the pilgrimage to a new mecca for hit-seekers, American Sound Studio in Memphis.

American Sound was an idea whose time had come to rock 'n' roll. The funky studio, located in an old brick building in a seedy part of town, was more than just four ceiling-tile-covered walls—it was producer/owner Chips Moman, producer/bass player Tommy Cogbill, guitar player Reggie Young, organ player Bobby Emmons, piano player Bobby Wood, drummer Gene Chrisman, and bass player Mike Leech.

"I wouldn't classify any of us as 'studio musicians,'" said guitarist Young. "It was like a group production company. Everybody was interested in the song, everybody wanted to cut a hit record. I think we put a little more into it than most people . . . We'd build an arrangement from the ground up.

"There really wasn't any other rhythm section doing that, except Rick Hall [in Muscle Shoals, Alabama]."

It seemed inevitable that the Memphis team would develop its own special sound working that way, and that's what happened. Among the flavors that went into their roots-oriented musical stew was Young's country-blues guitar stylings, Emmons' Ray Charles–inspired organ playing, and Chrisman's rock drumming.

Then there was the unique bass sound of Tommy Cogbill. An outstanding jazz guitarist, Cogbill originated the "busy," or "boogaloo," base line. His playing can be heard propelling "Respect," the R&B scorcher that transformed Aretha Franklin from a lounge artist into a star.

By January of 1969, the rich sound of American Sound could be heard on an array of hits: "The Letter" and "Cry Like a Baby" by the Box Tops, "Son of a Preacher-Man" by Dusty Springfield, "Angel of the Morning" by Merrilee Rush, and R&B charters by Joe Tex and King Curtis.

On the morning of January 8, Diamond, accompanied by Tom Catalano, strode in the back door of American Sound Studio for his turn. Among the several tunes he hoped to get down on tape during the two days he'd booked was a new gospel-flavored rocker that he figured would be right up the Memphis boys' alley: "Brother Love's Travelling Salvation Show."

The idea for a song about a revival preacher had been percolating in the back of Diamond's mind for a year or two, ever since he claimed he had attended some revival meetings down South. He said he had been originally struck by the "spectacle" nature of the events, even though he was incensed by the Brother Loves themselves, branding them as rip-off artists.

"But then," he said, "I went up to Harlem, 125th Street, to a church there, and I sat in on a meeting one Sunday, and it blew my mind. Because I realized for the first time that this was not a rip-off. These people were getting what they came for—they were finding answers, that there is truth in what these people say . . . And I started to think about it more positively." However, it wasn't until he was airborne and Memphis bound that he actually took pen in hand to write the celebratory "Brother Love" lyric to go with his already-composed melody.

After exchanging pleasantries with his new recording team, Neil sat down and played "Brother Love" for the first time. The gang at Memphis Sound were knocked out. As Tommy Cogbill and Chips Moman sat behind the glass manning the knobs, the group jumped in.

Boasting a well-crafted, electric lyric that seduces the listener into Brother Love's steamy tent, the song probably would have been a hit no matter who produced, arranged, and played on it. But it would be hard to imagine a musical team packing any more sparks into the three-and-a-half-minute track than the Memphis players—Wood with his thumping piano, Tommy Cogbill protegé Mike Leech with his pulsing bass, Gene Chrisman pounding out that good gospel beat.

Neil got religion singing—and in this instance, sermonizing—to his musicians' playing. His performance was flawless: sultry, sexy, and, especially when he becomes the supercharged Brother Love, totally convincing.

When he heard the record, Uni promotion manager Pat Pipolo was ecstatic, and relieved. He so dreaded having to tell an artist his record wasn't happening that he tended to pussyfoot around, painting the glossiest picture he could. The first and only time he tried that tack with Neil, Neil had cut him short: "Sounds like hype to me." Even a fairly straightforward "It didn't happen" wouldn't satisfy Diamond, Pipolo said: "He'd ask 'Why?' . . . Neil would be a great manager."

With "Brother Love," Pipolo was delighted to dish up the straight poop: The tune was guaranteed Top 40. Pipolo: "It was an exciting record to play for programming directors because it was an ear-grabber. I remember everybody gave their own interpretation of what they visualized when they heard the record. Everybody was saying, 'Elmer Gantry.'"

Released in mid-February, "Brother Love" shot up onto the charts, peaking nationally at number twenty-two. It was Neil's highest-charting record since "Kentucky Woman," almost a year and a half earlier. Suddenly, Pipolo said, the same radio station music directors who had dismissed Neil a few months earlier were singing his praises. "Everybody knew that Neil Diamond was about to explode."

Pipolo had fresh ammunition to contribute to the cause when he returned from Chicago, where he saw Diamond perform for the first time. "I was amazed at the audience—totally amazed," he said. "His demographics were total. I mean you'd see kids in the corner trying to light a joint, and the grandmas eating a sandwich. He was a rock 'n' roll star, he was an MOR artist."

Figuring that one good session in Memphis deserved another, Neil returned to American Sound at the end of February to record more tracks for his second Uni LP, "Brother Love's Travelling Salvation Show," released in mid-April. He returned again in May to lay down his next single.

The Memphis boys were higher than kites during those months. Four days after Diamond had left in January, Elvis Presley had checked into American Sound, where he cut the tunes destined to put *him* back at the top of the charts, "In the Ghetto," "Suspicious Minds," and "Kentucky Rain." ("What a funky, funky place," Elvis was said to have commented as he walked into the studio, followed by "Man, what's all that noise?"—directed at a rustling sound above his head. The musicians changed the subject rather than confess to Elvis that some mammoth Memphis rats, refugees from a garbage bin from the café next door, were dancing in the rafters.)

The studio high continued in May as Neil and his Memphis cohorts recorded a cheery country-flavored song of Neil's. If "Sweet Caroline" wasn't catchy enough for its infectious melody and instantly memorable chorus, organ player Bobby Emmons delivered the crowning commercial touch by creating the inventive lick that begins the record.

"'Sweet Caroline' was the first time I burnt up the wires," Pat Pipolo said. "I had a little office downstairs at Uni Records, and I was sitting there with Neil and Rick Frio. And I was on the phone calling every program director I knew. And it was the first time I remember Neil getting on the phone to say hello and do a couple of minutes with the guys. I think the program directors knew the record was a smash and they wanted to be in on the ground floor, to be able to say they had had a conversation with Neil."

In those days, Uni president Russ Regan would break out the champagne whenever the company sold 100,000 copies of a single in a week. Not long after Pipolo's phone blitz on "Sweet Caroline," the sounds of popping corks could be heard in the company's offices. Eventually, the song crested at number four. It was Neil's highest-rated single to that point—as well as the best evidence yet that a second Neil Diamond career explosion was imminent.

To help him capitalize on the sudden turn in his career fortunes, Diamond took on a new manager, Joe Sutton.

They had met early in the year. At the time, Sutton, a transplanted Brooklyner himself, was working as the vice president in charge of PR for Campbell-Silver-Cosby, a Hollywood-based entertainment company of which Roy Silver, the former partner of Fred Weintraub, was a principal. Also employed at the time by the company, as a secretary to Harry Ginnis, head of promotion and advertising, was Marcia Murphey.

One day, Murphey approached Sutton and asked him to meet with Neil. Sutton, who had just been hyped on Neil by his fourteen-year-old niece, said sure.

"We sat in the office and talked, and then we went to a coffee shop on Beverly Boulevard called Jan's and talked some more," said Sutton. "Neil said he wanted management, and he wanted to relocate here. His career was kind of [on hold], and he was having problems with his wife, they had just separated. I think he was going through a major change."

Even though the personable, upbeat Sutton found Diamond "very unsure and *very* wary," they hit it off. He suggested to Roy Silver that Silver take him on as a client.

Silver, however, nixed that notion: "I knew Neil . . . and knowing my style I knew we would not be able to work together . . . It was better for Joe Sutton, who wasn't as dictatorial as I was." Though the PR executive was just then breaking into management with his first act, Lou Rawls, Sutton pronounced himself eager and willing when Diamond asked him to be his manager. Displaying the wariness that Sutton saw in their first meeting, Neil refused to seal the deal with anything more binding than a handshake.

Sutton had his work cut out for him, which was partially his own doing: "I told Neil, 'I think you're gonna be the biggest boy singer in America.'"

Sutton's first order of business was to take Neil off the road. That was easy to do, since his band had walked out on him shortly after the release of "Brother Love," after he had turned a deaf ear to their ultimatum that he hire a roadie to lug their equipment (several members of the group went on to record an ill-fated album for Capitol Records as The Rig). Said Sutton, in explaining his move to cancel Diamond's pending dates: "Neil had been booked into some saloons . . . places that a Tom Jones would play, a Sinatra . . . And Neil's not a saloon singer." He kept Neil off the road, he added, for about six months, "'til the work was a certain fee."

"Sweet Caroline" improved Neil's fee picture overnight. By then

Joe Sutton and Diamond's agent, Burt Zell, had decided on their performance game plan for Neil: a steady diet of college gigs interspersed with a small number of key club engagements.

Before he could tour, however, Diamond had to hire a new band. He found his bass player, Randy Ceirley, through Joe Sutton, and he found his guitarist, Carol Hunter, and drummer, Eddie Rubin, through auditions he held at a rehearsal hall in Hollywood.

If he was striving for notoriety via his selections, he couldn't have done a better job. "Just in appearance alone, we were probably the farthest thing from anybody's idea of what Neil's backup band would be like," said Ceirley, laughing.

In those days, the affable bass player, from Bakersfield, California, sported a wild man's head of blond hair and a bushy mustache. "Neil referred to me alternately as looking like the Cowardly Lion or a *very old* baby," he chuckled.

He added that drummer Rubin, by contrast, favored the "reformed beatnik" look: turtlenecks, short hair, thin mustache. Personality-wise, Rubin was as inward as Ceirley was ebullient.

Then there was Carol Hunter—a woman.

It would be an understatement to refer to Carol Hunter as a pop-rock oddity in 1969. "She was *it*," said Ceirley. "No other chick played with a rock 'n' roll band."

If her sex wasn't novelty enough, Hunter had a cheeky sense of humor, which she displayed at her audition in August by picking out that summertime classic "Rudolph the Red-Nosed Reindeer" on her twelve-string.

The trio was fairly well seasoned. Ceirley had backed the Kingston Trio and was in the process of establishing himself as a studio player; Hunter, raised on Long Island, had played with Steve Stills and Richie Havens in the Village, and Rubin had performed with Johnny Rivers.

Ceirley, Hunter, and Rubin got a crash course in Diamond's repertoire at his home in Tarzana, in the San Fernando Valley. Neil and Marcia had recently moved to the hilltop ranch house on Caritina Drive from Hollywood, where they had briefly rented a cottage on Yucca Trail that Joe Sutton had formerly owned. Neil's Tarzana spread included a barn in the back, and that's where he and his new players worked up his show.

The first time they ventured from the barn was to play a nonadvertised shakedown gig at a club called Cisco's in Redondo Beach. "It was a surf crowd, and the show was pretty much a disaster," Ceirley recalled. Then Sutton booked Neil into the Golden Bear, a well-respected folk-oriented club in Huntington Beach, for four days. Ceirley, who had played the Golden Bear himself when he was a solo folk act, figured this would be the gig that would show him just what Neil was made of as a performer.

As he scanned the song order Diamond had scribbled out shortly before they went onstage opening night, Ceirley got his first inkling he was in store for a treat: "I went, 'Damn, this is real good pacing—realllll gooooood.'"

However, the bass player was not prepared in the slightest for the Neil Diamond he saw take the stage that night, a Neil Diamond who had learned a great deal about putting on a show since 1966. "I wasn't sure what was going on. All of a sudden this *performer* came out and he blew my socks off! And I just went, 'Whoooaaa,—this gonna be a *funnnnn gig!*'"

With no promotion, that show was sparsely attended. But the word got out, and Neil played to packed houses over the weekend.

Joe Sutton liked what he saw so much that he booked Neil in Los Angeles' then-premiere rock artist showcase: the Troubadour in West Hollywood. Opening night, the traditional press and music industry night, was a hot ticket, according to Uni's Pat Pipolo. "My phones were ringing off the hook," he said. "Everybody in the world wanted to go to the Troubadour. Judging from the requests that I got and Norman [Winter, the independent PR man who serviced the press for the Troubadour] got we knew he was gonna knock 'em dead."

Diamond, no doubt still haunted by the disastrous Hullabaloo experience three years earlier, didn't know that, however. A few days before the September engagement was to begin, he informed Joe Sutton almost nonchalantly, "I'm not ready for the Troubadour. Cancel it."

Sutton was in shock but he reacted with calculated good humor: "Cancel it? You can't cancel it. If you're not going on, I'm going on. And I'll lip-sync to your records and you'll *really* be embarrassed."

The approach worked; Neil immediately relented.

On opening night, Pat Pipolo was looking for a sign from Neil that he was going to be the smash the promotion man had predicted. He thinks he witnessed it in the fraction of a second before Diamond began singing his opening song—but he added that it could have been a figment of his wishful imagination: "I saw him taking a deep breath, hyperventilating, and then turning around—legs apart—and hitting that first chord on his Ovation."

The image seems reasonable. The audience saw and cheered a charged Diamond not only on opening night, but every night during the six-night stand.

This time the *Los Angeles Times* review was a rave: "Neil Diamond . . . is an excellent reminder of what made early rock such an exciting sound," wrote the newspaper's new pop music critic, Robert Hilburn. "[He] exhibited at his opening Tuesday the same strong vocals and pounding guitar-bass drum beat that ushered in the new era in pop music in the mid-1950s."

A few months before the engagement, and the raves, manager Sutton had had a hard time finding an agent for Neil ("I'd say 'Neil Diamond,' and they'd say 'Neil Sedaka?'"). That changed only hours into Diamond's week at the Troub. Suddenly, "everybody wanted to handle him, talk to him," Sutton mused.

"The same thing happened with Sammy Davis, Jr. at the Mocambo, Martin and Lewis at Ciro's. You can be a star in this town in one night if you do it right. And it happened to Neil."

Shortly after the engagement, Diamond began a seventeen-day tour.

As much *"funnnnn"* as he anticipated having with Neil, Randy Ceirley approached this first concert swing with some foreboding. The problem was, Ceirley, a confessed lover of pot at the time, liked to have fun offstage, too, and he wondered how much he was going to be able to get away with.

Although Neil had never requested that Ceirley and the other band members refrain from smoking marijuana as he had with his previous band, Ceirley said that Neil's reputation for being *"deatttttthh onnnnn druggggggs"* had inhibited him so far from lighting up in his presence. So, like naughty Midwest teenagers, he and the other smokers around Diamond had felt disposed to tiptoe behind Neil's barn-cum-rehearsal-room for a few drags while old man Diamond was otherwise engaged at his Tarzana home.

In his hotel room in Salt Lake City, the first stop on the tour, Randy decided that he had had enough of that sneaking-around nonsense. Gazing through the marijuana haze at a couple of other members of the tour party, he suddenly declared, "This is *bullshit*. I can't live like this anymore." Then the bass player dialed Neil's room. "Look, Neil, we got enough weed down here to get everybody stoned," he announced. "If you're not down here in five minutes it's all gonna be gone and you can forget it."

The others were still gasping in horror at what Ceirley had done when they heard a knock on the door. Sure enough, it was Neil. But, according to Ceirley, instead of laying down the law about drug use in his band, the writer of "Pot Smoker's Song," the founder of Performers Against Drugs, the man who had gone against the tide of the times by speaking out against marijuana, LSD, and drugs in general simply accepted a joint and began puffing away.

That fall, Neil had another reason to feel giddy: He had scored his second Top 10 tune of the year, "Holly Holy," which had been recorded in Memphis a month before his Troubadour engagement.

That it was even cut during his fourth visit to American Sound that year was a credit to the Memphis magicians.

"'New York Boy,' that was the song that everybody thought was the single of the batch," recalled organ player Bobby Emmons of the punchy, albeit somewhat trite country rocker about an Easterner who gets countrified. He did confess, however, that he and the rest of the band had their doubts about whether the tune was strong enough to follow "Sweet Caroline."

Then at a playback session for "Boy," Diamond took out his guitar in the control room, said "Tell me what you think of this one," and launched into the haunting, gospelly tune with the sensuous, mysterious lyrics. Suddenly, recalled Emmons, "the band came to life. We weren't planning on recording a new song that day, but we insisted we cut it." And they did, even though, Emmons added, "We almost had to convince Neil to do 'Holly Holy,' convince him that it was finished, that it sounded like a song."

While "Holly Holy" might have sounded like a song by the end of that session, it still didn't sound like a hit record. What the tune now needed was some "sweetening," with the addition of string, horn, and/ or background vocal parts. In the early part of the year, producer Tom Catalano and Diamond had been content to record those parts at American Sound as well. But, with "Sweet Caroline," he and Neil changed their modus operandi, hiring New York arranger Charles Calello to write string and horn charts, and then recording the parts in New York.

With "Holly Holy," Tom Catalano and Neil looked beyond Memphis again for just the right finishing touches. This time the call went to New York arranger Lee Holdridge.

The then twenty-five-year-old Holdridge was one of a new breed of classically trained arrangers who had begun to thrive in the pop arena in the late '60s, thanks to the Beatles. Holdridge had met Catalano in New York the previous year when he was engaged in one of his wilder undertakings, The Seventh Century, a loose association of fourteen studio musicians who composed and performed rock-baroque numbers, including a piece called "Ballet Trinity," which the Joffrey Ballet performed. But it was an arrangement that Lee had done for Peggy March's obscure cover of Diamond's "And the Grass Won't Pay No Mind" that he thinks won him the "Holly Holy" job, as well as an offer from Catalano to arrange some other tunes that Neil wanted to record in Los Angeles for his next album.

Twenty minutes after he agreed to fly out to Los Angeles and go to work for Neil, Holdridge got a second call from Catalano. "Tom says— and this was kind of funny—'I don't know where to record in L.A. I don't know what musicians to use. Do you know any people in L.A.?'" Lee really didn't—he'd only paid one brief visit to L.A. himself—but, wanting to be accommodating, he said he'd check and get back to him.

Holdridge didn't know where to turn except to his record library. "At the time I was a big admirer of Jim Webb's writings; he had just done an album with the Fifth Dimension called 'The Magic Garden.' It was a suite of songs and orchestral bits, and I was very impressed by the playing, and also the engineering. So I looked on the back of the album and I saw [engineer] Armin Steiner's name, and I saw these four or five rhythm players." To Holdridge's surprise, these same players were credited on the backs of several other of his favorite albums. "Hal Blaine was the drummer, Joe Osborn was the bass player, Larry Knechtel was the keyboard player," he said. "And there were two or three guitar players—it seemed to rotate around Mike Deasy, Fred Tackett, and Dennis Budimir. There was this nucleus."

Holdridge called Catalano back and reported his findings. Little did he know that the people he was recommending would—like he—play a key role in Neil's career in the years to come.

For several troubled days, however, Lee Holdridge thought "Holly Holy" would be his first and last assignment for Diamond; that's how long he listened to a cassette of the song in a vain search for musical inspiration. "I thought it was the most boring song I'd ever heard," he said, chuckling. "I mean it was just the same thing over and over and over."

But keeping in mind Catalano's suggestion that he think in terms of letting "Holly Holy" start the way it did on the tape and then building it into something big, Holdridge hung in with the song, focusing on the musical part he liked the most: Bobby Wood's piano figure. "After they go through the first sixteen bars, they come to the place where they go *dun-dun-dun-dun-dun-dun-dun-dun-CHOM-CHOM*. And I thought, 'That's an interesting little eight-note figure—it sounds gospel to me—where the voice sort of answers the rhythm section.' I then put some chords on that answer. The orchestra would play *CHOM-CHOM!* And then the piano *dun-dun-dun-dun-CHOM-CHOM!* And each time it kept building. And that became the seed from which the arrangement grew."

Still, Holdridge said "I didn't know what to expect, and I guess Tom and Neil didn't either" when he reported for duty at Armin Steiner's Hollywood studio, Sound Recorders, to record his string arrangement for "Holly Holy." Adding to the drama of the occasion, Catalano had gone all out by hiring a twenty-piece string section.

"We ran through the chart and it sounded pretty good," Holdridge said. "There were a couple of things we changed, and Tom and Neil said, 'No, go back to the way you had it.'

"Suddenly that song built, something it never did in its original format."

Fanning the new fire of "Holly Holy" was the sound of a black chorus, recorded soon afterward. Holdridge wrote their part as well, although, he said, "Being gospel singers they added a lot of little touches that you cannot write down. They were wonderful.

"What 'Holly Holy' became now," he continued, "was this simple gospel song that build into this tremendous explosion of Neil and chorus and rhythm section and orchestra. It became a very exciting record."

"Holly Holy," however, did have one drawback as a single as far as the Uni braintrust was concerned: It was a hefty four minutes and forty seconds long. "Russ [Regan] was scared," Pat Pipolo recalled. "He may have been president of the company, but he was still a promotion man, so he felt the same thing I did—'It's too long, we're going to have problems.'" Neither Regan nor he could persuade Diamond and Catalano to cut the song, however.

Soon after "Holly Holy"'s release in mid-October, Holdridge heard how at least one AM disc jockey had resolved the problem of length—by speeding up the turntable. "The song is in the key of E, and, all of a sudden, I'm hearing it a little more than a quartertone sharp, and I'm saying, 'What have they done to it?'" he said. "I was shocked."

After "Holly Holy" began to catch on, however, Lee began to hear the tune consistently in all its four-minute-and-forty-second glory. It peaked only two slots lower than "Sweet Caroline," at number six.

"Holly Holy," however, had something that its cheery-sounding, straightforward predecessor didn't—a powerful air of mystery that improved Neil's mystique quotient overnight.

"First of all, um, that's a weird song," Neil later responded when asked to explain "Holly Holy." "That's a very weird song—I don't even know if I can explain it. What I tried to do was create a religious experience, represent a religious experience between a man and a woman, as opposed to a man and a god. And, uh, that is essentially what this man is singing about."

To bass player Randy Ceirley, however, the man supposedly hell-bent on writing important songs gave a different answer, portraying himself, in the process, as the Brother Love of tunesmiths—dishing out sizzle instead of substance. Ceirley: "I said [to him], when I listened to it, 'What does this song mean?' And he went, 'Nothing.' I said, 'But it's a hit record.' And he said [amused voice]: 'Yeah, sure is.' He admitted to me that that song was a joke . . . 'Let's see what they make out of this.'

"And," Randy continued, "there were people coming up to him after a concert—'Neil, you don't know what that song did for my life.' We'd all be like this [stifling a smirk]."

In early November, "Touching You, Touching Me," containing "Holly Holy," became Neil's second LP release in seven months. It was a rush job, evidenced by the fact that four of the five non-Memphis–recorded tunes—"Mr. Bojangles," "Everybody's Talkin'," "Both Sides Now," "Until It's Time for You to Go"—were "covers." In fact, Diamond, presumably on the road at the time, was not even present for the recording of those tracks, dashing in only to lay down his vocals. Contributing to the sense that the album was hastily packaged and released to capitalize on his hot streak on the charts was the LP's title: The phrase was a play on a phrase in "Sweet Caroline," which wasn't even included on the album.

Still, "Touching You, Touching Me" became Neil's highest charting album to date, cresting at number thirty, fifty places higher than the "Brother Love" LP. And it passed muster with *Los Angeles Times* critic Robert Hilburn, fated to become an influential champion of Neil: "Diamond proves, perhaps more convincingly than ever, that he is an important talent on the contemporary music scene."

That Thanksgiving Neil had even more than his career rebirth to be thankful for. On November 25 his divorce from Jay finally came through.

It had been a protracted, difficult proceeding. Asked later about the beard he was wearing in the photograph that appeared on the cover of the "Brother Love" album, Neil replied: "I suppose [it] looked like I was getting hip or something. In reality, I was hiding from some private detectives my first wife had hired." Considering his fairly high profile at the time, growing a beard for disguise purposes seemed to be of dubious value, but Randy Ceirley seconded the notion that Diamond was behaving curiously. "All I know is when I first met him he was not an at-ease man at all; he seemed like a guy looking over his shoulder . . . And it was, 'Here's how to get to Neil's house, but make sure nobody else gets this address.' And at that time he wasn't that big a star yet, so I was going, 'Huhhhh?'"

During those trying months it was clear that Diamond's Tarzana home was his one sanctuary, and that Marcia Murphey had become the key person in his life.

Former Bitter End manager Stephen Prince, who had gone to work for Neil as his road manager, lived with Neil and Marcia at the time. "They were really into one another," he recalled. "And they spent a lot of time together alone . . . in the house. There were a few of us who were their friends who could enjoy that with them. It is nice being around two people who are really in love."

Asked to describe those domestic times, Prince talked about their three dogs, Neil's German shepherd, Shilo; Marcia's Lhasa-Apso, Cherry, and his own English sheepdog, Joshua, who systematically dug up the front yard (Prince: "Neil fell in a hole one day that Joshua dug. He thought it was pretty humorous that the dog could dig a hole big enough for a man to fall in"). He also talked about the many evenings spent "watching television, eating popcorn, telling jokes. Really down-home stuff."

Contributing to the sense of domestic bliss at the time was the fact that Marcia had become pregnant.

On December 4, nine days after his divorce was finalized, Neil and Marcia went to City Hall to obtain a marriage license. Witnessing their signing of the Certificate of Registry of Marriage were Tom Catalano and Jody Paonessa, a friend of Marcia's who had flown in from New York City.

The next evening they were married in their living room by the Rev. Stephen H. Fritchman, a Unitarian minister.

Randy Ceirley and his wife, Carol, were among the fifty or so mainly industry guests. He remembered Neil being casually attired—slacks and a silky, rose-colored shirt—and Carol Ceirley recalled Marcia looking beautiful in a pinkish dress that made no attempt to conceal her now-ample bulge. As for the ceremony and the celebration that followed, Randy recalled them "sort of running into each other. 'I now pronounce you man and wife, and let's a party.'"

Added Carol: "The party was off the wall. There were people getting stoned in the bushes, but not fried to where they were zombies. It was giggle-silly, a wonderful celebration. Wonderful food and drink. It was such a relaxed, fun feeling that I remember thinking, 'This is how all weddings should be.'"

·9·
DICHOTOMY

His glorious 1969 under his belt, Neil proceeded to start 1970 with a Bang. It wasn't the kind of bang he had in mind, however.

After presumably spending 1969 monitoring Neil's impressive comeback, Ilene Berns of WEB IV elected to return to the business of releasing Diamond products from the Bang Records vault.

Her first release of 1970 was "Shilo," the very tune that Neil claimed he had tried in vain to get Bert Berns to release as a single three years earlier, prompting him to leave the label.

Layering an irony upon an irony, Ilene Berns, who had put out a version of "Shilo" in 1968, only to see it bomb, journeyed from WEB IV's new headquarters in Atlanta to American Sound Studio in Memphis. There, on January 2, she engaged the same musicians who had cut "Brother Love," "Sweet Caroline" and "Holly Holy" to cut a new rhythm track to Neil's vocals!

The battle of "Shilo" was on.

"We were doing some sessions at the time, and suddenly Tom [Catalano] said, 'We're doing "Shilo,"'" Lee Holdridge recalled. "[He said] 'We want to do it just like the original record.' So I listened to the record and basically copied the arrangement. We did it in a great hurry."

Diamond and Uni decided to stick the tune on the newly repackaged "Velvet Gloves and Spit" LP. That way they could kill two birds with one stone: offer an alternative to would-be "Shilo" singles buyers, as well as move more copies of his first Uni LP effort, which, of course, had bombed in its initial release. (Uni followed the same strategy with the "Brother Love" album, repackaging and rereleasing it with a thirteenth track, "Sweet Caroline.")

While the "Shilo" affair had its amusing side, there was no mistaking the gravity of the larger war between Neil and WEB IV over the issue of who was going to profit from his Bang-era songs, music that, judging by "Shilo"'s success on the charts in the spring of 1970 (peak position: number twenty-four), was standing the test of time. As long as WEB IV's suit seeking a permanent injunction against Diamond recording for another label was still alive in the courts, Diamond seemed to have a built-in disadvantage: He was receiving none of his Bang royalties. The label was supposedly holding them in escrow.

That situation had to have perturbed Diamond. At the end of March he returned for another one-week engagement at the Troubadour with his three-piece band, as well as three backup singers. At a cost of $75,000, three of the performances were recorded by Armin Steiner for a live album, "Gold." Included among the LP's ten tracks were tunes Diamond had recorded for Bang: "Solitary Man," "Cherry, Cherry," "Kentucky Woman" and "Thank the Lord for the Night Time."

"Gold" was released in July. That same month, Bang rereleased "Solitary Man." Both shot up the charts.

It was showdown time once again.

In August, WEB IV moved for a temporary injunction in Manhattan Supreme Court enjoining the sale of "Gold," claiming that the album's release was in violation of a five-year rerecording restriction that Diamond had agreed to with the label. Neil argued, in turn, that the restriction was included in his separate agreement with Tallyrand Music only.

Judge J. Lupiano issued his ruling in September, the same month that a brand new re-repackaging of Diamond's Bang tracks, "Shilo," hit the charts: "Plaintiff does not establish clear legal right to temporary injunctive relief and risk of injury and irreparable damage is not demonstrated," Lupiano wrote. Motion denied.

It was a sweet victory for Neil: "Gold," which also included versions of his three 1969 hits, became his highest-charting album yet, cresting at number ten. Playing a role in the album's success, ironically, was Bang's rerelease of "Solitary Man," which this time hit number twenty-one.

Although his jousting with WEB IV might give the impression that Neil was forced to live in his musical past for much of 1970, the fact was that he was simultaneously writing, recording, and touring like a man possessed.

For much of the year, he divided his time evenly between the studio and the road, recording during the first several days of the week, then taking off on Thursday or Friday for a long weekend's worth of dates. By summer he was showing big results on both fronts.

Studio-wise, he served notice one day early in the year at Armin Steiner's Sound Recorders that he was plotting new directions for himself. He had brought along some African percussion instruments. "This is going to be an experiment," he announced to Steiner and the rhythm section of Hal Blaine, drums; Joe Osborn, bass; Larry Knechtel, keyboards; and Louie Shelton, guitar. He explained that he had a notion to record a song flavored with African rhythms. All he had at that point, however, was an idea for a guitar figure. "It started out as a total nothing," Steiner recalled.

In attempting to make a musical something out of a nothing, Neil had assembled the right recording team. Steiner was a legend of sorts on the local scene for his brilliant work on behalf of clients ranging from Motown to Richard Harris ("MacArthur Park"). Shelton, Blaine, Knechtel, and Osborn, meanwhile, ranked as the cream of L.A.'s studio musician crop. The latter three, in fact, had been dubbed the "Anonymous Kings of Rock 'n' Roll" by one local writer for their work on the likes of the Mamas and Papas' "California Dreamin'," the Fifth Dimension's "Up, Up and Away," and Simon and Garfunkel's "Mrs. Robinson." One of the reasons they were so in demand was their ability as studio players–plus. The "plus" meant that, just like the musicians at Memphis' American Sound, they threw in arranging and compositional work as part of the deal, all in the name of racking up hits for their clients—and keeping themselves booked solid at double scale.

"It was great fun, just wonderful," Blaine said of his first experience ever thumping on African log and hair drums.

"When we got finished," Steiner noted, "it was a collection of sound that was just electrifying."

Neil then penned a brief lyric for the track from the "Holly Holy" school of lyrical obfuscation. He titled it "Soolaimon."

The jarring yet infectious Afro-flavored rocker was released in April. While it did only moderately well on the charts, it fulfilled its function, serving as a musical calling card of sorts for a more daring Diamond. Neil demonstrated his pride in the tune by immediately employing it as his concert opener. He also began contemplating further forays into an African sound.

The next sound heard from Neil in 1970, however, was straight-ahead and totally irresistible pop. Bass player Randy Ceirley was present from the song's conception to its rush-recording:

"We were in Canada, Toronto I believe . . . And this girl came down from a local paper, a college paper or something, and was trying to interview Neil. Somehow she had gotten in. And I think the only reason she had gotten in was she was cute and bubbly, a good chick . . .

"And Neil used to have a trick he pulled on interviewers, which was . . . he would end up interviewing them. He started doing this to this chick. 'What goes on around here?' And I sat and watched . . .

"Somehow the conversation got around to these Indian reservations—and the ratio of like one woman to 100 men. And Neil said, 'How do these guys spend the weekend?' 'Oh, they go out with Rose.' 'Who?' 'Cracklin' Rose.' He said 'What?' And she said, 'They go down to the store and buy a bottle of Cracklin' Rosé wine and get mashed—that's their weekend. And their girlfriend is Cracklin' Rose.' And I saw a look in Neil's eye. I knew there was a song coming.

"We got back to L.A. on Monday morning. I got a call Tuesday, and he said, 'Get down to Armin's studio.' He couldn't get some of the regular studio players.

"So I showed up, and as I recall, it was [pianist/arranger] Don Randi, Hal Blaine, me, and Carol [Hunter]. And Neil did not have all the words to the song yet; he didn't even have the song put together. He did have an intro: 'Wait till you hear this.' And he had stolen that old lick from the Andrews Sisters' 'Beer Barrel Polka'!

"We cut 'Cracklin' Rosie,' in, I believe, four sections, because of the key changes. We'd play to a point, stop, change keys, start again, stop . . . As I remember, the reason why we did that was because Carol, playing the twelve-string, couldn't bar when we changed keys, 'cause it's really tough. So we'd stop and she'd put a capo on her guitar . . . Meanwhile, Neil was trying desperately to write down pieces of lyrics.

"Neil, I think, got all the words that night . . . He came in the next morning to do the vocals because he wanted his voice to be low [to sing], 'Oh, I love my Rosie child.'

"And then," Randy concluded, "we left this thing in pieces, man, and went back on the road."

Putting those pieces together in Neil's absence were Tom Catalano and Armin Steiner. Steiner said that their greatest challenge was in whipping up an ending. "The record came to a dead halt—there was no coda," the engineer recalled. "And Tom said, 'We're going to have fun with this.' And we pieced together the drum fills . . . and on the end Tom hit these big percussive cymbals . . . and we made a record."

"Cracklin Rosie" was released a few days later, on July 30.

"It was another record we knew was a smash," said Uni's Pat Pipolo. "And Neil knew he had a smash; he absolutely knew it. And he offered to do phone interviews with me again. And we sat in that little office of mine and called everybody I could around the country and put Neil on.

"Then Neil told me he would be available for extensive phone interviews with important stations. So I put together some very, very important stations, and I went up to Neil's house—he had just moved into Coldwater Canyon—and Neil did the interviews from his house."

A few weeks later, "Cracklin' Rosie" hit number one on the charts.

While "Cracklin' Rosie" was blaring from radios across the country, Neil could be seen in a new kind of venue that attested to his number-one rating as a concert attraction as well in the summer of 1970. Some weeks earlier, Randy Ceirley had gotten the word on Diamond's imminent jump from the "jerkwater college" circuit from Diamond's William Morris agent, Sherman Tankel. "He said, 'In about two months, the way we got it planned, Neil is going to be one of the biggest stars in the country.'

"And it was almost two months to the day that we played this ice hockey *arena*—I remember because the ice underneath was freezing my ass. After that our itinerary read the so-and-so *arena* in Memphis, the so-and-so *concert hall*."

It wasn't only Neil's high profile on the charts that had made the move to larger venues possible. A spate of guest appearances on network TV shows—"The Ed Sullivan Show," "Johnny Cash," "Johnny Cash Presents the Everly Brothers" (where Diamond finally got to meet his longtime idols), "The Glen Campbell Goodtime Hour"—also had served to enhance his celebrity, making it far more difficult for the mischievous Randy Ceirley and Carol Hunter to play "Being Neil," signing for the boss at hotel desks and car rental agencies.

Diamond approached his budding TV career in typical conscientious fashion. He acquired a video camera and set it up in his downstairs studio at home, and proceeded to shoot himself performing. Meanwhile, he hung mirrors on the walls, so that he could monitor his expressions. "There was no angle left unturned," said old friend Bobby Feldman, who got a look at the mirrored room when he visited Neil for the first time in California. (As for the show that Diamond began to stage at the dinner table for his Brooklyn pal that night, Feldman said: "[He] put out the good china, and everything was formal. And I looked at him and I said, 'You really don't need this for me, you know.' And he looked [at me], and we hugged each other. And we got rid of the china, took off our shoes, and we sat on the floor and ate.")

Gung-ho as he seemed to be about TV, the fact was that Neil was miffed about his inability to wield the kind of control over his appearances that he'd come to exercise in other career matters. Feldman recalled him griping about the way he looked on one of his "Glen Campbell" guest slots, and his frustration came through in a letter he penned at the time to Rachel Ames, daughter of a movie producer friend, Saul David: "Saw myself on TV the other night and barfed all over my German shepherd. If I have to walk down one more long, winding staircase singing 'Kentucky Woman,' I'm either going to die of embarrassment or a nosebleed."

Neil's most maddening TV experience, however, was his first, and last, appearance on "The Joey Bishop Show." Randy Ceirley was an eyewitness:

"I know personally that before the show, Joe Sutton, Neil Diamond, and whoever was head of the account at William Morris at the time went into Joey Bishop and said, 'We will do the show. There is only one requirement that we ask—no mention of drugs. It's a bogging [down] issue, Neil does not want to talk about it' . . . Because this was after . . . 'The Pot Smoker's Song,' and I think Neil was starting to change his views as to the dangers of smoking a little weed . . .

"Everybody kept *assuring* Neil that everything was OK. So we did a song, the band sat down on the side, and Neil went over and sat down with Joey. The first thing Joey said was, 'Well, how do you feel about drugs, Neil?'

"All of our toes curled up. To this day, I have no idea what Neil answered . . . You could see him just shrink, and just get sick to his stomach . . . I heard him start to mumble—and I didn't want to see the rest of it." Ceirley and the rest of the band beat a retreat to the Green Room. He does remember Neil's words when he joined them there: "I will never ever do another television show where I do not have complete control."

For a short time in the spring of 1970, that's what Diamond thought he was going to get as the host of Glen Campbell's summer replacement series. But, according to Joe Sutton, certain CBS higher-ups had last-minute qualms about whether Diamond could carry a series, "so we shined them on."

Having already gotten what he wanted from the medium—arena-sized celebrity—Neil found it easy to shine on TV in general for the time being.

In the fall, Diamond played his two most important dates yet. The first was a one-night stand at Southern California's 9,000-seat Anaheim Convention Center on September 26, exactly a year after his first engagement at the 300-seat Troubadour. The show sold out a week in advance.

In her review, *The Hollywood Reporter's* Sue Cameron described an artist who had become one with the stage: "In a big concert it is difficult to achieve a rapport with a crowd and make each member . . . feel as if you are singing to him. Diamond does . . . He talks to the audience between numbers as if it is a living room conversation."

A month later, Neil flew to New York for a pair of performances at Carnegie Hall, his first dates in Manhattan since pulling up his New York stakes. Among those in the audience opening night were an immensely proud Kieve and Rose Diamond.

One of the few constants of Diamond's tumultuous recent life had been his continuing close bond with his parents and number-one fans (Diamond even gave a special concert at the Manhattan Beach Hotel in honor of his mother's fiftieth birthday two years earlier, calling for her to join him onstage to conduct his backup band for a number). At the world-famous New York auditorium, Neil treated them and the other 2,700 in attendance to a "Night to Remember," which just happened to be the title of an account Kieve penned for his son's fan club newsletter:

The lights dimmed . . . and we sat stoned with great expectations of Neil's performance. Neil came on and was very warmly received. The audience seemed to know what song he was going to sing just by hearing a few bars of the introduction. It seemed to us that they loved him—we did. His comments were humorous and witty and his explanations to some of the songs were a revelation and added to the excitement.

Now came 'Brooklyn Roads,' our favorite. Rose and I clutched hands so tight . . . [but] the pain from our nails digging into our skin was unimportant. This was our song, our memories—our tears. Yes we cried, but they were tears of Joy . . .

It seemed that every song brought the house down, but the last number, 'Brother Love,' was so full of feeling and excitement, it brought all of Carnegie Hall to their feet for a standing ovation.

Thrills of thrills for parents to witness this phenomenon— again, tears of joy. Rose and I looked at each other in disbelief. Can this be happening to our son? To us?

By the time Neil played Carnegie Hall, the two collections of employees in his life, his studio team and his tour team, had had ample opportunity to draw a bead on him. Each saw a strikingly different man at the precipice of superstardom. Randy Ceirley, one of the rare ones to view Diamond both on the road and inside the studio, capsuled the contrast in Jekyll and Hyde terms: "It was two faces."

According to Randy, Neil began wearing the on-tour face that he would come to know and love almost from the start. One could hazard a guess why the highly charged Diamond had come to enjoy himself on the road. For the most part there were no managers, agents, lawyers, accountants, or record company executives to contend with; no producers, engineers, arrangers, and high-powered studio musicians to ride herd over; no heavy decisions of any sort to make. The only business he had to conduct each day was a ninety-minute concert, and that was increasingly becoming an ego trip as his audiences became more and more demonstrative. The rest of the time was his own, to gather his thoughts; to write, which he loved to do, Solitary Man–style, in his hotel room; or to air out with fans and the slightly wacky cast of characters he had assembl d. "Other than the parade of towns and colleges and motels and airplanes and waiting rooms, nothing much happened other than when we started making our own fun," Ceirley commented.

So relaxed did Ceirley & Company come to feel around Neil that they even directed some of their twitting at him. For example, after Neil had struck a few wrong chords on his guitar during one show (Ceirley: "He would grab a handful of strings and you'd never know what would come out"), he and Carol presented him with a batch of guitar picks that they had had made up, inscribed with the words, "Wrong chord, stupid!" To commemorate the simple chord progression that cropped up in many of his songs, meanwhile, they dubbed him Mr. E-A-D-A-E. (Commenting on the musical similarity of his tunes, Ceirley added: "I do remember a couple of times starting a show with one song, like 'Kentucky Woman,' and Neil would have a change of heart from the wings and yell out 'Cherry, Cherry'! And all we'd have to do is move up a key and go into a slightly different riff.")

Neil seemed to enjoy the ribbing. He also enjoyed cracking up Ceirley and Hunter on occasion. Hunter recalled one notorious TV interview he did backstage after a concert in Canada, when "we were all just wasted . . . And the last question was, 'If you could say anything you wanted to say on television, something you had never said before, never been given the opportunity to say . . . what would it be?' And Neil looks into the camera and says *'Fuck you!'* "

Neil's most memorable stunt occurred after a concert in St. Louis, in a nearby International House of Pancakes. "We ask for a table," Ceirley recalled. "So what do they do—they give us this huge table right in the middle of the restaurant. And Neil was at the end of this long table, in full view of everyone in the restaurant, most of whom had been at the concert.

"So we're starved and we're trying to get through dinner, and everyone in the restaurant is going [imitates enthusiastic whispering]. Nobody came up, it was just all this turning and whispering . . .

"And then Neil calls the waitress over and he whispers something to her. She goes, 'Right now?' And Neil has this look in his eye—I didn't know what was happening.

"A couple of minutes later, the waitress returns with this big goblet full of ice cream and whipped cream and nuts, and with a cherry on top. And, very, very animatedly, Neil takes this goblet, lifts it up, shows it to everybody in the restaurant, sets it down in front of him, spreads his arms out and dumps his face right into it—and comes up with this big grin!

"It stopped everything. And, of course, all of us were under the table—it was just priceless. We gave him a hand. So incongruous to his quote 'image.' "

The fun quotient rose even further in the summer of 1970, when Diamond, probably harking back to the late nights he used to spend at the Bitter End being royally entertained by the antics of the Drop In improv players, began hiring comedians as his opening act. "It was like a pressure valve, I think, especially for Neil, to have these guys around," speculated Jefferson Kewley, Neil's new roadie at the time. "When you were waiting at an airport at six in the morning, or when cars weren't there or airplanes were canceled, these guys would just always bring you up."

Of the three comedians—Fred Smoot, Albert Brooks, and Sandy

Baron—who took turns playing jester in the Court of Diamond, Smoot, who had portrayed Trivers in the TV series "Wackiest Ship in the Army," was the most audacious. Not sated by his opening slot on Neil's show, he would steal a little piece of Neil's onstage thunder with one of his wacked-out cameo appearances. One night, he managed to stick his legs in a loose toilet backstage and wriggle the length of the stage behind Neil as he was taking his bow.

Offstage, Smoot was wilder yet. Occasionally he would parade about as the Foamy Monster, naked save for little clouds of shaving cream, strategically placed. After a while, Jefferson Kewley said, the Foamy Monster "got very brazen and started showing up at Neil's press parties."

No one, not even Diamond, got a bigger kick out of Smoot than the roadie. Soon after the comedian's arrival, they became the Laurel and Hardy of the road team.

They made quite a sight. Smoot was five-foot-eight and slender, while Kewley boasted stereotypical roadie dimensions: six feet tall or so and a strapping 250 pounds–plus. Kewley also did Randy Ceirley a few curls better with an amazing mass of blond hair.

Their specialty was mooning. Smoot introduced the sport during a concert one night, dropping his drawers at Neil and the band from the wings. Neil, he recalled, "saw me out of the corner of his eye and broke up a little bit—but he kept up with the song." But Kewley, who was playing congas that night, couldn't muster the same self-control. Convulsed in laughter, he fell off the riser.

Their favorite moon was the "pressed ham," for which Kewley had an awesome built-in advantage. The duo performed the ham against the back-seat windows of limos on the major highways of America, typically when they were passing the limo Diamond was sitting in.

Neil returned the fire. "I saw Neil's tush many times," Smoot chuckled, adding that Neil, however, never pressed his flesh: "For some reason, he was very fast!"

Neil occasionally took part in other shenanigans staged by Smoot and Kewley. He accepted one of the "poo-poo cushions" the duo had picked up in a toy store and sat on it in a commercial airplane or two. He was spotted flinging an occasional spoonful of mashed potatoes during restaurant food fights. And once, according to Kewley, he participated in a game of Beer Bottle Bowling in a backstage dressing room, "and actually carried on and enjoyed it."

Mood elevators that they were, Smoot and Kewley, who would later serve as the inspiration to Neil's tune "Captain Sunshine," found themselves welcome between tours at Neil's house. "He always had cold beers waiting for us because he knew that we loved beers," Jefferson recalled fondly. "And we'd sit around the kitchen just talking and laughing it up, telling road stories. Or we'd go downstairs, where he had a little work room and a pool table, and we'd play pool and listen to new tracks he'd recorded.

"And you'd never have to worry, 'Well, I've got to be careful about this, I can't say anything about that.' Being with him was just like being with a pal, it wasn't like your usual employee-employer relationship . . . We could have been stringing wire together for the phone company!" With that, Kewley unleashed a hearty laugh.

No one who inhabited the same studio as Neil during that time could have conjured up such down-home imagery in describing him. In fact, to members of his recording team, he was "Mr. Gloom," a dour, demanding boss.

"The first hour he loved what we were doing, the second hour it was *terrible,* the third hour it was 'Let's go home.' And the next day, 'Let's try it all over again.' But after a playback . . . Neil would look around at everybody and say, 'Jesus, this is great—there's nothing we should do to this,'" said drummer Hal Blaine of Neil's "teeter-totter" way in the studio.

Engineer Armin Steiner put it more bluntly: "Neil is the most incredible mass of self-torture that I have ever seen in any individual, bar none."

Tales of Diamond the Difficult during the recording of his 1970 album, "Tap Root Manuscript," were many. One of them involved a new face, Marty Paich, the well-known Hollywood arranger.

Paich had been called in to perform an important mission for the album: tie together a handful of African-type tunes—among them the folk-flavored instrumental "Madrigal," the choral piece "Missa," and the child-sung "Childsong" (a timely tune considering the birth of Jesse Michael Diamond on April 30)—which Neil had written after "Soolaimon." The result was Paich's orchestral piece, "African Trilogy," which wove strains from the tunes with new melodic lines into a summing-up musical statement. Tom Catalano had hired a forty-piece orchestra to record the piece at Western Sound on Sunset.

Armin Steiner recalled the notorious session:

"Marty comes in. Now here he is going to have to do something with this track and make it into what you hear on the album . . . And I remember Neil pacing up and down the control room: 'It isn't going to work. It's terrible. He didn't do the right thing. It's not the right melody. What is he doing here? I've got to change it all around.' Over and over. And Tom says, *'Give the man a chance, for God's sakes!* You've only heard the first few bars.'

"Now he goes out and he starts to converse with Marty. I turn to

Tom and say, 'I hope he isn't going to blow it because if he does not allow this to go through, the whole piece is going to be ruined, it'll never be tied together.' And he starts changing [things] with Marty. When I say changing, I mean he starts singing, because Neil cannot write music in a formal sense. 'No, Marty, I think it should be [sings] *Dah dah dah, de de de.*' OK, Marty writes it down, and he changes it. 'No, I don't like that—[sings] *Dah dah dah, de de de.*' Here, we're sitting with a forty-piece orchestra.

"I think we finally came back to what Marty wrote originally, after going full circle . . . suffering for four hours."

Steiner added that he had a sneaking suspicion about why Diamond had behaved so boorishly: "I just think that it [what Paich had written] was probably so overwhelming to him that he didn't know in his own mind whether he should take the credit for it, or Marty . . . I mean, Neil has a big ego." (As it turned out, Diamond had no problem in taking credit for his "crowning delight" of a suite in interviews—while tossing a bouquet to the Beatles: "They opened the door for everybody . . . I never could have attempted 'The African Trilogy' if it hadn't been for [them]." However, in the booklet that accompanied "Tap Root Manuscript," there was a brief note of thanks to "Marty Paitch" [sic], for his "exceptional musicianship and insights in helping to bring the african suite to fulfillment.")

There was blood on the tracks of "Tap Root Manuscript" as well for arranger Lee Holdridge, who worked on most of the other tunes. He mentioned "Coldwater Morning," inspired by Diamond's move into the Beverly Hills canyon of that name, as a vexing case in point: "We spent days and days on that song . . . And the musicians were soooooooooo tired of it; they were playing it mechanically. To this day, I listen to it and I say, 'Gosh, that song should have been thrown out.'"

As for "Done Too Soon," a charged song with an inventive lyric consisting almost entirely of names of famous figures throughout history, "when we played it in the studio it was right the first time." But, the arranger added, Neil insisted on applying the same kind of maddening scrutiny to it: "We played with it, did this and did that. Finally, after a couple of hours, it was getting to the point where we had tried it every possible way—it was ridiculous." It was then, Lee said, that he took a stand: "If you want any more changes," he told Neil, "why don't you come on the podium and do them yourself?"

Some hushed arguing ensued between Diamond and Catalano, he added. "Finally, Tom came out [of the control room] and said, 'Do the chart the way you wrote it.'"

Neil waged a different kind of battle entirely on the album's one tune he didn't pen himself, Bob Russell's and Bobby Scott's "He Ain't Heavy . . . He's My Brother." He strongly resisted recording it, despite being lobbied by Catalano and Armin Steiner. It wasn't until a prere-cording meeting in Neil's home, Holdridge explained, that Catalano finally succeeded in getting him to at least try the song.

"So we went off to the studio. Because of all the indecision, I didn't have a chart, so we basically scratched out a lead sheet in his key . . . and just started playing through it."

At the session, Neil did something rare for him: He laid down his vocals live with his rhythm section rather than return to the studio to overdub them later. While that may have been his way to give "He Ain't Heavy" the bum's rush, in this instance it turned out to be a stroke of genius. Holdridge: "You could sense that the musicians responded by having him [there] singing; I think they felt the song more, and they put that into their playing. When it was all done I thought it was beautiful. Tom did, too. And I think Neil liked it."

But Lee couldn't be sure because Neil didn't say as much, and his somber face—a face that was already becoming disturbingly familiar to the arranger—didn't betray any positive emotions. "It was the start of a very difficult period," Holdridge added.

Uni released "He Ain't Heavy" as a single in October. Considering that the Hollies had enjoyed a Top 10 hit with it earlier that year, Neil's rendition did very well, cracking *Billboard*'s Top 20 in December.

By then, "Tap Root Manuscript," also released in October, had set a new chart standard for a Neil Diamond studio LP, peaking at number thirteen.

Mainly because of the curiously titled "The African Trilogy: A Folk Ballet" (actually composed of seven tracks and six different numbers), it also set a new standard for Diamond praise in the press. *Time* maga-zine lauded the "Trilogy" as "a stunning example of pop crossbreed-ing." And a profile in Britain's *Melody Maker* noted that "things are changing for the good-looking American singer-composer. Now, he is a name that can be mentioned to intellectual friends . . . It took a seven track Trilogy dedicated to Africa to place his name on the quality list."

In the piece, Neil was quoted as saying, "It's a nice feeling to be taken seriously."

·10·
I AM...

"I spent my whole life preparing a defense of myself and never open-
ing up to anybody . . . My attitude, in purely intellectual terms, was
'screw you.'
  "[But] being a relatively closed person is like reveling in your
own dirt . . . You're better off if you can open up, give freely and
without insecurities . . . [That's why] this acting thing, these offers,
have been a godsend. It's more than therapy, it's a colossal new can-
vas. And I have a rainbow to paint with now."
                    —Diamond, from a press release, circa 1969

Committed as he was to being taken seriously as an artist, the fact was
that Neil's new career canvas contained but one acting splotch by the
end of 1970. That had come on a segment of the TV show "Mannix,"
in which he appeared as himself, singing several songs in a club. As he
was midway through one of them, "Raisin' Cain," Joe Mannix (Mike
Connors) wound up at his feet—courtesy of a punch—cuing the put-
out Diamond to utter the one line he'd spoken as a professional actor,
"Hey, man, do you mind if I finish the set by myself?"

Yet Neil did seem sincere about forging an acting career. One person in an ideal position in the late '60s to gauge his interest in acting,
as well as his potential, was Saul David, a Universal-connected movie
producer *(Von Ryan's Express, In Like Flint)*. The two were introduced
several years earlier when an agent friend of David's brought Neil over
to David's Beverly Hills home.

That get-together didn't begin very promisingly. David failed to
mention to his then-twelve-year-old daughter, Rachel, a big Diamond
fan at the time, that Neil would be joining the family for dinner, and
when she was called into the living room to meet him she was so shocked
that she burst into tears and ran upstairs. "It embarrassed Neil so badly
that he couldn't talk for a while," recalled Totty Ames, Rachel's
stepmother.

Neil managed to regain his composure, and in the course of that
evening and subsequent dinners, a friendship with David was born in
which he revealed other sides of his complex self.

On the surface, it seemed an odd pairing: the pop star and the middle-aged, rock-loathing movie producer. But David recognized that the two of them had things in common, including their roots. David, too, had been born in Brooklyn.

"We talked about where he came from," David said. "And I think it was probably true of Neil's generation as it was of mine, of loving and accepting what you came from and at the same time being a little ashamed of it and wanting to be part of the larger, brighter world. And it's a part of what I guess is generally conceived of as Jewish guilt."

It followed that he and Neil would discuss Diamond's flight from Brooklyn roads. "We talked about the business of the remarriage, and the kind of world he had left and whether he could make himself feel at home in the world he was embracing," David confirmed. "And that was easy for me. My own parabola may have been a kind of reassurance to him at the time—that it is possible to change [to a] world . . . that suits you better intellectually and emotionally without just feeling endlessly guilty about the one that you left. Maybe that may have been part of the attraction that I had for him."

David added that he was taken by the "Byronic" persona that he saw that Neil had fashioned for himself. "I do remember that the first thing I thought about him was that he was a little awkward, and clearly a very romantic figure to himself and perhaps to others. He dressed almost all in black. He wore boots. And when he would come to your house he would do that thing which is so endearing in a young man— and, in a way, very European—which is, get up from a conversation and go stare out a window . . . He was always kind of romantic."

David's fascination with Diamond's adopted image didn't stop him from ribbing him about it. He was amazed, for example, to see that Neil persisted in dressing the part—black boots included—in Jamaica even, where he visited David on the set of *Skullduggery,* an action thriller the producer was filming at the time. "I remember we used to twit him a lot, sitting there in the heat in his black boots," David recalled. "I was constantly trying to get him to take off his boots and wear sandals. I was sure he was uncomfortable."

David doesn't recall whether or not Neil ever did peel off his boots, but he does remember Diamond's reaction to his kidding: "He thought it was funny, too."

That he did was necessary for their friendship to take root, David added. "If he had been totally caught up in playing Lord Byron, without any sense of himself that it was a performance, we probably couldn't have been friends—he would have been offended." But instead, David said, Neil and he shared an appreciation for "the momentary absurdity of things . . . We laughed a lot together."

They enjoyed hours of conversation. "We just talked about everything: books, history, politics, philosophy," David continued. "Neil was interested in conversation in the old-fashioned sense . . . where the assumption was you could use quotations without being accused of being bad company. He was a pleasant person to have around in a community where people tend to be often intensely parochial, talking very specifically and internally about deals and dates."

Saul added that he and Neil, in fact, seldom discussed their respective careers: "And it may have been that one of the reasons that Neil enjoyed my company was [that] everybody else he talked to wanted to talk to him about his career or how they could get a part of it. And, you know, I just liked him for the way he was, an interesting fellow who was fairly talented and had a lot of ideas."

Some ideas that Neil did voice, however, had everything to do with his career. "He wanted to try acting," David said. "He was like a lot of other guys; he wanted to try things, and particularly he wanted to try movies."

As much as he wished he could be, the producer found he couldn't be particularly encouraging. He said that he had qualms, dating back to their first get-together, about Neil's ability to make the plunge from the concert stage to the screen. "I think that an actor has to have the ability to abandon himself to the thing he is doing," he explained. "I just thought Neil would have a very hard time letting go to the extent an actor needs to be able to do it.

"On the stage, for example, he was letting go and not letting go. What he does on the stage is really very studied, a very controlled emotion and manipulation of the audience. It works, because what you do theatrically is quite different from what you do in front of a camera. And the reason why so many stage actors don't work too well in movies is because the very theatricality which works for them on stage looks phony in the enormous magnification of a camera. A camera really worships normal, whether it is true natural or not . . . And I thought Neil would be stiff in front of it."

Also lurking as an obstacle to Neil's ability to surrender to the camera was what Saul David perceived to be the "double image" he had cultivated for himself. David said he sensed that, unlike other popular figures in music he had met, people who felt that "how they looked was far less important than what they felt," "Neil saw himself as a figure in a drama . . . so that the figure that he was cutting, how he looked, was something that he was always aware of." This constant monitoring of self, he added, made Neil "a little graver, perhaps, than necessary at some times." Certainly, it didn't enhance his chances, in the producer's mind, of becoming a good actor.

Despite these reservations, Saul David saw which way the wind was blowing at Universal in 1968, and that was toward giving Neil a crack at a film. It just so happened that, at the time, he had a film project, *A Stretch on the River,* that was entering the screen-test stage. With the strong encouragement of Universal executives, David agreed to test

Diamond for the lead role, that of a young man in 1950s America who takes a job on a Mississippi towboat as a means of hiding from the draft, only to mature sufficiently during his stretch on the river to face life's challenges. David: "I think that *Stretch on the River* was more a vehicle for Universal to see what he tested like than a totally serious consideration of him for that part."

The test, which took place on a Universal back lot, was an elaborate one. A portion of a river boat was used, a then-up-and-coming Universal actor by the name of David Hartman was called in to perform with Neil, and veteran Gordon Douglas directed.

"He was not as bad as I feared, or as good as I had hoped for," David recalled. "He was stiff. But, you know, Neil is smart. When you tell him to do something over again and, this time, do it this way, he can." Still, the producer added, he didn't think Neil possessed the "incandescence" that he felt the part demanded.

David shared his feedback with Neil. "He accepted it. He accepted it and talked about next time."

But there were to be no more next times at Universal, its studio brass cooled to the notion of Neil Diamond, movie star. So Neil cast around for film offers from other quarters. It wasn't until 1970, however, that he got a bite.

The interested party was producer Marvin Worth. The former manager of Lenny Bruce was working at the time on a film bio of the late comedian for Columbia Pictures, and he and his director, Tom O'Horgan, were having difficulty finding an actor to portray Bruce. "Nobody wanted to touch it," O'Horgan said. "At that point it was too touchy a subject for some of the major names." So they had gradually extended their search to less likely candidates; one of them was Diamond.

Demonstrating his enthusiasm for the project, Diamond booked himself into the Bitter End West on Santa Monica Boulevard for one night for the sole purpose of showcasing his ability to handle Bruce-style comedy. His performance turned Worth and O'Horgan into believers. Said Worth: "He did Lenny, and he was terrific." Said O'Horgan: "He had all the qualities that we were looking for . . . somebody who could do the humor, and who had some kind of performance charisma."

The next step was a screen test. O'Horgan had a couple of friends of his (including future San Francisco Supervisor and gay activist Harvey Milk) coach Neil with his lines. Neil later spoke of the profundity of those rehearsals: "He [Bruce] was just saying all those things I had been holding in . . . 'fuck' and 'shit' . . . and 'death' and 'kill' . . . It was frightening because I had never been willing to admit this part of my personality."

The role, now that it seemed to be a distinct possibility, might have suddenly seemed even more frightening to Neil for another reason as well. In O'Horgan's words, it promised to "turn [his career] upside down . . . It surely would have taken him on a different trip." The question was, could Neil, always aware, in Saul David's words, of the "figure that he was cutting," allow himself to go through with a part whose consequences he couldn't begin to script?

It turned out that he wasn't sure he could. Before he agreed to do the *Lenny* screen test he requested that producer Worth insert a back-out clause in their agreement. "You don't test anybody unless you make the deal first and he'll do it," Worth commented. But he made an exception and granted Neil his out.

In Worth's and O'Horgan's opinions, Neil's ensuing test was an unqualified success. "I probably liked him better than all the tests," Worth said. For his part, O'Horgan marveled at Diamond's "freshness . . . He had that performer quality which is what Lenny had, yet he wasn't a stand-up comedian. In that he was a singer, essentially this was kinda like a fresh bend; it made him very right . . . I think he could have been quite extraordinary."

Neil didn't think so, or so he claimed to concert audiences. His account of his *Lenny* screen test became familiar concert fodder, serving to introduce a certain song that he said he began to write that day. In 1971, for example, he told a Los Angeles audience:

About a year ago I went to Columbia Studios . . . to do a screen test for a film that was scheduled to be made, which never was made; it became a Broadway show called *Lenny.** And the film was to be about a man named Lenny Bruce, and I wanted to do the part because I believed in the man and what he had to say, and also the tragedy of his life . . .

[And] they said, "Study these three scenes, come in, we'll film you, we'll see if you're right." And I really worked on it, I prepared myself. And I came in the morning of the screen test about five o'clock—which is a ridiculous hour . . . [and] they put on makeup and everything, did that whole thing . . . And we went in front of the cameras at seven.

The first scene that they wanted me to do was a love scene, which is just *impossible* to do at seven in the morning, just *impossible*. Really impossible. I tried, the girl tried, the director tried, everybody tried. But I couldn't—I guess partly because of inexperience and partly because of the hour, I couldn't involve myself in it. But I felt OK, I had two more scenes to go and "you'll just do everything you can with those two scenes and there will be no question because you'll be so good that you'll get the part . . ."

And I came back after a short break for the second scene,

* *Lenny*, the film, starring Dustin Hoffman, was finally made in 1974.

which was to be a nightclub monologue . . . which is extremely difficult if you know what Lenny Bruce is about . . . But I was ready for it and felt that I could do it.

Just before I went in front of the cameras the director came over to me and said, "Neil, I'd like you to meet Sally Marr." And as it turned out, Sally Marr was a very attractive middle-aged lady who turned out to be Lenny Bruce's mother. And meeting this woman before going in front of the cameras to portray her son, her dead son, was just something that left me—it broke my concentration completely. I felt for what she would be going through watching *me* speak her son's words. It just freaked me out. I'm trying to give her the best that I could. I wasn't happy with the way it came out . . .

Now, I figured, "Well, it's two scenes and you blew it." I was super-depressed, I mean really depressed . . . And I went back to my dressing room, took a break for an hour, and I, uh, picked up my guitar, started to write a melody and some words. And, uh, I'd like to do it for ya.

The song was "I Am . . . I Said."

The long and winding in-concert intro Neil gave to the quasi-auto-biographical tune reflected the importance he attached to it. Guitar player Carol Hunter observed his delight with "I Am . . . I Said" even before he had finished it. "I had already heard the first verse," she said. "And we were in a hotel in St. Louis. We had gotten there an hour earlier. And I got out of the room to go to the ice machine. And all of a sudden Neil came *rushing* out of his room and *grabbed* me by the wrist and *dragged* me in to his room, and said, '*You've got to hear this!*' And he sang me the 'frog-king' verse. And he was *so* happy with it. I've seen Neil real happy a lot of times . . . but never more so than at that moment. He *loved* that verse."

Arranger Lee Holdridge also got a taste of Neil's excitement all the way from Costa Rica, where he was spending the Christmas holidays with his parents (his father, a research scientist in tropical forestry, was working there at the time). "They called me and they wanted me to interrupt my vacation, come home and write the string arrangement," he recalled. "And I said, 'Could you wait another four days, until the second [of January]? I haven't seen my folks in a while.'" But Holdridge was told that Diamond couldn't, and arranger Marty Paich was hired in his stead.

As it turned out, the recording of "I Am . . . I Said" took weeks. Playing the studio malcontent once again, Diamond tabled Paich's work and brought in another arranger, Larry Mahoberac, to do a new chart. Little did he know, however, that Armin Steiner, who happened to love Paich's work, revived it on his own and blended it with the Mahoberac arrangement. "That's why the sound of the record is so huge," he confessed. (Steiner added that he and Tom Catalano also stuck to their own judgment on the English horn solo during the "frog-king" verse: "Neil hated the solo—*'I don't ever want to hear that.'* Tom and I left it in because it was beautiful.")

The resulting record, released in March of 1971, marked a milestone in Neil's recording career, according to its composer. Tapping his now-well-publicized downbeat view of his Brooklyn past, he would label it "a statement on my part, for the first time in my life, which said essentially *I am, I exist,* I recognize it, and love me, accept me. It said all of the things I needed as a child—all of the schools that I had been to that I was never accepted in, all of the times that I had spent alone at home. It was the self-esteem that I never had that I wanted."

Not every listener, however, was willing to follow Neil Diamond out onto his quasi-confessional artistic limb. Songwriter/performer Jake Holmes, his Bitter End–era acquaintance, was one who drew the line.

Holmes recalled an ironic conversation he had had with Neil several years earlier: "We were driving in a car uptown one day, and Neil looked at me and said, 'You know, your songs—you've *got* to write more simple.' And I looked at him. I didn't understand what he was talking about! I mean to me, he wrote *too* simple . . . I considered myself a 'heavy' writer, writing meaningful stuff . . . I said, 'This is crazy. I don't care if I don't get hit records, I can't write those type of songs."

Holmes flashed on Neil's advice when he heard "I Am . . . I Said." "Talk about being simple—that was the most complicated song I ever heard. He should have taken his own damn advice!"

(Years later, Jerome Kass, the first screenwriter on *The Jazz Singer,* would have a similarly befuddled reaction to the lyric, which he studied in preparation for writing his draft: "I tried and tried to understand what that song was about . . . I have a feeling he's not very clear in his thinking. I think he's kind of muddled, in fact.")

Indeed, Uni's Pat Pipolo confessed he did encounter a somewhat subdued reaction from radio programmers. "I don't think everybody felt it," he said, "but it was a Neil Diamond record and they could not afford to not play it."

Also, skeptical programmers could take heart in the fact that "I Am . . . I Said" certainly had the sound of a hit, with its majestically plaintive melody, Neil's charged vocals, a dynamic build, and the exquisite Paich-Mahoberac arrangement that merged pop and classical strains.

"I Am . . . I Said" turned out to be a major seller, peaking at number four. Its impressive showing couldn't be attributed to the record's "hit" sound alone. That, in turn, said something significant about Neil's audience.

What it demonstrated was that Neil and his record buyers had come to a special place in their relationship by 1971. Conditioned by his previous confessional tunes, his fans, apparently, weren't confused in the least by "I Am . . . I Said." They could identify "lonely" and "emptiness" as Diamond buzzwords, and they could make the jump from point *A* to point *B* in the sketchy lyric. To them, Neil was singing poignant self-truths directly to them. And they were eager to indulge this self-crowned "king" of pop. Now, and in the future.

·11·
IN THE
FAST LANE

Having tabled his acting plans for the time being, Neil had time in early 1971 to continue dealing with what had been his one professional Achilles' heel: his tour operation.

During 1970, he had finally made important strides on the tour front, hiring a roadie, Jefferson Kewley, who was worth his salt (among many other foul-ups, Kewley's lackadaisical predecessor had crashed a truck into a backstage wall), and contracting regularly for his sound with Stan Miller of Kearney, Nebraska, then in the process of making a name for himself as one of the best sound men in the concert business. Speaking of the four-column Shure system Neil had been hauling around when he came aboard, Kewley chuckled, "It was like one step above a lounge act."

Another favor Neil did for himself in late 1970 was to add Joe Gannon to his tour payroll. At the time he still was in dire need of a crack road manager, a resourceful lighting director, and a savvy show consultant. In Gannon, a veteran of tours with such disparate acts as Tiny Tim, Bill Cosby, and the Kingston Trio, he found all three.

Guitarist Carol Hunter talked about the impact of Gannon the road manager: "Before he came along I'd have to call the office and say, 'I know I have to be at such and such an airline at six A.M. Friday, but are we going to cold places or warm places?' And then I'd have to get to the airport myself.

"But when Joe came onboard the *limo* picked us up. A day or two before we left we got the itinerary in the mail which said exactly where we were going, where we were staying, who the local contact was, where you could get something to eat afterward.

"Joe," she added, "made touring almost a pleasure."

Gannon the lighting director turned out to be just as indispensable. Recalled bass player Randy Ceirley: "There was a joke that somebody— it may have been me—started about Joe: 'If you give Joe Gannon a piece of colored paper and a flashlight, he'll put on a helluva show.'" In the early going with Diamond, especially when they were playing college sports arenas, Gannon claimed he didn't have a great deal more than that to work with: "Lights—we'd request folo spots . . . 'We don't have any of those.' So I'd spend time going to the college theater people and yanking and doing . . . every day."

When he had all the lights he wanted, which was the case more often than not by early 1971, he proved a whiz. "Joe *knew* lights," said Jefferson Kewley. "He knew *different* lights, not just 'I want a green here' . . . He added a dimension of real showmanship to Neil's concerts, which, of course, enabled Neil to get more and more confident because the show looked so good.

"And you could feel it on you when the lights are working well—you look around and you see how it looks. That got Neil going to where he was realizing what he really could do in his performances. I'm sure he would have gotten into it on his own eventually, but Joe gave him that great shortcut. He probably saved him another year and a half of getting it together."

Still, lights alone didn't make the man in concert. Enter Gannon the show consultant.

Gannon happened to boast a recipe for pacing a concert; he called it The Formula. "It's in play format," he explained, in describing how it came to be applied to Neil's ninety-minute show. "You can't start the show out really high, you start it out fairly high, to give 'em a goose; and you do it with an overture, an opening piece of music. You start with an overture for a couple of reasons—to build up the anticipation in the audience for Neil, and to give the sound man a half-assed chance at mixing it."

For the first "scene," Diamond would take the stage and perform his first few numbers . . . the first two medium fast, the third a ballad, and the fourth "a gangbuster kind of a light tune, like 'Kentucky Woman.'"

Then, Scene II: "You sit on a stool. The minute you do that the set changes before your eyes . . . the audience feels more familiar with you." In this section, Neil would croon several of his lighter songs.

"Serious business" would then take place in Scene III—"whatever serious tunes he had in his catalogue at that time." The next to last song in this final segment would be Neil's latest hit single. And the last song would be the kind of rocker that would allow Neil to exit in a blaze of glory. Invariably, that tune was "Brother Love."

And, according to Gannon's Formula, that was all the show that was needed. In other words, no encores, other than Neil returning, perhaps, to reprise a portion of "Brother Love." "You have to leave them wanting more," Gannon reasoned. Anyway, as he explained to Neil, "When you do 'Brother Love,' how are you gonna top it? You'd have to get the 1812 Overture with the Brass Bucket Choir and the Norman Luboff Choir."

Diamond, who Gannon was surprised to see had a pretty fair grasp of pacing already, went along with almost all of The Formula, including, for a time, the no-encore rule. (It was relaxed by 1972 when Gannon saw that even after Neil performed an encore number or two, "the audience would still want more.") However, Joe, like others before him, found out early that Neil didn't just accept his theories on face value. "I came in as sort of the fastest gun in the West and I think Neil wanted me to know that even though things may have seemed screwed up, he had some ideas," he said. "We would sit and argue—not in the sense of *arguing*, but I'd say, 'I think this,' and he'd say, 'Well, I dunno, why don't we do this?'"

One of the first things Gannon recalled hearing from members of Diamond's tour party when he reported for duty was "Hey, we got to do something about the drummer." Once he began to weave his magic on Diamond's show, the focus returned to Eddie Rubin.

The 1970 "Gold" album had showcased the play of Neil's backup band. None of the players had sparkled on the LP, but, of the three, drummer Rubin's mechanical play certainly was the most suspect. "In fact," said roadie Jefferson Kewley, "when Eddie didn't show up in rehearsal some times, I played drums. Neil used to laugh and say I played better than Eddie."

In the forefront of the replace-Rubin movement was Randy Ceirley, who even had a new drummer in mind: Dennis St. John. The bass player had worked with St. John in Los Angeles, and had found the Georgia-born drummer to be a "dead beat—by that I mean he stuck his foot in it and the tempo was there and you never ever worried. And he had the great licks besides."

Ceirley finally finagled an audition for St. John in Hollywood, "and the look on Neil's face when Dennis started playing—it was heaven."

The next weekend Neil went out, he had St. John in tow. "All of a sudden, the band got ten times better," Ceirley said. Little did he know at that time that St. John would soon figure into his own dismissal.

"From what I understand," said bass player/guitarist Emory Gordy Jr., an old friend of St. John's, "Neil set Dennis down on the airplane [that first weekend] and says, 'Dennis, what do you think about the band?' And Dennis says, 'Personally, I feel the band sucks.' And Neil says, 'OK, get me a better band.' And Dennis says, 'Are you serious?' And Neil says, 'Yes.'"

It was a great opportunity for the ambitious, yet outwardly laid-back Dennis St. John to immediately cement his power in the tour hierarchy. And exploiting opportunities that lay in his career path just happened to be another of his talents.

Gordy, who a decade earlier left an Atlanta party band called Wayne Lockadisi and the Kommotions to join the drummer's rival band, St. John and the Cardinals, recalled his pal's savviness: "Dennis was an excellent organizer . . . a go-getter. I felt real comfortable working for him. I knew I'd get paid, I knew that he could get the bucks, and I knew that he had a strong sense for where he was going."

St. John and the Cardinals became the hottest local band in Atlanta, dispensing its versions of the R&B-flavored hits of the day nightly at the Kitten's Korner on Peachtree. During the day, and occasionally after their 9 P.M.–2 A.M. club gig, St. John and Gordy played on sessions at Master Sound Studios. Among their credits was the Classic IV's first hit, "Spooky," as well as records by Billy Joe Royal and Roy Orbison, the latter of whom they toured with.

However, finding Atlanta too small for his ambitions, St. John made his pilgrimage to Los Angeles in 1969. There he became drummer and manager of the house band at Producer's Workshop, a Hollywood recording studio. A year later he persuaded Gordy to join him.

Gordy was the first musician St. John tapped for Diamond's new band. It just so happened at the time that Randy Ceirley was in the most vulnerable position of the remaining three players (keyboards player Mark Kapner had been added to the lineup in 1970). By Ceirley's own account, the road had turned him into a "lost ship . . . I was snorting cocaine, snorting methadrine, smoking weed, taking Valium, and basically becoming a basket case." He added: "I think Dennis saw me disintegrating."

Randy claimed he was about to call Neil to give his notice when Neil called him to tell him he couldn't use him anymore. (Soon afterward, Ceirley said that he and his wife retreated to their mountain cabin where, *sans* drugs, "I chopped wood, walked, drank water, ate good food, took *the cure*.")

Next, the ax fell on Mark Kapner, the gangly keyboards player who liked to appear onstage wearing a dog collar. His replacement: Alan Lindgren, a young player from Riverside, California, who had caught Emory Gordy's ear. "Alan went straight from playing Holiday Inn lounges to going on the road with Neil and flying in Learjets," Gordy said.

That left Carol Hunter. The way she described her state at the time, she, too, seemed ready for a pink slip: "I was kind of spaced-out and doped out . . . [although] I could play just fine. But my attitude was not always on." But Neil, who had more of a one-to-one relationship with her than with the other band members, wanted her to remain in the band as a guitarist/background singer. So instead of replacing her, St. John hired nineteen-year-old Richard Bennett of Arizona, another player at Producer's Workshop, as a second guitarist.

(Regarding Hunter's relationship with Neil, Randy Ceirley noted: "He was patient, kind, indulgent to her. I never quite understood it." Hunter commented: "I always felt like he was a big brother. Rumor to the contrary, woman *banging* on my door after the gig, saying, 'Let me in—I know he's in there!'—well you can't do that . . . Neil's a very attractive man; he was a *boss*, and he was my pal.")

Emory Gordy remembers well the first weekend he went out with Diamond in 1971. He particularly remembers a moment during the second gig, at the University of Indiana on March 14:

"I had already played with a bunch of people. And I was thinking, 'What is Diamond? Is he happening today? Where is this gig going?' You can't believe how beamed in your thoughts are when you're playing onstage—the audience disappears, everything disappears except what you're doing.

"But I think maybe the third or fourth number into the set I had enough time to just look up and absorb some of the audience. And I said to myself, 'Yeah, this is happening.' What I felt was a charisma— this guy has charisma. And this audience—there's a rapport there. They are getting off on what he's doing and he's getting off on what they're doing."

Once the new backup band was constituted, there was no doubt that it was happening, too, musically. Roadie Jefferson Kewley, however, admitted to a little sadness about the turn of events. "I don't know why, but Dennis [St. John] took over . . . Neil just thought, 'Well, this is OK. It's easy. I don't have to think about it. I'll let Dennis be in charge of the band.' I'm not saying that anything changed in the way he cared about the band. But members changed, so then the whole thing kind of changed a little bit. It lost its initial family feeling."

Kewley still had reason to laugh on the road, however. His buddy Fred Smoot, who continued to open the show for Neil on occasion, helped see to that. And so did Joe Gannon, who, Jefferson was delighted to find, "was as crazy as the rest of us."

Getting loose once in a while, it turned out, happened to be a part of another Joe Gannon formula, this one for maintaining one's sanity on the road. Kewley: "After the show was over, the show was over to Joe . . . He would get Neil out of his hotel room . . . and we'd go out."

(Back home, Gannon tried to get Neil to hang loose on at least one occasion as well, when he and Smoot coaxed Diamond onto a golf course for the first time in his life during a trip to Palm Springs. Smoot: "He had a good swing, there was potential, and I'd encourage him— '*Come on, come on, get into it!*' But he just lost his crazy patience immediately . . . he became so damn frustrated trying to hit the ball." Smoot added that when they finally got through the nine holes, Neil took off by himself on a motorcycle, *his* way of unwinding in laid-back Palm Springs.)

Given the post-concert party atmosphere on the road after Gannon's arrival, it was only natural that some serious mischief be stirred occasionally. And, in fact, in Nashville one night, Gannon and Smoot conceived what they instantly knew would rank as the Neil Diamond prank of a lifetime. Their accomplice was an actor friend of theirs, Joe Higgins, whom they happened to butt into in the lobby of the Holiday Inn where they were staying.

Although Higgins' name wasn't well known at the time, his face was, thanks to his portrayal of the burly Southern sheriff on a series of Dodge commercials. In fact, he was at the hotel to perform as his sheriff character before a convention audience.

As Smoot and Gannon got a load of Higgins in his uniform, they looked at each other and Smoot blurted out, "Joe, you gotta bust our party! You have to bust our party because Neil is sitting in the room, and everybody"—Freddy pantomimed a deep drag on a joint—"is wacked completely."

"I'd *love* to!'" Higgins said.

Barely able to contain themselves, Smoot and Gannon returned to Neil's hospitality suite. By this point, Smoot said, "the room was *filled* with smoke. Remember when you were in the Army and you had to go in that room, and they'd set off the gas and you'd have to put on your mask? Well, the room looked like that." Meanwhile, Gannon managed to spot the unsuspecting Diamond through the haze, chatting with a couple of female fans.

"All of a sudden," said Smoot, "The door *crashes* open, Joe comes in, *he blows his bloody whistle!* and he says, *"Awright, everybody's under arrest!"'*

"My eyes were glued on Neil, and he shit blue apples," said Gannon. "And it was beat one, beat two, beat three—all of the blood is now out of Neil's face, his eyes are wide open."

"It was the first time I'd ever seen Neil's jaw kind of quiver and drop," said Smoot.

Jefferson Kewley, who wasn't in on the gag, said the stunned silence in the room lasted for a few seconds—the time it took for everyone to focus on Joe Higgins' familiar mug. "And then," Jefferson laughed, "The place went nuts!"

In May and June, Neil took his band to Europe. A consistent seller overseas ever since his Bang Records days, he had traveled to England twice previously, in 1967 and 1970, but only to do interviews and perform on TV. Although press and television appearances also comprised a considerable portion of this tour, his new manager, Ken Fritz, had scheduled eight shows, three in London, and five in Germany.

The day after performing on the BBC's "Top of the Pops," Neil opened the tour portion of the trip with a date at Annabel's, a posh watering hole of the young British elite. A prestige gig, it was the first club date he had done since the Troubadour, and the last he would ever do. "The audience went crazy," guitarist Carol Hunter recalled.

But not as crazy as the crowd that packed Royal Festival Hall two nights later for Neil's two shows there. To look at the audience, made up largely of screaming teenage girls, was to take a trip down Memory Lane to Diamond's performances at the Good Guy Hop.

As Neil left the theater that night, dozens of those fans gave him a scare. Arranger Lee Holdridge, who had been invited along on the tour, recalled the incident: "We just started walking to the limos, and suddenly all these girls started crowding around . . . One of them jumped on Neil . . . he got a bit of a scratch on his face, and they tore a part of his shirt. I got kicked a few times. Then we started *running* for the limousine."

Holdridge made it into the same limo as Neil. "He was very shaken up for a while." The incident, coupled with the response Neil had received in concert earlier that night, made a deep impression on the arranger: "It was the first time that we had a sense that we had a superstar here."

Those were precisely the sentiments of Phil Symes, writing in *Disk and Music Echo*: "Neil Diamond promised 'a few surprises' for his London Festival Hall concert . . . and we got them! The biggest of all was the man himself. Offstage he's reserved and soft-spoken, so you expect him to appear on stage with just a guitar and sit there and pour his heart out to you. Not the case. He's quite the most exhibitionist showman since Tom Jones, and roars songs like a lion with a thorn in his paw."

Fearing a similar response from his German fans, Neil tightened his security. As it turned out however, he didn't have to. At his June 9 Munich date, in fact, Holdridge noted that the audience was so polite, "it was like they were at a classical concert."

While band members were free to travel on their own or stay at a seventeenth-century estate Diamond had rented for them in the English town of Crowborough, Holdridge tagged along with Diamond while he did press and TV. He was with him in Milan, where Neil taped two television shows, and in Paris, where he appeared on the Sunday TV staple, *"Tele Dimanche."* Lee had a funny memory of the Paris experience:

"This TV show was sports, news, and entertainment . . . [it] went on for hours. I've never seen anything so crazy in my life. And I remember we were in the dressing room and they told him he would go on at a certain time to sing 'Done Too Soon'—he had the track and he was going to sing it live.

"All of a sudden someone came running into the dressing room and said, "You've got to go on now!' And Neil said, 'But it's ten minutes early.' 'Yeah, but the tennis match finished early.' So everybody went running out. The guy had already started the 'Done Too Soon' tape . . . the first eight bars had gone by before Neil even got in front of the camera! It was good of him that he kept his cool and picked it up from the second verse. But I was laughing . . .''

Lee wound up laughing a lot on what, for him, was an immensely enjoyable trip. However, he said the only laughing he did around Diamond was at his expense one night—when Diamond ordered a steak at a ritzy London restaurant they and Tom Catalano were dining at, and then smeared it with catsup. "The maitre d' came over and said, 'Is there anything wrong with your steak?,'" Holdridge recalled, chuckling. "In Europe, if you put catsup on the steak, they're mortified." For the most part, Holdridge claimed that, around him at least, Neil wasn't at all the at-ease person that the likes of Randy Ceirley had talked of, but rather the same "stiff, uncomfortable" man that he had seen in the studio: "You just couldn't talk to him about the weather, or tell jokes."

Carol Hunter saw a clipped Diamond as well at the end of the tour, a June 21 taping of an "In Concert" special for the BBC in London. An interview that Hunter had done with *Melody Maker* had just appeared, and Hunter, who had told Neil she wanted to pursue a solo career after the Europe tour, had been quoted as making some comments that fell outside the Diamond party line. In describing the band, for example, she reportedly said it was "essentially made up of session men who play the same note, all the notes every night. Having been a performer it's hard to be bound to such a rigid formula."

At the end of the "In Concert" taping, her last performance with Neil, Carol went over to him to say goodbye. She said, "If there's anything ever that I can do or help you with—" at which point Neil interrupted, saying, "Don't talk like that to interviewers anymore."

(Hunter claimed she was "mortified" by the article, and that she apologized profusely to Neil for granting the interview. She also maintained that she had been misquoted.)

Neil's seriousness about his press, his European mission, and his career in general at the time was reflected in an interview that he granted to the British magazine *Sounds*. The interview was the first of many that he would give in the next year in which he would respond to questions about his career explosion with you-ain't-seen-nothing-yet braggadocio. In the article, for example, he talked about his renewed interest in film, making note of a screenplay he claimed he had been writing for the last year and a half, and his plans to get it filmed; his intentions of writing the score for John Huston's new film, *Fat City;* and his desire to land the film rights to *Death at an Early Age,* Jonathan Kozol's book about a Boston schoolteacher in a black ghetto ("I'd work my ass off to get that!"). The author, Penny Valentine, was suitably impressed: "That Diamond will eventually succeed within the cinema world is obvious. He has the air of confidence about him that signifies him being picked from the class of '71 as most likely to succeed."

Seemingly lost in the shuffle of Neil's touring and cinematic scheming in 1971 was his songwriting. When he resumed work on his fifth studio album for Uni Records in the summer of 1971, upon his return to Los Angeles, the only original song he had in the can was "I Am . . . I Said," already a hit. The other tunes already set for the LP were "covers"—including Joni Mitchell's "Chelsea Morning," Leonard Cohen's "Suzanne," Tom Paxton's "Last Thing on My Mind," and Roger Miller's "Husbands and Wives."

Diamond needed a couple more original songs, preferably a single. He had at least one candidate, a ballad. The problem was he only had the kernel of the melody, and was apparently stuck for inspiration. So he elected to do what he had done in the studio with "Soolaimon": He brought in the few bars he had written and he tapped his accommodating musicians, arranger Holdridge, and producer Catalano for their help in molding the rest of the melody. Holdridge: "We were able to extrapolate a four-bar phrase or an eight-bar phrase and make a song out of it. And that's what we did with 'Stones.'"

But just because he had the track down didn't mean that Neil was out of the woods yet with "Stones"; he still needed to write a lyric. This process became an ordeal, not only for him but for members of his recording team who were forced to sit idly by as he spent weeks struggling to scratch out the verses at Sound Recorders. "When you are in the studio for two or three months on a simple lyric, it is hard to fathom," said engineer Armin Steiner. It is also very expensive: in the case of "Stones" alone, tens of thousands of dollars.

But then, of course, by 1971 money was no longer an object with Diamond. "You're talking about the heyday of record companies, when they were making a fortune," said Lee Holdridge. "And they were not about to complain to an artist like Neil Diamond about his budget."

Neil took a break from "Stones" the song and "Stones" the album-in-progress in August to play the most important concert stand yet in his career, a seven-night engagement at the prestigious Greek Theater, in Los Angeles' Griffith Park.

From the moment the dates were booked, he was determined that they be an event. That meant adding some extraordinary touches to the proceedings.

Neil had had one previous experience which had emboldened him to think big for the Greek: For his first night at Carnegie Hall he had arranged for the Howard Roberts Chorale, a gospel chorus, to join him onstage for "Brother Love." "It was one of the crystalline moments in my life, and I'm sure in his," Carol Hunter recalled. "Randy and I just *whirled* around and stared. It was the most show-bizzy thing I've ever seen."

For the Greek, Neil settled on other firsts, among them a thirty-five-piece string section, with Lee Holdridge handling the special arrangements as well as conducting. He also decided to use background singers, which he hadn't done since his second Troubadour appearance; this time he decided to hire six.

And, for the first time, Neil engaged a set designer. Manager Ken Fritz made the contact, hiring Jim Newton, the assistant art director on the Smothers Brothers TV variety show (Fritz also managed the Smothers Brothers). Newton came up with two sets: an abstract design utilizing wooden slats that resembled an undulating train track, and, for "Brother Love," an abstract country church. (Said Newton: "Neil was concerned that what we were doing was going to be so overwhelming that he wouldn't stand a chance in front of it. I told him that would never happen because he's such a dynamo that you could do a hurricane behind him and no one would notice.")

If all these preparations weren't enough, Diamond assigned his now-resident sound wizard, Stan Miller, to devise a stereo sound system for the Greek, the first time that that feat had ever been attempted.

Helping to launch the engagement—it was not a complete sellout beforehand—was a profile on Diamond by Robert Hilburn that appeared in the *Los Angeles Times* on the eve of his first performance. The empathetic piece, which carried the headline FROM BLACK SHEEP TO WHITE KNIGHT OF POP, revealed how adept Neil had become in projecting a more confessional—and thus sympathetic—image.

Diamond had first taken his more personal, open interview stance a couple of years earlier, renouncing in the process his former rebel pose, best evidenced by this testy 1969 quote: "I never wanted to expose myself completely and that's nobody's goddam business but my own . . . Even poets have secrets." In one of the first interviews he gave after softening his sullen solitary pose, he talked about the song that had given him an image in the first place: "I never really considered a song a reflection of myself . . . but when 'Solitary Man' came out, the first question people started asking was 'Are you really a solitary man?' And I thought the question was ridiculous. But I thought about it for a while, a year, two years, and I began to realize that, yes, songs are reflections of people, their attitudes . . ."

Flash ahead to 1971 and his interview with Hilburn, and Neil sounded like he was discoursing from a psychiatrist's couch: "I've been a victim of myself. I've been running through life, taking it so seriously." But now, he assured readers, he was a much happier person. Then, he tied a ribbon to his neat little word package with another dose of you-ain't-seen-nothing-yet: "People tend to think of me as someone who has been around a long time. But I've only scratched the surface."

The next night, after the intermission following opening-act Odetta's set, the strains of "Missa" could be heard filling the open-air amphitheater. When the band—now including Jefferson Kewley on congas and Danny Nicholson on guitar—launched into "Soolaimon," Diamond, a fashionably mod figure with his now-shoulder-length hair and Bill Whitten-designed denim suit and necklace, took the stage.

"This is going to be a special show, I'll tell ya that," he said shortly into his set, nervous excitement coloring his voice. After a few cracks, including one about the freeloading "tree people" ("I wonder if, when Liberace plays here, all the tree people are eighty-year-old ladies"), he turned the show into something special.

The triumph of the concert was that Neil was as compelling in his intimate segments—regaling the crowd with snippets of several "dumb" songs he had written in Tin Pan Alley, introducing "I Am . . . I Said" with his lengthy account of his *Lenny* screen test—as he was when he rocked out on "Brother Love." Other factors, such as the retooled arrangements of past hits like "Cracklin' Rosie," the surprise selection of "He Ain't Heavy . . . He's My Brother" as one of his three encore numbers, Lee Holdridge's strings, Clydie King's backup singers, Stan Miller's stereo sound, Joe Gannon's lights, and Jim Newton's sets served to give the show a stunningly fresh, dynamic air.

Los Angeles critics sang themselves hoarse in their praise, among them the *Herald-Examiner's* Frank H. Lieberman: "Until Monday, Neil Diamond appeared to be just another top-flight contemporary artist on the Greek Theatre's summer lineup.

"At about 10:30 P.M. Monday, following a couple of encores and standing ovations by the audience, he became number one, having presented the finest concert—in artistic and production sense—in Greek Theatre history."

Sans orchestra, backup singers, and set, but infused with new confidence in his performing abilities, Neil took to the road in October for a tour of the East and Midwest. During the course of the tour, "Stones," the LP was finally released.

Only three of the tunes were originals: "I Am . . . I Said," the light-rocking "Crunchy Granola Suite," and the nightmarish "Stones." (Marcia Diamond provided an assist in Diamond's completion, finally, of the "Stones" lyric, according to one informed source. One night, she reportedly visited him in the darkened studio, and after Neil requested that the monitor be turned off, engaged him in a romantic interlude.

129

Very soon after that, the source added with a chuckle, Neil crashed through his writer's block and completed "Stones.")

While one could argue that "Stones" wasn't a serious LP project for the preponderance of non-original tunes, it seemed to serve its purpose, buying time for Diamond the songwriter, without embarrassing him, artistically speaking. And, in Lee Holdridge's judgment, the title song added to Neil's growing reputation as a serious pop writer: "Whereas 'Cracklin' Rosie' was flashy, clever, 'Stones' shows a certain maturity, wisdom, depth. It garnered a respect for him."

Certainly Lee's classically flavored arrangements for "Stones," one of the best things about the LP, solidified his position in the pop world. Diamond paid homage to the arranger in an interview Uni Records produced for distribution to radio stations around the country: "Lee did . . . a fantastic, beautiful job." He also implied they would be enjoying many more projects: "We think alike in many ways."

"Stones" the album, as well as "Stones" the single, spent the rest of the fall nestled high on *Billboard*'s charts. Even though his contract with Uni still had more than a year to run, Neil decided that the time was ripe to land himself a new multimillion dollar recording deal.

·12·
"HOT AUGUST NIGHT"

Diamond decided to keep the hustle and bustle to a minimum in his quest for a new record contract, limiting his negotiations to Warner Brothers, Columbia, and MCA (Uni's new name).

Even though Diamond and MCA had grown into industry mainstays together—by late 1970 the record company's artist roster also included a promising singer-songwriter by the name of Elton John—MCA was the longshot of the three. "What more could he accomplish with MCA?" argued Pat Pipolo. "Perhaps when an artist is with a company too long, complacency sets in. And who wants to fight advertising budgets every time? Who wants to deal with people who are above the president of the record company that you're recording for? Imagine how a new label would be treating him . . . a superstar at the time. Much, much better than MCA could afford to." Not helping MCA's chances in the least was new label president Mike Maitland's apparent decision not to vigorously pursue Diamond's re-signing.

By contrast, Warner Brothers and Columbia made it clear by their bids that they were hot on adding Neil to their rosters. In fact, Columbia's Clive Davis—who, in the interest of business had forgiven Diamond for allegedly walking out of his handshake deal with Columbia four years earlier—tendered Neil the biggest offer of his presidency: a $2.5 million guaranteed advance for ten albums. He had to have been shocked, then, when Warner Brothers did him $1.5 million better, offering a cool $4 million—which, next to the Rolling Stones' $5 million deal with Atlantic Records, was the most money ever offered to a recording act at the time.

The problem, if "problem" was the word for it, was that Neil preferred Columbia for its superior marketing and distribution setup. So, he authorized his attorney, David Braun, to deliver a parry to Clive Davis: Match Warner's offer, and Neil Diamond was a Columbia artist.

Davis said yes on the spot.

To avoid embarrassment to MCA, for whom he was in the midst of recording his sixth studio LP in early 1972, Diamond and Columbia didn't publicize their deal at the time. Neil, however, couldn't resist marking his passage into the ranks of superstar-priced recording artists at the signing ceremony with his stamp of the dramatic.

Set designer Jim Newton was a party to the plan. The day before the Saturday night contract signing at Armin Steiner's Sound Recorders, he was hired by Diamond manager Ken Fritz to transform the studio into an elegant Victorian-era drawing room. He paid a visit to a couple of prop houses, returning with a number of striking pieces: pedestals with busts of Beethoven and Schubert; an exquisitely carved wall piece featuring ribbons intertwining a mandolin, an oriental rug, and, for the signing itself, a huge library table that, in Newton's words, "looked as if the Declaration of Independence had been signed on it." Said Newton: "He didn't want it to appear that he was just a country-and-western singer who had blundered into the studio. He wanted them to know that he had a great sense of class."

When Davis and aide Elliot Goldman arrived at Sound Recorders, Neil, doing his best to cover up his extreme nervousness, welcomed them into the control room. There he played several of his songs-in-progress. Then, he turned on the lights in the darkened studio on the other side of the glass, revealing to Davis a scene that would have done Lord Byron, or any "king" of pop, proud.

In his 1972 interviews, Neil became more expansive yet to the press about his grandiose plans and bullish view of his talents.

In March, he announced to *Billboard* that he would be taking a one-year sabbatical from performing following his return engagement at the Greek Theatre that fall. He had decided on the move, he explained, because he wanted to study music theory and composition—training that would help him write "a great symphony. The mere thought of just doing songs for the next ten years is not enough."

He also said he wanted to write a Broadway musical, book, music, and lyrics. He gave himself three years to turn that trick.

(Evidently Neil had swapped big music plans for big film plans, since no mention was made of the goals he had voiced in his *Sounds* interview less than a year earlier—getting his screenplay filmed, snagging the film rights to *Death at an Early Age*, and writing the score to *Fat City*. Regarding *Fat City*, another writer wound up getting the assignment, producer Ray Stark reportedly commenting on Diamond's offer, "Who is he? I've never heard of him.")

Then, in April, Neil invited *Crawdaddy* writer Michael Ochs on the road with him for a weekend. When Ochs turned on his tape recorder, Neil gifted him with some of the choicest quotes of his career, including his intriguing explanation for his "consistency" as an artist: "I have a lot of confidence, but little self-esteem. This has given me a tremendous creative spark because it forced me to keep proving myself."

On the subject of his accomplishments and potential versus his public image, Neil hit his impassioned peak, tailoring his blunt comments to *Crawdaddy*'s hip readership. "I don't think I'll be a phenomenon until I'm dead," he railed, "because then someone will turn around and say, 'Jesus Christ, look at what that man wrote' . . . Right now I have the problem of not being in, not being new . . . I still have to live down that whole early part—the teenybopper thing.

"Shit, you'll look back later and say the Beatles did this and Neil Diamond did that, and I don't know who is going to come out ahead . . . I have complete control over what I do. And now I want to do more extended works . . . I feel really close now to a suite for Beethoven."

There was an underlying irony to Neil's vigorous sell of himself in 1972. At the time, the man who was scheming on symphony- and suite-composing had settled into the comfortable practice of walking into the studio with song *fragments* rather than completed songs. "I think that he was kinda tapped out as a writer in that he didn't come in with ten tunes finished and do an album," said guitarist Louie Shelton. "I remember he would have a double session booked every day with me, and Hal and Joe, and a piano player or Lee Holdridge. And he would come in with just an idea for a tune. And he would say, 'I've got this idea for a song. And I'm not sure whether I want to do it in two-quarter, four-quarter, or three-quarter time. And I'm not sure whether I want the chords to be A, G and C or D, F and E.' In other words, he didn't have anything set on the song. So what we would do, we would . . . try different progressions, different rhythms to the tune and we would gradually mold the tune into a record, develop it as we went along."

To arranger Lee Holdridge, Diamond had become a victim of his lack of musical craftsmanship: "Neil, I think, was capable of tremendous inspiration. [But] there were times when he had great ideas and he just didn't know how to execute them. He did not have any compositional knowledge, any harmonic knowledge, any contrapuntal knowledge of how to extend a theme. These are all things that come from craftsmanship . . . And I think that he kept coming up against walls. And that's where he had to start turning around to musicians, arrangers, and record producers to help him." Further, to Holdridge, at least, Diamond didn't display a sustained interest—contrary to his public declaration—in expanding his musical horizons, spurning the arranger's suggestion, for example, that he take guitar lessons so that he could learn some new chords and harmonies. "It takes a certain kind of understanding of yourself to admit that you might need lessons after many years of success," Holdridge commented.

Given Diamond's musical limitations coupled with his apparent need to compensate for them with his brash goal talk, it was no surprise that his recording sessions in 1972 were the same trying affairs for all concerned as in the days of "Tap Root Manuscript."

To keyboards player Larry Knechtel, for example, the prerecording skull sessions were "like pulling teeth. You knew it was going to be an agonizing time mentally. It meant going microscopically through a part." Compounding matters was Neil's penchant for using vague words such as "rainbow" to describe what he wanted to hear musically. Commented Knechtel, sarcastically: "What kind of rainbow? How big you want it? Over what? You'd tend to make fun of him later on."

As if the players weren't stressed enough, Neil would persist in goading them. Even bass player Joe Osborn, the most soft-spoken and taciturn of the bunch, was fair game. "Joe would start playing harder . . . hitting the strings harder," Knechtel recalled, chuckling at the way his silently fuming friend would simultaneously vent his anger and react to Diamond's demand that he play a part differently. "He would even play the series of notes Neil told him to try, but he made sure that they sounded like shit!"

Knechtel had a vivid memory of one near run-in with Neil himself, after Neil critiqued his play on one middle-of-the-roadish song with the words, "That's schmaltzy." The prideful Knechtel, who had won a Grammy the previous year as one of the arrangers of Simon and Garfunkel's "Bridge Over Troubled Water," claimed that he almost fired back, "Goddamn, Neil, this *whole song* is schmaltzy." He bit his tongue, however, although, "I could have punched him in the mouth." From then on, whenever Knechtel—who preferred boogie woogie to Diamond's brand of pop in the first place—was struggling with a middle-of-the-road passage, Osborn and Hal Blaine would tease, "Hey, that's a little too schmaltzy."

A good-natured jibe here, a joke there, played a crucial role in a Diamond recording session, serving to defuse the constant tension. Among the musicians, drummer Blaine was the unquestioned dean of the timely one-liner. At a particularly uptight moment, he was prone to look up from his drums and, in his booming voice, announce, "Hey, look, we didn't come in here to have fun." He also had an unerring ability to keep a session moving, grandly declaring, in one instance, that a musical idea that Diamond had was absolutely marvelous when it was evident to everyone in the room, except, perhaps, Diamond, that the idea was largely Blaine's. In that regard, Armin Steiner maintained, "Hal was the ultimate psychiatrist."

Steiner wasn't a slouch himself as a mood manipulator. Possessor of a basso-profundo voice as well, Steiner indulged in reckless confrontational humor, often targeting Neil himself. One of his favorite stunts was taking whatever Diamond melody was being worked on and regaling everyone by crooning his own filthy lyric to it. He would also taunt Neil with such cracks as, "Your lyrics are so bad that the pimples on your ass are better than what you've written." Steiner: "Tom [Catalano] used to say to me, 'How the hell can you say those things to the poor guy?' I'd say, 'It's good for him; he needs it.' I played with his emotions to the extent of keeping him from self-destructing." Neil, he added, often responded with a smile or laugh.

Effective as Blaine and Steiner were at times, the man who did more in the studio to rein in Diamond at critical junctures, making it possible for projects to be completed, was coproducer Tom Catalano.

"Tom was a very relaxing influence on Neil," explained Larry Knechtel. "Sometimes when you're as intense as Neil you're not quite sure how you want the song to go. And so Tom had a calming effect . . . Basically he would confirm, 'That sounds real great,' when Neil was in doubt."

Catalano's role, of course, bespoke an unusual bond between him and Diamond—Neil couldn't be soothed by just anyone. Arranger Lee Holdridge was aware of their special relationship: "I think Tom Catalano was his best friend . . . It's almost like they were brothers in a strange way." Songwriter/producer Al Kasha, who knew both well in the '60s, could see why the pent-up, moody Diamond would be attracted to a man who, by contrast, seemed to be enjoying life immensely. "It's funny, there was kind of a reversal in personalities there . . . Tom really lived his life for him, in a way . . . It was like having an alter ego who was a swinger."

Indeed, Neil trusted Tom implicitly, allowing him to go beyond a producer's call of duty in looking after his interests. Armin Steiner, a good friend of the producer himself, went so far as to refer to Catalano as Diamond's "front man" in any and all business matters. "Tom was a wonderful businessman," the engineer said. "He took Neil by the hand and negotiated a lot of the deals . . . Neil didn't speak unless it was through Tom, in many cases."

Uni's Pat Pipolo came to appreciate just how formidable a customer Catalano was when he took up a cause on Diamond's behalf. "Neil would never deal with me or anybody at the record company from a negative aspect," Pipolo said. "We wouldn't even hear from management. We'd hear from Tommy . . . He would come in with a big smile—he was always smiling—big blue eyes battin' at ya, with a handshake, and a slap on the back. Then he'd smack me with a ton of feathers. For example, he'd have a chart from WLS, Chicago, and a chart from KYA, San Francisco. And he'd say something like, 'What's goin' on? Do you mean to tell me this record can go to number three at WLS and you can't get it on KYA?'"

Although they didn't know it at the time, the album this assortment of talented, harried studio denizens cum amateur shrinks were recording in the first half of 1972 with Diamond—the aptly titled "Moods"—would be their last hurrah together.

Several tunes made it a hurrah to remember. Lee Holdridge related the recording saga of "Song Sung Blue":

"Neil walked in, he played it for Tom and me, and we looked at each other and we said, 'That's a hit song.' We cracked up at the same time because we said, 'But it's also Mozart.' It's true. Tom found out later that Neil had watched the movie *Elvira Madigan,* in which the Mozart piano concerto No. 21 is used. Mozart has that wonderful little chromatic in it, which Neil doesn't know from . . . so he goes to the block chord. But it's the same melody. Listen, if you're going to be influenced, Mozart is certainly a great place to start! And there was no question about it in our minds—'*That's* a hit song.' I mean it was like instantaneous . . . it sounded like one of those classic Tin Pan Alley hymns.

"Neil, by contrast, didn't have a lot of faith [in it]. So that was one of the few times that Tom and I really took the song out of his hands.

"We jumped on it. We took it in the studio—I remember it was a 10 A.M. session at Sound Recorders—and started recording it. We cut the rhythm track to it in two hours, and it was wonderful. Larry Knechtel did that marvelous electric piano introduction, that descending line—he improvised it on the spot, it totally came out of his creativity. And then we said, 'Let's break for lunch.' And Neil said, 'I want to come back and work on it some more.' And we said, 'Neil, it's wonderful; don't touch it!' He said, 'Well, I want to try to do some more.'

"We went to lunch, and Armin, Tom, and I ganged up on Neil: 'Leave it alone, it's *perfect.* It's a great track, it's a terrific song, it'll be a hit—Mozart will thank you!' He still didn't know why we kept throwing Mozart's name in there! We were kidding him, but at the same time we were saying, 'Look . . .' Finally he agreed . . . 'All right, all right.'"

Holdridge was also enthused about the romantic ballad "Play Me" and "Morningside," a tale of a master carver's passing that Neil would say was written in tribute to his grandmother, "who died alone in a New York hospital with no one even caring." "Upon hearing that song," the arranger said, "I felt it was important enough that I wanted to write that little prologue to it, 'Prelude in E Major,' so that the orchestra could quietly say, 'Now pay close attention because you're going to hear something.' Neil and Tom liked that idea a lot."

Not all of the songs they worked on had the transcendent pop qualities of those tunes. The cuteness of the nonsensical "Gitchy Goomy," Neil's musical gift to his son, Jesse, for example, disappeared after the first couple of listenings (Larry Knechtel: "That was one that made me cringe"). Yet even the weaker tunes at least *sounded* good, and distinctively Diamond. Holdridge: "You see the creativity that I got going was that Neil used so few chords in his songs—you had a C chord for four bars, for instance—that you had to do something with that chord or you would go nuts . . . So I did a lot of experimenting with suspensions against the chords, where the violins might start out on E in the first bar, move to a D in the next bar, and then maybe down to a G, so that in the chord they're not just striking the notes that are in the C chord, they might be passing through notes outside of the chords. And we developed a sound that, I think, became very striking . . . definitely a symphonic approach, which was not found in a lot of pop music before then. 'Moods' was the culmination of that."

Diamond worked on "Moods" through the very morning in May of 1972 that he caught a plane to London for the start of his second May–June tour of Europe in as many years. The next night, Tom Catalano and Armin Steiner—who had spent the intervening twenty-four hours putting the LP to bed while not going to bed themselves—hopped a jet to join him.

Engineer Steiner's presence on the tour in England was one indication that Neil had planned something special for his first date, at London's prestigious Royal Albert Hall; the presence of the baton-carrying Lee Holdridge, and the deathly-afraid-of-flying Marcia Diamond were other clues. (Huddled under a blanket with Joe Gannon and her friend Totty Ames, recently divorced from producer Saul David, Marcia was able to make the eleven-hour flight in one piece.)

In fact, Neil was regarding Royal Albert Hall as a kind of super-shakedown for his second stand at the Greek Theatre that summer, an engagement, he was bound and determined, that would set the music world on its ear. Using the nickname those future Greek dates would later be tagged with, Steiner declared: "Royal Albert Hall was the beginning of Hot August Night." He had come not only to help sound man Stan Miller rig the enormous auditorium with Miller's imported sound system and handle the sound for the forty-piece orchestra, but also to make mental notes for his own role during the Greek stand—engineering the best live recording ever.

Weaving some of the new songs from "Moods" into his set—"Song Sung Blue" had just been released in the United States and Great Britain and was sailing up both charts—Neil gave Steiner, as well as the 8,000 Britons, an earful. "The crowd just about tore up the place," he recalled.

At the post-concert celebration at Indigo Jones, an exclusive London restaurant, a giddy Lee Holdridge played a musical prank on his boss. Slipping out of their private room after the main course, the arranger sat down at the harpsichord downstairs and began to play Mozart piano concerto No. 21. Hearing the piped-in strains of the concerto in the dining room Neil, obviously pleased, turned to Tom Catalano and remarked, "Oh, they're playing 'Song Sung Blue.'" Catalano, who was in on the gag, managed a straight face as he replied, "No, they're playing Mozart." "Neil even laughed about it," said Lee. (It wasn't until 1976, four years later, that Neil would confess publicly that he had lifted his "Song Sung Blue" melody from Mozart.)

Neil's mood stayed light as he toured elsewhere in England, and in France, Holland, and Germany, before returning to the Royal Albert Hall for a tour-ending encore date. Helping see to his high spirits were comedians Albert Brooks and Fred Smoot.

Originally, Neil had only intended to take along his friend Brooks, and then only as a guest, eschewing the idea of an opening act for the tour. But Smoot, who had been the life of Neil and Marcia's New Year's Eve party at their new Holmby Hills home, where he arrived in a tuxedo and sneakers with a roomful of balloons, and, later, streaked through the backyard, finagled an invite as Neil's "tour photographer." Roadie/conga player Jefferson Kewley recalled the after-show party scenes with both of them on hand: "It was constant one-upmanship. I mean you'd return to the hotel, and you'd be worn out from laughing."

During his show at the Odeon in Birmingham, Neil decided to share his tour party's private comedy team with the audience, first bringing Brooks out to perform a guest set, and then calling for Smoot to join him. After Smoot walked out, Diamond left the stage with his other good-humor man, Jefferson Kewley. "Neil and I went back to the dressing room, turned on the intercom so we could hear what was going on, had a few beers and sat there hysterical for like an hour and a half while these two guys were trying to one-up each other," Kewley recalled. "The funniest part about it was the audience didn't have any idea what was going on—a lot of the stuff they did they didn't understand a bit."

In Germany, all the Brooks- and Smoot-inspired foolishness got to Diamond. The moment came at a park where Neil encountered a large statue of a gorilla. As "tour photographer" Smoot aimed his camera, Neil accommodated him by mugging with "King Kong." Said road manager Joe Gannon: "It was like he got into Freddy's pants and transisted for about twenty seconds."

Doing nothing to dampen Neil's spirits in Europe was the news that "Song Sung Blue" had hit number one in the United States.

Back in Los Angeles in July, he had the pleasure of watching "Moods" take its turn in storming the charts. That month he returned to the road for dates in the United States and Canada, culminating in a five-night stand at Detroit's Pine Knob Amphitheater in early August. Then he returned to Los Angeles, where he began final preparations for his ten-date return engagement at the Greek.

For two weeks straight in Los Angeles, Neil drilled his band, now seven members strong: Dennis St. John, drums; Emory Gordy, electric guitar, mandolin, acoustic six-string and twelve-string guitars, ukulele, vibes, and glockenspiel; Alan Lindgren, acoustic grand piano, electric piano, organ; Richard Bennett, electric guitar, acoustic six-string and twelve-string guitars; Danny Nicholson, electric guitar; Reinie Press, electric bass, and Jefferson Kewley, congas, shakers, tambourine. While he honed his 110-minute show, other members of his team worked furiously on their assignments.

For clothes-designer-to-the-stars Bill Whitten, the second Greek Theatre stand meant dressing up Neil like a "Renaissance prince," a far cry from his all-black Solitary Man threads of yore ("It was a protective thing," Diamond would later say of his black get-ups, adding that his eventual embrace of a full range of colors, including white, symbolized his "opening up" as a person). As Whitten would later tell an interviewer: "His clothes have to be romantic. He is a lover who projects that love in his songs. He's earthy, not flashy." Whitten described the embroidered tapestry shirts, buckskins, and Indian-style necklaces he designed for Diamond as "elegant funk."

For Lee Holdridge, meanwhile, the Greek engagement meant dressing up Neil's show with an opening music piece, as well as some new string arrangements. As for the former task, Holdridge explained that Diamond "wanted something special for the opening. He said, 'Lee, write a prologue.' He was going to open with 'Crunchy Granola Suite,' which has a nice, interesting guitar vamp lead-in. So we devised an idea whereby I wrote a piece that started with a solo cello and gradually added instruments. It became a quartet, then a sextet, then gradually the entire string section was in. Then we added an organ line against the strings, and gradually the percussion came in, and it swelled and swelled and swelled. And then, in a huge downbeat, the entire rhythm section came in with this vamp to 'Crunchy Granola.' We extended the vamp to make it really exciting, and we just had everything going at once."

Lee also focused his attention on the end of Neil's show by adding strings to "Soolaimon," which Neil planned to use as his first encore. "I mentioned to him, 'Even if you don't hear the strings, visually you should have everybody on that stage singing, playing, whatever, so that the last thing the audience sees is the whole stage going.' And he said, 'You're right; put the strings on "Soolaimon."'" It worked great."

For Diamond's sound man, Stan Miller, the Greek engagement meant going one step beyond the stereo sound of 1971 into the uncharted realms of quadraphonic sound, designing the first quad system ever used for a live show. To accomplish that, he positioned speakers on the sides of the theater and in the back.

Another of his charges was assembling an even bigger sound wattage-wise than had filled the outdoor amphitheater the previous summer. That meant assembling two immense columns of Crown DC300 speakers, one on either side of the stage. The Crown DC300 was selected, Armin Steiner, Miller's associate on the project, explained, because it was the "first high-powered amplifier that didn't blow up." Still, as extra insurance that the wrong kind of explosion wouldn't occur at the Greek, Miller and Steiner created their own air conditioning by placing blocks of ice and fans in front of each column. Steiner: "We were running something like 20,000 watts of power. It was the most spectacular sound system, in my opinion, that has ever been created for a live performance."

For Armin Steiner, the engagement meant much more than helping Stan Miller set up the PA, it meant making the recording of his life for the planned release of a double live album. To prepare for that challenge, he arranged with Miller for a totally separate sound feed into his sixteen-track remote recording van, which he'd rented from Wally Heider Recording.

Then there were the inspired miking touches, most notably his decision to record the audience by stringing a piano wire the width of the theater above the audience and hanging three battery-powered U-87 microphones from it. "Wally Heider didn't want me to do that," Steiner recalled. "Finally I told him I'd pay for the mikes, because I couldn't take them down every day."

While Miller and Steiner covered the sound and recording bases, producer Joe Gannon and set designer Jim Newton plotted the show's look. For Newton, the engagement meant topping his 1971 abstract wood-slat design, which Neil wound up taking to Royal Albert Hall. He succeeded, his most clever creation being a series of ten mirrored panels simulating two huge hands. By his plan, the two movable "hands" would be pointed downward over the stage as Neil made his entrance, and then would lift up as he began singing "Crunchy Granola Suite." They would remain in that position for portions of the show, functioning as divine protection of sorts. Finally, as Neil left the stage after his second encore, "Brother Love," the song that inspired their creation, the hands would point down to signal the show's end.

Newton also labored to turn several of Joe Gannon's scenery notions into reality, including a mirrored panel design in the shape of a sunburst for "Morningside" and another wood-slat abstract church design for "Brother Love." He also followed Gannon's instructions in designing a permanent set for the back of the stage that simulated scaffolding. The design satisfied Gannon's desire to position segments of the thirty-five-piece string section on several tiers, as human scenery.

For Joe Gannon, the Greek Theatre engagement also meant coming up with one stupendous effect that would make the audience's socks roll up and down. He hit on an idea one day when he came across some old 2K "sun beams" at Olson, a Hollywood firm that rents theatrical lighting. He decided to rent twenty of the blindingly bright lights, string them up in a row on a pipe, position the pipe at eye level behind the band, and at two peak moments of the set—when Neil took the stage and when he yelled out "Brother!" at the start of "Brother Love"—shock the audience with a 40K blast of light. To enhance the effect for blast number one, Joe rented some smoke machines.

With an extravaganza like this taking shape, Neil evidently saw no need for sharing the evening with an opening act. So the Everly Brothers, the duo that the young Diamond had idolized, were informed that their services would not be needed after all at the Greek Theatre from August 18 through August 27.

Then, with fascination surrounding his sold-out stand peaking in Los Angeles in the several days before opening night, Neil delivered a deft PR touch to the engagement. In an interview with the *Los Angeles Times*' Robert Hilburn, he renewed his pledge to take a one-year or longer "sabbatical" from performing soon. "I want to study piano," he declared. "I want to learn the technical language of music . . . I want to read."

Not all the preparations for the Greek engagement went swimmingly. MCA, for example, turned Tom Catalano down on his request that it spring for a crew to film the event. With Diamond apparently unwilling to pay for a film crew out of his own pocket, none was hired.

And on opening day, the stage was set, literally, for a self-described "temper tantrum" by Lee Holdridge that, for a few minutes, threw the entire production into tumult. At issue was the "scaffolding" set, with its rows of seats for the string players, the highest some thirty feet off the ground. After taking one look at the set, Holdridge announced, "There's no way I'm going to send my friends up there." He wound up issuing an ultimatum to Diamond: Either the orchestra stayed put or he would take a walk. "Diamond sort of got upset," Holdridge recalled, "and then he said, 'Can we compromise?'" Eventually, Holdridge and Gannon did work out a deal: Three-quarters of the string section, including all of the older members, were grounded, and the remaining players were positioned only partway up.

Neil, laying his eyes on the scaffolding for the first time himself that day, voiced his own strong opinion to Joe Gannon: "That's the ugliest fucking thing I've ever seen in my life." Gannon assured him that during the concert, with the lighting he had planned, his opinion would change.

That night, Gannon was standing in the wings, stage right, as the sound of a sole cello joined the din of the audience. As Gannon had the lights brought down slowly, the audience quieted, and the cello became a string quartet. Meanwhile, behind the giant fire doors, which still closed off the stage, he directed that the smoke machines be activated, and the row of 2K lights turned on.

The quartet became a sextet, and in a moment the rest of the thirty-five-piece string section—twenty violins, six violi, six celli, three basses—joined in. Alan Lindgren contributed his organ line, and Jefferson Kewley began tapping a tattoo on the congas. Time seemed to stand still as the sounds swelled and swelled and swelled, creating an almost overwhelming sense of anticipation in the hushed audience.

And then the downbeat, and the release. As the band began its extended opening vamp to "Crunchy Granola Suite," the huge fire doors cracked, and the crowd got its first glimpse of white light and smoke. (Jefferson Kewley said the band members were relieved to see the smoke escape: "Gannon used this spearmint-flavored smoke . . . and it was terrible. We were all dying back there.")

Two roars followed—that of the clanging doors opening ever so slowly, and that of the 5,000-plus in the audience reacting to the shockingly surreal scene of blinding light and billowing smoke.

In the wings, Neil Diamond, dressed in a dusty rose Western outfit, strode confidently by Joe Gannon, a smile on his face. "Have a good one," Gannon told him, with a slight nod of the head.

And then, Neil walked onstage through the smoke and white light looking like a pop god walking on Cloud Nine.

For the most part, the show had Joe Gannon's Formula written all over it.

In the "give 'em a goose" Scene I, Diamond performed a string of mainly "up" tunes with the band: "Crunchy Granola Suite," "Done Too Soon," "Solitary Man," "Morningside," "Cherry, Cherry," and "Sweet Caroline."

In the lower-keyed Scene II he got intimate, regaling the crowd with his "obscure song" segment ("I have a whole closetful of songs that are obscure and deserve every inch of that obscurity," he joked by way of introducing his "newly written obscure song," "Porcupine Pie"). Then he moved the crowd by crooning ballads like "Red Red Wine" and "Girl, You'll Be a Woman Soon" to the sparest of accompaniment.

In the serious-business Scene III, Neil performed the likes of "Play Me" and "Canta Libre" and then began his four-hit countdown to encore land—"Song Sung Blue," "Cracklin' Rosie," "Holly Holy," which earned him his first standing ovation opening night, and "I Am . . . I Said," which he introduced with the words, "My name is Neil. And I weep, and I care, and I love, and I want, and I need . . ." Standing ovation number two.

The band had already begun "Soolaimon" when he returned to the stage. He steamed through the song, and then, with a primal yell of "BROTTTHHHHERS!," segued into "Brother Love's Travelling Salvation Show." The encore blast of white light jolted the crowd, by now limp with excitement.

Displaying his offstage delight at moments of triumph has never been Neil Diamond's way. He made an exception back in the dressing room, taking a cake in his hands and heaving it against a mirror, setting off, in the words of Jefferson Kewley, "a mass-hysteria food fight."

On Monday, August 21, Neil's fourth date at the Greek, the fun began for Armin Steiner. With Diamond and band having presumably worked out all of the show's bugs, he turned on the tape recorder for the first time. He recorded the next four shows as well.

They were Hot August Nights in more ways than one for Neil. By Tuesday he was fighting a virus, reporting for duty that night with a 102-degree temperature. "He was very ill," Steiner recalled. "They pumped him full of antibiotics." After the show, he departed from his post-concert ritual of hosting the inevitable stream of Hollywood celebrities, and immediately returned home and went to bed.

Although his voice still possessed a nasal quality, he was on the rebound by Thursday, just in time to make a little recording history.

Guitarist Emory Gordy felt it from the stage: "Thursday was it for me . . . Neil getting off, the interplay between the audience, between the lighting people, between the stagehands, between the musicians, between the string players . . . Lee Holdridge . . . there was a click. It was like K-Y jelly had been thrown over the whole night."

Armin Steiner felt it in his recording truck: "It was magic and sparks. Neil created his life right there in that performance."

After the final show on Sunday, August 27, after the last member of the audience had left and the doors to the Greek Theatre had been closed, Lee Holdridge asked Neil to return to the stage. When he did, he was surprised to find that the members of the string section were still in their seats, and that the rest of the show personnel were crowded around.

"This is yours—my gift to you; thanks for a great engagement," Holdridge announced. He then took baton in hand and led the orchestra in a performance of Tchaikovsky's rousing *Andante Cantabile*. As Neil stood and listened, tears streamed down his cheeks.

BROADWAY

When he first aired his dream of writing a "special one-man show" for Broadway to an English reporter in early 1971, it seemed an audacious notion, even for the free-talking Neil. No rock-dabbling pop star, after all, had ever concertized on Broadway, and the number of entertainers who had performed in "one-man" shows there, legends all, could be counted on the fingers of one hand: Garland, Kaye, Jolson.

However, turn the calendar ahead to those magical Hot August Nights of 1972, and it was clear that Neil's 102-degree temperature wasn't the only fever gripping him. Caught up in his most glorious personal triumph ever—with fans, the music community, and the press heaping the kind of Serious Artist praise on him that he'd been lusting after for years—Neil felt emboldened to go for more. Now. Before his "sabbatical." As he considered Broadway "the ultimate . . . I didn't care whether it was dead or dying," that meant only one thing.

The word filtered down from Tom Catalano to members of the tour team during the Greek Theatre engagement. On September 9, *Billboard* reported the news: "The Shubert Organization will present Neil Diamond in a one-man show at its Winter Garden Theater," commencing October 6.

In the hectic weeks before the three-week Winter Garden engagement, Diamond made it clear that he viewed the stand as the showcase gig of his life, his superstar bar mitzvah.

Among his preparations was his decision to doll up the old, drab Winter Garden at his own expense. Overseeing the project was a new key employee, his and Marcia's friend, Totty Ames, whom he had recently hired as his first executive assistant. Ames had most of the theater's interior repainted, replacing the institutional gray and green that Neil abhorred with a more palatable gray. She also gave his dressing room a new look, directing that the windows be washed, the yellow draperies cleaned, and the walls painted beige; renting a new dressing table and furniture; and stocking the room with candles, plants, and flowers—mostly daisies, the Diamonds' favorite.

Meanwhile, Neil demonstrated his keen interest in who would be filling up the newly redone theater by compiling a long, intriguing list of people from his past whom he wanted invited. Among them were his

NYU fencing coach, Hugo Castello, as well as all of his Violet team-mates. That made sense: Even as Neil was rising to new public heights as the Solitary Man, he remained caught up with his fencer persona. Backstage before a show, he was not above adopting an *en garde* pose and leaping across the room at some unsuspecting soul in his retinue, a stunt he'd been pulling since his days with Jack Packer ("He'd poke me with his finger. 'Go ahead, try and stop me,'" Packer recalled).

Then there were the dozens of music-biz acquaintances dating back to his earliest days in Tin Pan Alley—fellow tunesmiths, publishers, record company executives, studio musicians, Bitter End hanger-outers. Some of them, such as Hal Fein, former president of Roosevelt Music, he hadn't talked to in years. (No invitation, however, was extended to former partner Packer, much to his disappointment. Said Jack, who had left the entertainment business the year before after performing in the Starlight Theater chain: "I would have liked to have just shook his hand and said, 'You really did it, kid. All those nights in the basement.'")

As for those who did make it to Diamond's list, one of the most surprised had to have been disc jockey and hop host Jack Spector. Spector had firsthand knowledge of just how sudden, and seemingly final, partings with Neil could be.

"I had cancer in my left eye in 1968," he said. "The word got out in the industry very quickly. But I hadn't seen Neil. And the day before the operation at New York Eye and Ear, in walks Neil Diamond, into my private room. It was about noontime, and he's all alone, wearing a black leather jacket. 'Hey, Neil, how ya doin'?' 'OK, Jack. Jesus, I heard you were sick.'

"At this point a nurse came in, and she wanted to take some blood. And I complained—'My god, I feel like a pin cushion . . . Well, OK, there's this large vein at the back of the hand.' And I look the other way, at Neil. And he's crying. Tears were just pouring down his face. And he said, 'Hey, I can't watch this,' and he turned around and left the room. And he didn't come back." That was the last Spector heard from him until, four years later, he received Neil's Winter Garden invite.

Another who hadn't been expecting Diamond to call was Herb Rosen, the former A&R man at Mercury Records who had kicked Neil out of his office some seven years earlier with the choice words: "Neil, Neil, until you bring me some good material I don't want to see your ass in here again." Rosen was so sure that he had burned his bridges with Neil, in fact, that when Neil rang him up several weeks before his Winter Garden engagement and identified himself, he didn't believe him. "Come off it, who is this?" he demanded.

As it turned out in Rosen's case, Neil had something more in mind than to simply invite him to see the show. But he was cagey over the phone, asking Rosen, who was then working as an independent record promotion man, "Can you come over to the hotel?"

The puzzled Rosen arrived at Diamond's suite at the St. Moritz, where he found a Ping-Pong table set up in the living room. Obviously not ready to talk yet, Neil handed Rosen a paddle; they wound up playing two hours' worth of table tennis for a dollar a game. Then Neil got down to business.

"He had a schedule of radio buys that he wanted to make [to promote the engagement], and he wanted me to go over them to find out if they were right," Rosen recalled. "I think it was something like $30,000 worth of time he was buying."

Rosen informed Diamond that it was unnecessary to buy so much time. What he suggested, instead, was that Diamond buy minimal time—$7,000 worth—and reap a harvest of free publicity by granting live and taped interviews to a number of New York deejays.

Neil, not surprisingly, loved the idea. The next thing he knew, Rosen had been hired by Neil to help arrange the interviews.

The resulting radio campaign, which included an hour with local legend Murray "the K" Kaufman, formed an important part of Neil's pre-show interview blitz.

Neil, of course, didn't have to twist any arms to be interviewed; his Brooklyn-to-Broadway tale was ripe for media exploitation. For good measure, he gussied up his story further by making note of a couple of fetching ironies attached to the engagement: The last performer to play the venerable theater was none other than Al Jolson, whose "Mammy" Neil claimed to have made his public singing debut with in the first grade. Also, the theater was located in the same building as Sunbeam Music, where Neil had toiled exactly a decade earlier.

Diamond was happy to oblige his interviewers by delving into his Solitary past. He was at his hammy best with Murray the K in capturing for the umpteenth time the moment he wrote his first song as a lonely teenager: "It was a stunning experience to me because I had a voice, I had *wings.*" Marveling over the "two lifetimes" he'd lived in the last six years of his career, he worked his way to the matter at hand with the deejay, sounding every bit the absorbed artiste: "I've been obsessed with the feeling that I want to play all the great concert stages of the world, so the bookings took on a different character. We started to play concert halls in Germany . . . We played Royal Albert Hall—I couldn't begin to describe it. Suffice it to say—the Greek Theatre in L.A., Carnegie Hall.

"Of course, the ultimate for any artist, for any performer who walks onstage is Broadway, right here, right here at home in New York, Broadway. And, uh, there's no better way for me to close out my concert career than to do it on Broadway."

With less than totally empathetic interviewers, however, a different Diamond emerged—this one sounding clipped, strident, and cocky. When, for example, one reporter at a group interview noted that NBC had suggested an alternate producer for a TV special he was said to be planning at the time, Neil snapped, "Mal Stuart does the special and that's final." Grace Lichtenstein of *The New York Times,* meanwhile, didn't endear herself to Neil for suggesting that the "almost childlike" "Song Sung Blue" was the work of "a real Gershwin!"

"No, a real Beethoven," he corrected. He went on to say: "I don't dream of being George Gershwin. I dream of being Beethoven and Tchaikovsky and Robert Frost. That's how much I think I can do muscially."

Thanks in part to Neil taking to the hustings, New York got a case of Diamond fever: All seats to his twenty performances were sold out in advance of opening night. "They were the hottest tickets in town," recalled Herb Rosen. As the man charged with servicing the radio stations with tickets, he was in a position to know. "I got my records played pretty easily for those few weeks," he chuckled.

With twenty sold-out houses and an army of show-me New York critics awaiting him, with a Clive Davis–arranged benefit opening night for the Robert F. Kennedy Memorial and the Bedford-Stuyvesant Restoration Corporation that promised to lure Ethel Kennedy to the Winter Garden, Neil had cause to be climbing the walls with anxiety as the engagement neared. But even to Totty Ames, he seemed "really very cool."

It was an act. Shortly before he was scheduled to take the stage on opening night, Neil's facade of calm was shattered.

Delivering the telling blow was comedian Sandy Baron, one of his former opening acts. Baron, who had flown out from California to root Diamond on, had brought along *his* ideas about the kind of show Neil should be doing, ideas that were based, presumably, on his own recent experience on Broadway in the play *Lenny.* What he told Diamond was strong stuff, indeed: The extravaganza that he had staged at the Greek Theatre, which Neil had planned to repeat at the Winter Garden, wouldn't work on Broadway for the more sophisticated crowds. He was much better off scrapping the fancy sets, the smoke machines, the 2K lights, and *really* doing a one-man show, in front of a stark black curtain.

Musician Emory Gordy, one of those standing around as Baron went on and on, said that the comedian even suggested a new opening number to replace "Prologue/Crunchy Granola Suite": "The Singer Sings His Songs," an obscure, anemic ballad of Neil's that Neil, for some unknown reason, had announced was his favorite song pre-"I Am . . . I Said." "I remember distinctively [Baron saying that] in that New

York voice of his, which was very nasal," said Gordy disgustedly. "It came out 'The Singah Sinnngs His Saahhnnngs.' And we all turned to each other and said, 'No, this is not true.'"

But, evidently, Baron did succeed in getting Diamond's ear, as Joe Gannon, the show's producer, found out at noon on opening day: "Neil gives me a call at the Winter Garden: 'Hey, really, I got to see you. Right away.' So he comes over, we go and sit outside the Winter Garden. 'Listen,' he said, 'I talked to Sandy Baron . . . and I want to change everything.'

"I said, 'Look you're on Broadway, it's now. I think the show works, it worked fine at the Greek.' He said, 'I know, but this is Broadway. Sandy knows Broadway.' So he said, 'This is how it's gonna be.'"

Stunned, Gannon returned inside. After dispatching Jefferson Kewley for a bottle of tequila, he obediently launched into the awesome task of redoing the lights and hauling off the scenery—only to find, after a while, that his slow burn over Neil's last-minute decree had now engulfed him in rage. "Look, guys, put every fucking thing back the way I had it!" he suddenly exclaimed. As members of the road crew applauded, Gannon declared, "I'm going to go back and talk to the cat. And if he don't want to do the show that way, then I ain't showing up!"

Confronting Diamond, however, proved to be easier said than done. When set designer Jim Newton visited Gannon in his hotel room at 5 P.M. he still hadn't called Neil, and Newton found him "in tears . . . he really was in a state."

Finally, Gannon screwed up his courage and dialed Neil's hotel room. "Look, Neil, it's no threat," he said. "If you want to do that other show, that's your prerogative. But I'm not gonna be there. And none of the other people that I brought over are gonna be there. It's no threat—it's just that they have too much integrity, like myself, to let you do such a stupid thing. There is *no threat*—you can definitely get through the show. Lights will go on and off. But why don't you do this? Why don't you think it over, and see whether you want to do it my way."

A whole hour passed before Joe heard back from Neil. The call, in fact, didn't come until 7 P.M., fifteen minutes before Diamond was due to hit the stage. "I think we'll do it your way," Neil said in a subdued voice.

"So I practically hop, skip, and jump over to the theater," Gannon recalled. "I got there about ten after seven. I walked onstage. Everybody was there, just sort of *looking*, man, nobody knew. I said, 'We're gonna do it *my* way, guys.' And the band, everybody stood up and cheered."

Un-Broadway-like as it may have seemed to Sandy Baron, Neil Diamond's entrance onto the Winter Garden stage that night caused the same stunned reaction in the 1,479-seat theater as it had at the Greek. Artie Kaplan, another '60s-era acquaintance of Neil's whom Neil had hired to contract the string players, described the moment: "Neil walks on through the smoke in an all-white outfit, very Elvis Presleyish. The audience was just electrified. My hair stood on end; it was just the most wonderful thing I ever saw in my life."

A few minutes later the sound of Diamond's first words came through the twenty-one loudspeakers: "My name is Neil Diamond, and I have come to Broadway to own you. I will accept nothing less." Although he quickly quipped that he'd settle for a year's lease, his unqualified statement of purpose seemed closer to what he really felt his Winter Garden engagement was all about.

Neil celebrated the inauguration of his Broadway run at a post-concert party at Sardi's. While the party was still going on, the first edition of *The New York Times,* containing his review, hit the streets. A photograph that later appeared in *Life* magazine recorded the ensuing scene for posterity . . . the cigar-puffing Diamond sitting next to his radiant mother at a Sardi's table packed with relatives, his ear cocked in the direction of his high-priced new PR man, Paul Wasserman, who stood reading the *Times'* verdict.

After Wasserman got through reading, Neil had reason to beam himself. Don Heckman's review was largely a bouquet of praise: "Call it an idea whose time had come, call it the right performer in the right circumstances, call it the final stage in the mass popularization of rock. Neil Diamond's one-man show at the Winter Garden is all those things, and more."

But if Neil thought that on the basis of the *Times* review he was destined for the kinds of raves his Greek Theatre engagement had elicited, he was mistaken. While the critical reaction was generally positive, reviewers did find fault with his show—as did key members of his own team.

One of the negatives both critics and such associates as Armin Steiner agreed upon was the bone-crushing sound. "[Diamond's] electric rock and I had electric shock," Earl Wilson complained in his column, while Steiner said he was enraged: "The sound just about sterilized everybody in New York City . . . I kept going back and telling him [sound man Stan Miller], Tom kept telling him, 'This is not the outdoors. You don't need in an indoor environment 125 db sound pressure.' He ruined the performance, in my opinion."

The most notable negative criticism, however, had to do with Neil himself, specifically with his onstage persona. *Newsday*'s Robert Christgau heard it in his rendition of "I Am. . . I Said," when "his enunciation slips into the high-tone ridiculous"; the *Hollywood Reporter*'s Ben Wasser noted it in Diamond's penchant for referring to himself in "revered, institutional terms. It is 'his,' 'my,' 'mine,' and 'me'." And Joe Gannon, who thought Neil "had all the charm, all the charisma, all the aplomb" at the Greek Theatre, felt it throughout the performances: "I think he started to take on a 'star' attitude . . . He was a little caught up with what he was doing."

Self-indulgent as his shows may have been, one only had to peek backstage at the Winter Garden during the stand, however, to find that Neil's conquering-hero stance was playing big with fellow stars, family, friends, fans. In fact, the nightly post-concert backstage scene, in which would-be Neil-greeters had to run a carefully set-up gauntlet to get to him, was a spectacle in itself.

"Producer" of the post-concert events was executive assistant Totty Ames. Since so many people wanted to come backstage each night—a "great number [of whom]," she said, "Neil wanted to see, a great number that he didn't want to see, and some he was just kind of *asi asi* about"—Ames was charged with developing a strategy to keep people moving—or in their place. Making clever use of the backstage design, she decided on a three-level plan of action: "I had one group, the C group, on the main floor, in a room there, with champagne and nuts and candies. Then, on the next landing, there was another room, where I had the B group. Above that, on Neil's floor, was his dressing room, a little anteroom, and another dressing room, from which I could filter the A group into his room, a few at a time."

Ames added that certain members of the B group also gained passage to Neil's inner sanctum, but "the poor fools in the C group," she said, laughing, "never got up to the second floor."

The A group, of course, was largely limited to VIPs like Ethel Kennedy, Columbia's Clive Davis, and the seemingly endless parade of celebrities, ranging from Elton John to, as Totty Ames put it, "all the people who were appearing in town at the time." But Neil also made a point of spending a few minutes with the various former acquaintances/colleagues of his that he had invited.

For some of those people, like his former songwriting partner Carl D'Errico, seeing Neil again was a poignant experience. Since they had last been in touch, some five years earlier, D'Errico had left the business and gone to work as an office manager. "[He said] 'Hey, Carl, come back here,'" D'Errico recalled of their backstage encounter. "And he chased everybody out of the dressing room, and we started chatting. 'How ya doin'?' That kind of stuff. Unfortunately at that time in *my* life I wasn't prepared for [that] . . . We didn't have much in common in terms of music anymore."

D'Errico's private trauma, however, couldn't have been any more severe than that of Neil's former drummer and band manager, Tom Cerone. Unlike D'Errico, Cerone had not left the business. In fact, in an amazingly ironic twist of fate, he just happened to be drumming next door, at a joint called the Hawaii Kai. There, Cerone was a member of the house band, Frank Son and the Fabulous Son Brothers, which performed "Korean-American" music nightly. Thanks to Stan Miller and his high decibel count, the Son Brother could hear Diamond performing "good and loud" through the walls . . . "maybe louder than it was."

While he and Diamond chatted backstage, Cerone said, it was "like the old days." As he watched Neil converse with others in the room, however, the drummer saw a new Diamond: "[He was] now much more reserved in his actions, much more aware that he was being watched . . . [He was] doing Neil Diamond product."

Comedian Mike Mislove concurred: "He was going around like the Man of the Year." The Bitter-End–era acquaintance of Neil's was amused by the sight, as well as his exercise of unearthing and inviting acquaintances from his dim past to bear witness to his Broadway triumph: "I think what he was saying was, 'Look, here I am—and *good-bye!*' That was the last time I ever saw him."

While the above types were being granted their dressing-room moments with Neil, family members, save for Marcia, were usually contained—at Neil's request—in the B area until after all the A visitors had left.

Neil had a reason for this: He didn't want to be embarrassed by the horde of boisterous Rapaports who descended nightly on the Winter Garden, led by Rose Rapaport Diamond, bejeweled, coifed, and dressed to the nines, and looking young and striking enough for her fifty-four years for the likes of set designer Jim Newton to do a double-take. ("The first time I met her I wondered who she was. I assumed it was his mistress. She's a very attractive lady, and full of energy.")

At the Winter Garden, that energy was channeled into playing Jewish Mom of the Year to Diamond's Man of the Year. And Rose was a smash, signing autographs nightly and proclaiming to one and all that her son was her "biggest production."

With Neil firmly ensconced on his Broadway musical throne, it took an invitation from royalty of another kind to lure him out of town for a special performance nine days into his run.

The invite, from Ethel Kennedy, was for him to play at a Sunday fund-raising party for Democratic presidential hopeful George McGovern and his running mate, Sargent Shriver, Kennedy's brother-in-law, at Shriver's rented estate in Rockville, Maryland.

The Kennedy family extended Diamond the royal treatment, sending their plane to New York for him and his party. When the plane landed, Ethel Kennedy was there to greet them, insisting on personally driving Neil and Marcia to the event in her Chevrolet.

Abraham Lincoln High
School graduation photo,
1958.

As a member of Lincoln's championship fencing team, 1957–58.

Jack Packer, the "Jack"
of Neil and Jack, at age
twenty-two.

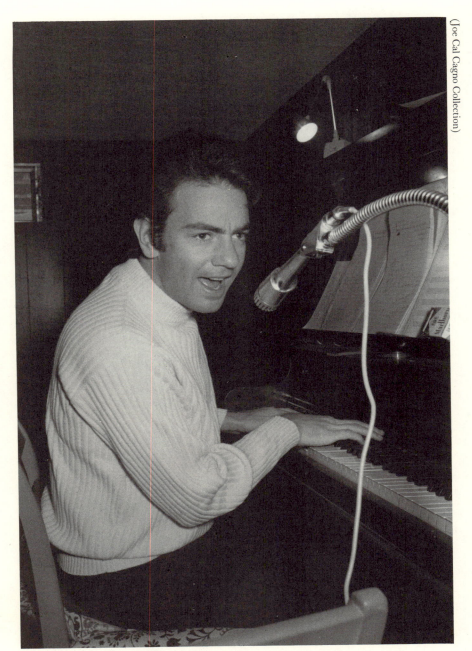

Pounding out a new tune at home in Massapequa, Long Island, 1967.

With first wife, Jay, 1967. They seemed "the *happiest* couple," according to his then-PR man, Joe Cal Cagno.

Neil, Jay and daughter Marjorie.

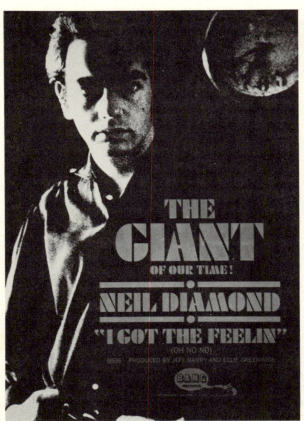

Trade ad promoting
Diamond's third Bang
Records single.

In the studio with producers Ellie Greenwich and Jeff Barry, 1967.

Celebrating his Troubadour triumph backstage, 1969.

Performing with one-time idols the Everly Brothers on the duo's 1970 summer-replacement TV series.

Mugging with "King Kong" in a West Germany park, 1972.

Autographing a fan's
painting, Los Angeles,
1972.

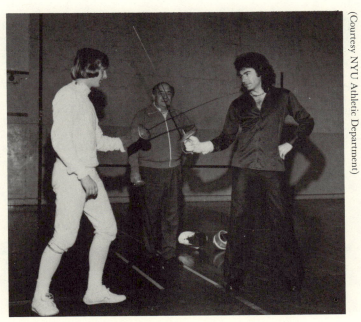

Taking up foil again with student James Bonnacorda
during a 1972 visit to NYU; coach Hugo Castello
looks on.

Onstage at the Greek Theatre, 1972.

Jim Newton's limited-edition rendering of the set he designed for Diamond's Greek Theatre and Winter Garden engagements.

At Sydney, Australia, press conference, 1976. "I've read a lot, I've met more people, I've grown up," he said of his performance "sabbatical."

Meeting Princess Margaret after 1977 London Palladium concert. At left is his second wife, Marcia.

With Barbra Streisand backstage following their surprise duet of "You Don't Bring Me Flowers" during the 1980 Grammy Awards.

Arriving at December 17, 1980 Century City benefit premiere of *The Jazz Singer* with Marcia and daughter Elyn, 12.

With Marcia, at *Jazz Singer* premiere.

Rose and Akeeba (Kieve) Diamond.

With son Jesse, 10.

Diamond's brother, Harvey, and his wife, Alice.

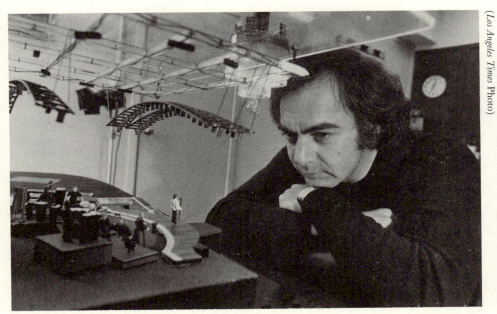

Inspecting a model of the stage he used for 1983 engagement at the Forum in
Los Angeles.

Meeting Prince Charles and Princess Diana before July 6, 1984
Birmingham benefit concert. The Garfield doll was a gift from
six-year-old Micah Diamond to two-year-old Prince William.

Striking a Christ-like pose during *Jonathan Livingston Seagull* segment, 1983.

Bantering with the crowd, 1982.

Pulling out all the glitzy stops during "America," 1985.

April 1986.

(Linda L. Perry)

Soaking up the cheers after performing "I Am . . . I Said," 1983.

Rocking out with "Brother Love," 1983.

(Donna Vazquez)

In his Melrose Place office, May 16, 1986: "I have to go out there and . . . live life to the fullest."

This was royal treatment that Neil could have done without. Totty Ames, who was in one of the limousines trying to keep pace with Ethel's "accordion-pleated" Chevy, described the scene: "I never saw anybody drive like that in my life—I mean they went out of the airport in that car in a two-wheel drift . . . My heart was going da-banga, da-banga, da-banga." Her, and Neil's, nerves weren't helped when Ethel zoomed through a couple of red lights.

An excruciatingly long fifteen minutes later, Kennedy's Chevrolet came to rest at the Shriver estate, but not before she announced her arrival by driving through a sawhorse that had been placed across the road to the house.

Diamond had a chance to regain his composure at a private lunch that followed with assorted Kennedys and Shrivers. Then it was on to the stage that had been constructed in the back of the house, on a large expanse of land peopled with the thousands of supporters who had paid ten dollars apiece.

Neil's ensuing performance was as memorable as his ride; a little competition that Ethel Kennedy and her sister Eunice Kennedy Shriver dreamt up saw to that. Informing the crowd that her favorite song of Diamond's was "Sweet Caroline," while Ethel's was "New York Boy," Eunice Shriver introduced Neil with the words, "I've asked him to sing the song first of the woman he loved most."

"This is a terrible predicament," Neil commented after taking the stage. A few songs later, however, he broke into "Sweet Caroline."

Ethel Kennedy did not take her defeat sitting down; she walked onstage behind Neil and poured a paper carton of beer over his head. "Neil had to go with it, and laugh," Totty Ames said.

To executive assistant Totty Ames, Neil's Broadway engagement didn't build to any one climactic moment. "He started off at a high-fevered pitch, and *every* performance was that way," she said.

On Saturday, October 21, Neil took the Winter Garden stage for the final two shows, a 2 o'clock matinee and the 7:15 P.M. final show. "This is the last of twenty performances tonight," he said shortly into the evening show, "and I welcome you all to share this special, special performance with us. I want to make the most beautiful music that we can make."

He proceeded to deliver virtually the same immaculately paced twenty-song set that he had delivered the previous nineteen shows. The audience was wildly receptive throughout. Two-thirds of the way into the show, one particularly enthused member of the crowd yelled out between songs, "Talk to us!" Without missing a beat, Neil responded, "I am."

After the theater was cleared, Totty Ames staged a party in the lobby which, she said, featured "the most grotesque cake you've ever seen: a carousel with tiers, and musicians all around, and Neil standing up." Afterward, Neil took his band to dinner in Little Italy.

"He was very pleased with the way the entire show came off, the way it was handled, the publicity that was done," Ames commented. "All of it. He was on a real high."

However, several of the people who had labored to get Neil Diamond to Broadway did not come home on a real high.

In Joe Gannon's mind, Neil's last-minute decision to redo the show that he had helped him painstakingly piece together over the last two years was proof that "Diamond didn't know what the hell I did [for him]." Gannon added: "As far as he was concerned . . . his talent came out on his own, and had virtually nothing to do with what I had done."

They would never work together again.

Even before embarking on the Broadway project, Lee Holdridge, meanwhile, harbored the same kind of bruised feelings as he read Neil's self-touting interviews: "He was mentioning all of this glorious music without ever mentioning he did have his helpers put it all together for him." His Broadway experience with Neil only served to solidify his growing dismay: "In New York, suddenly it was like 'Well, I'm too good for all of you.' He would come in wearing sunglasses in the middle of the night in the fall. It was like, 'Who is this guy? Does he know any of us? Should we reintroduce ourselves?'"

·14·
JONATHAN

His Broadway run made Neil a superstar. But after it ended October 22, it was history.

His second Greek Theatre stand, however, continued to live on into his performance "sabbatical," thanks to "Hot August Night," the two-record set memorializing his ten-day engagement. Culled mostly from his magical August 24 show—the one that musician Emory Gordy said had been coated with K-Y jelly—the superlatively recorded LP package came with an arresting cover shot, of a hot-and-bothered Diamond who looked like he was wailing on an invisible sax. (A reviewer for *Coast* magazine snidely suggested he was holding an "imaginary cock.")

"Hot August Night" was an immediate hit; by December it was nestled in *Billboard*'s Top Five. Meanwhile, the engagement paid off for Neil in another way: It led to a job offer from Hollywood movie producer/director Hall Bartlett.

Hiring Diamond to score one of his pictures had been in the back of Bartlett's mind since he had seen him perform at the Greek in 1971. But it wasn't until the following year that the producer, whose credits ranged from *Crazy Legs,* the 1953 film biography of football star Elroy Hirsch, to *The Caretaker,* a 1963 look at the issue of mental health, had a potential project in mind: *Jonathan Livingston Seagull.*

Bartlett discovered the sleeper of a tome by Richard Bach in February of 1972. Thrilled by the mystical saga of an outcast seagull, he had made an impassioned bid for film rights to author Bach, vowing to eschew animation and humans in favor of seagull "actors." Only weeks away from signing his formal contract with Bach, he attended several of Neil's "Hot August Night" performances. Watching Neil perform such Solitary Man standbys as "I Am . . . I Said," he decided that Neil would be the perfect composer for *Jonathan.*

But Bartlett couldn't persuade Diamond to meet with him at the time. Unwilling to write him off, he tabled his search for a scorer until after the movie was shot. On October 30, he began filming in the Big Sur area of California.

While the producer was out of town, Neil reconsidered. He did so from an appropriate roost, a Malibu beach house he and Marcia had rented. "There were seagulls everywhere, wheeling and diving and strutting along the sand," he would say. He had to be seeing dollar signs in those fluttering wings, given the fact that *Jonathan Livingston Seagull,* at more than one million hardcover copies sold, had by then become a publishing phenomenon, with a November *Time* cover story to prove it.

Diamond called Bartlett and asked for a screening. Bartlett was happy to oblige, fashioning a presentation from the 800,000 feet of film he'd shot, and as Diamond would later say, "I was knocked out . . . The scenic value and majesty of it were beyond belief." A couple of days later, he called Bartlett back. "Let's do it," he said.

Easier said than done. At the first negotiating session, Diamond's team of lawyers, headed by David Braun, served notice that Diamond wanted nothing less than a tradition-shattering deal for a scorer. Among the demands was that Bartlett *guarantee,* without hearing a bar of music beforehand, that he would use forty-seven minutes of Neil's original work, a concession that not even Hollywood's legendary film composers had ever won. The producer's attorneys advised him to begin looking for another scorer.

However, the strong-willed Bartlett, being one filmmaker who gloried in marching to his own drummer, agreed to the forty-seven-minute guarantee. The producer, a student of psychology, made that decision after meeting Neil—whom he found polite but wary—and concluding that such was Neil's lurking insecurity that he wouldn't commit to the project unless he, Bartlett, made some special show of faith.

However, Bartlett wasn't content to have Diamond's signature on a contract, which he got February 8, 1973; he also wanted Neil, like other key associates, to become a devoted member of his filmmaking family. Said one former employee: "Hall took sort of a possessive feeling toward all the people on his team. But he was certainly one of the people . . . who really knew how to handle men . . . And many times it wasn't obvious; he was just the type of man [who] just pumped your ass with sunshine. In other words, he built you up so that you . . . did your best work."

Bartlett's nurturing of Diamond began with an open letter in the form of a trade ad he took out announcing Neil's signing. "It all began . . . when I heard you communicate with an audience of all ages at the Greek Theatre . . . feelings," the ad read. "You shared the living of your life—the pain of it, the joy, the dreams, the challenge, the questions, the memories. You are a true poet of our times, Neil. You have reached out to people everywhere . . ."

In preparation for his *Jonathan* writing, Neil embarked on a self-styled study of philosophical and spiritual thought.

Among the books he acquired were *Religions of the World, The*

Aquarian Gospel of Jesus the Christ, and *The Sermon on the Mount According to Vedanta.* He also latched on to a young Hare Krishna convert. "The kid would come in and talk to him for hours," executive assistant Totty Ames recalled. "He was around for weeks and weeks and weeks."

Diamond later likened his research to "trying to fill up the well before the writing so the water would be clean and pure and cold and right." However, his frivolous use one day of an Indian yogi he had hired raised questions about how much of his study was sincere and how much of it was for show. The yogi's special mission: checking out Hall Bartlett's "aura" as the unsuspecting producer sat in Diamond's sitting room. (Diamond later confessed to the producer what he'd done, adding with a smile that the yogi told him that he, Neil, was going to learn a lot from Bartlett.)

Finally, some six weeks after he embarked on his study, Neil claimed he closed his books, dismissed the yoga master and the Hare Krishna devotee—whom he thanked with a Bill Whitten–designed suit and money for a one-way plane ticket to India—and began to write his first song. And "absolutely nothing came. It was because I had not really solved the crux of the story."

He didn't experience his breakthrough, he said, until he wrote the words "God Being" in his notepad, followed by just the word "Be." Suddenly, "I knew how I wanted to approach it all. Everything seemed possible. My heart started to palpitate."

While Neil gave the impression that his study and early songwriting struggles were all-consuming, the fact was that he was simultaneously debating walking out of the project. "Shortly after the contract was executed," he later maintained, "I realized that Mr. Bartlett expected far more of me in connection with the picture than the creation and composition of the musical score. He asked me to perform tests as Jonathan's voice and to write sample dialogue for Jonathan, as well as to perform numerous other functions . . . I realized that far more was expected of me . . . than I had previously understood, and I told Mr. Bartlett that perhaps it would be appropriate to simply call the entire transaction off."

Bartlett, however, had a totally different recollection of his difficulty with Neil in March of 1973: "He said he had a terrible wrenching feeling inside because his children [that is, his songs] had been torn from him and given over to someone else," the producer later wrote. "He said that he wanted me to return all publishing rights which I was to have under the contract . . .

"Diamond told me that he would stop working on the film if I did not change the contract. I said to Diamond that I was shocked and dumbfounded. I did not know what to say. The publishing rights which he was demanding that I give up could mean income to *JLS* of over $500,000.

"Neil said that he knew that this was a big blow, but he said, in effect, 'I think you can work it out. When someone wants to do something, they can find a way to do it.'"

In their accounts, Diamond and Bartlett did agree on one thing: that the matter was resolved through compromise. According to a letter of confirmation that the producer sent Neil on March 23, "The JLS Limited Partnership will receive no percentage of the music publishing revenue derived from the sale of your album 'Jonathan Livingston Seagull' until it has sold one million copies. You and the JLS Limited Partnership will share fifty-fifty . . . on all album sales over one million."

Neil returned to his composing work on *Jonathan* in April. He continued to be coddled by Bartlett, who adhered to a controversial method of working that flew in the face of filmmaking tradition.

In short, the producer disdained the practice of "locking in"—or completing the editing of—*Jonathan* before putting Diamond to work. Instead, after finishing reels of rough-cut film, he would put them on cassette and deliver them to Neil, who would then screen them in his office for song and music inspiration. Because the exact times of the musical sequences weren't yet set, Diamond didn't have to be burdened, for a while at least, with any timing requirements.

Meanwhile, Neil made his life easier yet by hiring Lee Holdridge to arrange and orchestrate his *Jonathan* work.

Holdridge entered the project with a mixture of great excitement and aggravation—excitement because the project represented his first important foray into film work, aggravation because of the hoops he claimed that Neil made him jump through before finally giving him the job.

"Tom calls me and tells me they're going to do *JLS*," he recalled. "At that time Neil was talking about getting Leonard Bernstein or André Previn to score the picture with him. So that's a little subtle putdown, like, 'We've decided we're moving on to bigger names.'"

But, eventually Neil brought him out from New York to discuss his participation. The arranger, still smarting over what he perceived as Diamond's new "star" attitude, had a premonition about the meeting when he walked into Neil's new office: "On the wall—I'll never forget—there were four drawings some school child had sent him. There was Bach, Beethoven, Brahms, and Diamond, all framed. And I remember looking at them and saying, 'Oh, oh, we're in trouble here.' It reminded me of the old school quiz, 'Which one of these doesn't belong here—*a, b, c,* or *d?*'"

At the meeting, Lee claimed, Neil greeted him with the words, "I don't know if you're capable of doing this." He added that many talks among him, Diamond, and Tom Catalano ensued: "It was very uncomfortable because Neil was putting me in a position where I was almost going to have to audition for him—and here I had been working for him for almost four years." But after repeatedly insisting he could handle the assignment, Holdridge got the job.

Knowing that Neil did not have the technical training to actually compose a background score, Lee entered the project with the assumption that his "score" would consist solely of songs. Then he viewed a three-hour version of *Jonathan Livingston Seagull* at Goldwyn. "I'm telling you, the film went on for days," he chuckled. "Shots of the ocean. Shots of the mountains . . . I suddenly realized sitting there that, even shrunk down to a couple of hours we're talking a *lot* of orchestra." Just as suddenly, he saw his role in the project expanding. "Right then, I should have hired the best lawyer in the country, and the best agent, and said, 'Work this deal out.' But I didn't. I [thought], 'Well, I'm here for the ride—I'll just see where the boat goes.'"

As it turned out, Neil and Lee glided along on a glass-smooth sea with *Jonathan* for a while. The only discord came, according to Holdridge, when Neil announced his intention of smoking pot during their sessions—to which the arranger calmly replied, "Well, when you decide to do that, I'll get up and leave." Diamond never lit up in his presence, Holdridge added.

The arranger's first order of business was bringing some life to the songs Neil had written. As Neil awkwardly plunked out the songs on the piano, Lee jotted the melodies down.

The first song Neil played was "Be."

To Holdridge, the melody was shades of "Holly Holy" in that "It was really strange; it never changed chords." He did, however, note the "nice little hook—*DEEEN-da-da-DEEEN-da-DEEEN-da-da-DEEEN-da-da-DUM-da-dum.*" He built his arrangement around this leitmotif. To give the monotone "Be" some semblance of depth, meanwhile, he had the strings "weaving all over the place, trying to create countermelody."

As for Neil's two-chord rendition of "Dear Father," Holdridge immediately appreciated its beautiful melody. "I said, 'You know, this kind of makes me think of Mozart.' And he said, 'Well, can you play it in that style?'" Lee did, moving the harmonies through different inversions, putting countermovement into it, and introducing new chords—in other words, playing "Dear Father" like it wound up being heard. "It became a lot more classical and elegant," he noted.

Holdridge also worked with Diamond on "Lonely Looking Sky" as well as musical fragments that would become "Skybird." As he did so, he felt renewed pangs of uneasiness. "We're into the summer, and the ship is sinking a little bit, because there is no score materializing, [only] a couple of nice songs," he said. "It was now getting to the point where deadlines were starting to appear and we were beginning to book orchestras."

While Lee Holdridge was growing anxious, *Jonathan Livingston Seagull* music editor John Hammell was sweating bullets. Keenly affected by Hall Bartlett's don't-bother-Diamond-with-technical-requirements edict, with which he strongly disagreed, the veteran editor (Francis Coppola's *The Godfather,* Cecil B. DeMille's *The Greatest Show on Earth,* Frank Capra's *Riding High*) nevertheless had by necessity begun submitting cue sheets to Neil detailing the precise length of each scene as well as the timing for the dialogue, if any. Each time he tried to explain to Neil the importance of having his songs and background music follow the sheets, however, he said Diamond brusquely put him off: "I think what Diamond was really concerned with was writing the songs. He didn't know how one of them was going to fit into a sequence which ran for six minutes and eight seconds."

When Neil entered Studio One at Warner Brothers in June to begin recording, Hammell had another surprise in store: Neil regarded the exercise as no different than recording a studio album.

"His technique I had never seen before," Hammell said. "Those first sessions he would come in by himself in the morning with his guitar, and he would go out there in the studio and form his song on the stage." Accustomed to recording a musical score in no more than three days, four if the score included some songs, Hammell nervously settled in for a long haul. "*Weeks* went by," he said. "*Months* went by."

Eventually, the music editor saw Tom Catalano act to deal with the timing requirements. According to Hammell, after Neil recorded the basic track of a song, Catalano would send the tape to Holdridge, asking him not only to orchestrate the song but to make it fit the particular cue. Holdridge verified the process: "Little by little, it started to be, 'Well, maybe you should take this [song] and extend it over here, Lee.'"

One of the first such assignments Holdridge got was "Dear Father." Diamond had written twelve bars of original music, which clocked in at roughly one minute. The time of the cue: five minutes and twelve seconds.

By the time he was through with the assignment, he was both elated and troubled. He was elated for the major contribution he felt he had made to the cue, and he was troubled because, in his mind, he had become the cue's cocomposer in the process.

Holdridge played the "Dear Father" cue off the soundtrack album, providing a running commentary in which he made his case for cocomposer status:

"[Track begins with instrumental.] I made up this intro in order to lead you into the melody. [Diamond begins singing.] There's that Mozartian piano thing . . . And it's lovely, works perfectly. Gives it a classical flavor, gives it a poignancy, an elegance. [Orchestra comes in.] So now we add strings, we repeat the phrase. Countermelody, a different new melody, for transitional purposes. Now, I'm going someplace else compositionally. [Diamond speaks.] He added those words later, after he heard the music. This is where Jonathan, I think, is trying to lift himself out of the water. A little Stravinsky-ish, perhaps. This is all original composition [by me] through here. [Thumping piano, horns, building strings.] See how nicely this leads you back to that melody. I brought back the 'Be' melody here from the opening; orchestrated it a little differently. It's my attempt to make a score out of it, by weaving some of the melodies together. And, now, a nice key change coming up [cymbals crash—return to 'Dear Father' melody]—it gives you a nice lift at this point. [Sweeping string sound; Diamond reprises vocal; strings become moody.] This is all something new I added. [Back to 'Dear Father' melody, sad, soft this time.] The point of introducing all that outside music is obviously it gives the piece growth and development and takes it someplace [Diamond sings again], so that when he comes back to the melody, it's fresh to you again.''

Holdridge was anxious enough about the kind of input he had had in the "Dear Father" cue, and anticipated having again, that he approached Tom Catalano. Holdridge: "I said, 'You know, Tom, I'm doing a lot of original composition.' And he . . . agreed with me, he said he understood, and 'Don't worry about it, I'll work it out.'

"So," Holdridge continued, "I didn't worry about it . . . But the truth of the matter is that I didn't stop doing it because I wanted the score to . . . work as well as possible."

As the *Jonathan* score began to take shape, so, finally, did the Neil Diamond–Hall Bartlett relationship.

In fact, Bartlett's frequent visits with Diamond in Diamond's office in the wake of their March imbroglio became a highlight of the producer/director's work on *JLS*. Although he never found Neil particularly loose at the sessions, during which Neil would play his latest creations, he was pleased to detect Neil's friendlier bent, as well as his excitement over the way the movie and his score were progressing.

Neil demonstrated his goodwill toward Bartlett on several occasions, including one time when he solicited the producer's opinion on the Excalibur, an automobile he was thinking of buying at the time. When the producer expressed his unfamiliarity with the car, Neil had one of his gofers drive a couple of them over to Bartlett's Bel-Air home on successive Sundays so the producer could get a look. On the third Sunday, Diamond surprised Bartlett by having his assistant drive over a rare Dual Ghia, the one car that Bartlett told him that he had always hankered to buy. The Dual Ghia, which belonged to Lucille Ball, happened to be for sale, and, encouraged by Neil, the producer wound up purchasing it.

Bartlett's close associates, however, never did warm up to Diamond. Music editor John Hammell, for one, confessed that he took a dislike to Neil from their first meeting, a curt how-do-you-do at Armin Steiner's Sound Labs. From there the relationship slid into oblivion. "I lost him very early . . . I don't imagine that Diamond and I had twenty, thirty minutes of conversation on the whole picture," he said. The little bit that Hammell said was accomplished in the technical area was because of Tom Catalano's cooperation.

One of the film's two editors, James Galloway, was similarly alienated: "He was extremely arrogant with people whom he felt were performing functions less important than his own." Galloway recalled Neil visiting the dubbing room one day, and ordering one of his gofers to buy him some candy. "And the runner came back with plastic bags, probably a whole grocery store's [worth] of candy," Galloway recalled. "And instead of offering them to us, he sat there pitching them to us. [It was] the type of thing that would turn you off a bit."

Galloway also was disturbed by Diamond's proclivity for having members of his ever-present entourage—usually Catalano—"do his thinking and pushing for him," as well as the "aura" Neil and group emitted. "When they walked into the room it was a little bit like the scenes from *The Godfather*," Galloway said. "That was not a happy crew . . . They were all afraid of one another; it was clearly part of the operation. And not comfortable to be around."

The editor paused for a moment. "It doesn't say a whole lot for being at the top, does it?" he said.

By the first of August, the songs and score to *Jonathan Livingston Seagull* were, for the most part, completed. Still blowing in the wind, however, was the matter of Lee Holdridge's credit, much to his dismay.

In Lee's mind, he had delved even further into actual composition since his work on the "Dear Father" cue. Specifically, he considered the three-minute-nineteen-second "Prologue" and the nine-minute-twenty-eight-second "Odyssey," to be, on the whole, new and original works that he rather than Neil had composed—despite the obvious presence of themes from "Be" in "Prologue," and "Be," "Lonely Looking Sky," and "Dear Father" in "Odyssey."

Holdridge's campaign for cocomposer credit for the score received a crucial boost when Hall Bartlett took up his cause personally with Diamond. Maintained Holdridge: "By now, Bartlett understood that I was really the mechanic, the one that was making it all happen." But it was a conversation with John Green, a cochairman of the executive committee of the music branch of the National Academy of Motion Picture Arts and Sciences, that compelled the producer to action. Green informed Bartlett that, under the Academy's rules, the *Jonathan Livingston Seagull* score would not qualify for consideration for an Academy Award in either of the two scoring categories—Best Original Dramatic Score and Best Scoring: Adaptation and Original Song Score—unless Diamond and Holdridge were given a joint composing credit. Green referred to Paragraph Four of the Special Rules for the Music Awards, which states: "In the case of a solo composing credit (other than song writing) the Executive Committee . . . shall define a composer as a person who can compose music and commit it to paper in a form more detailed than a simple lead sheet . . ." As for the investigation Green made into *JLS*, Holdridge hypothesized: "He could put the pieces together . . . It was all over town that summer about Diamond and *Jonathan Livingston Seagull*. Everybody knew . . . I was scoring the picture. Who was standing at the podium conducting the sessions?"

After Bartlett pitched the idea of joint credit to Diamond, Diamond agreed to convene a meeting with both Bartlett and Holdridge in his office in the hope of arriving at a mutually acceptable resolution of the problem.

At the meeting, Bartlett unveiled a specific credit that he explained had passed muster with the Academy, and which he considered fair:

Songs Written and Performed
by
Neil Diamond
Music Score
Composed and Adapted by
Neil Diamond
and
Lee Holdridge

Lee Holdridge: "Neil said to me, in words or in effect, 'Is it OK with you?' I said, 'Yes.' Neil then said . . . 'It's OK with me, too.'"
Holdridge then left the meeting and breathed a sigh of relief.

Later in the month, Bartlett gave Holdridge the opportunity to compose a crucial cue by himself.

The situation arose because of Bartlett's dissatisfaction with "Sanctus," the song that Diamond had written and submitted for the "New World" segment of the picture in which Jonathan ascends into the heavenly reaches. In the producer's opinion, "Sanctus" was copped from Catholic ceremonies, and, in addition, was pretentious sounding.

However, Bartlett's claimed attempts to get Neil to submit another song were unsuccessful. Needing, then, to keep "Sanctus" in the picture not only to meet his obligation to use forty-seven minutes of Diamond's work but also for Oscar score-qualifying purposes, he decided to move "Sanctus" to a less conspicuous part of the film. To fill the musical gap in "New World," he then quietly asked Holdridge to compose a new cue.

"Bartlett really wanted the music to take us into that other world," Lee recalled. "So I came up with the concept of leaving all the earthly-type instruments, like drums, bass, and keyboards, and going into a very pure classical form . . . a solo violin and orchestra . . . so that the music made a spiritual transition." Holdridge named the twelve-minute cue "The Other World."

"The Other World" turned out to be just what the producer ordered, and Holdridge recorded it immediately. Editor Jim Galloway, who had been a Juilliard piano major, was there: "After the first run-through, the members of the orchestra *applauded,* and you don't see that very often on a scoring stage. It was one of the best cues I have ever heard for a film, one of the saddest and most beautiful melodies I know . . . The whole sequence with that score behind it was devastating."

The *Jonathan Livingston Seagull* score was dubbed to the film in August and September. According to John Hammell, who was accustomed to having the composer present to offer input and to safety-check the process, Neil didn't attend any of the sessions.

Shortly after the dubbing was completed, Neil resurfaced, asking Bartlett to arrange a screening of the now-finished and soon-to-be-premiered film for him and some friends. The producer complied, obtaining the Samuel Goldwyn Theatre for the night of September 27.

At the time Bartlett got back to Diamond with the place and date, Neil invited him to a post-screening meeting at his house. Bartlett was pleased by the gesture, as Diamond had politely asked him not to attend the screening itself.

He arrived at the Diamonds' home on Ladera Lane in Holmby Hills at the appointed time, 11:30 P.M. Neil and Marcia had not yet returned from the screening, so he was shown to the study, where, with great anticipation, he awaited their arrival.

Twenty minutes later, he heard their car come up the driveway. A couple of minutes later they burst into the study.

"Marcia was still crying," he later told columnist Joyce Haber. "Neil told me the film was an all-time classic and would live forever . . ."

·15·
FLAP

In stark contrast to the praise Bartlett claimed that Neil heaped upon *Jonathan*, there were no bravos from author Richard Bach when he attended a screening of *Jonathan Livingston Seagull* the next night.

At a meeting with Bartlett the following morning, Bach, who wrote the screenplay and whose deal included approval of the script, musical score, and final cut, handed the producer a note listing thirty-three objections he had. The complaints ranged from the inclusion of "Sanctus" in the score ("music is unacceptable") to Bartlett's "arrogant" dedication of the film to the people who worked on it. But most of the criticism dealt with changes Bach claimed that Bartlett had made in his screenplay. "Overall my objection is that the major theme of the story is changed," Bach wrote. "The book says: be yourself, practice it, no matter what others say and the byproducts will be skill and adventure and a few who will be interested in learning what you've found, and that it's fun to share learning with these few.

"The film says, maybe you can be yourself if you don't 'hurt' anybody and if you later apologize for being different and learn to relate to others and go out and try to change the way they want to live. This latter is the missionary zeal that has destroyed millions of people.

"It's a pretty major change in the theme and message of Jonathan Seagull, and I cannot give my approval to it."

Several days of talks between Bach and Bartlett ensued, during which the author presented a formal list of changes he wanted made in the script. But on October 6, a little more than two weeks before the film's scheduled October 23 premiere in New York, the talks broke off, Bartlett holding to his interpretation of *JLS* as a Christian parable.

As the producer braced for a suit, he had other fresh concerns. On October 4, *Jonathan* was screened for the press at Mann's Village Theater in Westwood, and the response, according to music editor John Hammell, was a bad one: "You could tell right away: When those birds started to talk, it was finished."

Then on October 8, Neil hit the producer with a thunderbolt of his own, in the form of a David Braun–authored telegram. It read:

I HAVE BEEN INSTRUCTED BY NEIL DIAMOND TO ADVISE YOU THAT IN VIEW OF YOUR MANY BREACHES OF THE EXISTING AGREEMENT BETWEEN YOU AND NEIL DIAMOND, INCLUDING FAILURE TO GIVE APPROPRIATE CREDIT, INCLUSION OF ADDITIONAL MUSICAL MATERIAL WITHOUT KNOWLEDGE OR CONSENT OF MR. DIAMOND, IMPROPER EDITING AND FAILURE TO ACCORD MR. DIAMOND PARTIC-IPATION IN EDITING, MR. DIAMOND WILL SEEK, AMONG OTHER REMEDIES, TO ENJOIN ALL SHOWINGS OF MOTION PICTURE JONATHAN LIVINGSTON SEAGULL.

"Bartlett was furious," recalled editor Jim Galloway.

On October 11, three days later, Bach filed suit in Los Angeles Superior Court seeking to halt the release of *Jonathan Livingston Seagull*. In his application for a preliminary injunction, he claimed that Bartlett and codefendants Paramount Pictures, the movie's distributor, and the JLS Limited Partnership were guilty of breach of contract, and unauthorized use of his *Jonathan* screenplay.

Bach also sent telegrams to film reviewers around the country, requesting that they delay their reviews until the picture was "available to be seen in its final form." By then, *Daily Variety's* review of the picture had already appeared, authored by the influential "Murf," Art Murphy. Murphy sounded a doubtful tone, praising Bartlett for his "consistent concept and execution" and the film's "superb" nature photography, while making note of the film's "teenybopper psychedelics, facile moralizing, [and] Pollyanna polemics." He also was not impressed with Diamond's "formula melodies" and "monotone nasality." The outlook for the picture, he summarized, was either boom or bust.

As for the fledgling Bach-Diamond-Bartlett paper war, it was definitely boom. On October 12, as Bartlett and his attorneys read through Bach's suit papers, he directed his counsel to fire a reply to Diamond declaring him in breach of his contract with the JLS Limited Partnership. Among the charges leveled in the telegram were Neil's alleged failure to deliver the required forty-seven minutes of original music, provide proper credit on the soundtrack album and liner notes, and refer to the picture when promoting the album.

Giving rise to speculation that Diamond's displeasure with *Jonathan Livingston Seagull* was a very recent development—perhaps linked to fear of a hostile press reception—was an interview that he granted to the *Los Angeles Times'* Robert Hilburn in early October. The only difficulty Neil spoke of in connection with the movie was the angst he experienced in coming up with his songs. As for his relationship with Bartlett, Diamond termed it "very special."

The day after the October 14 article appeared, Neil filed suit in Los Angeles Superior Court against Bartlett, JLS Limited Partnership, and Paramount Pictures. Like Bach, he asked for a temporary injunction preventing the defendants from releasing *Jonathan Livingston Seagull.* In his complaint he charged breach of contract, citing the same particulars he had alleged in his telegram.

Neil also filed a personal declaration. In it he provided an account of his September 27 screening and his post-screening meeting with Bartlett that was poles apart from that of the producer's: "When I viewed the photoplay, I learned for the first time that major and substantial changes . . . had been made in the musical soundtrack which I had previously submitted to Mr. Bartlett. At the conclusion of said screening, I voiced to Mr. Bartlett my objections to those changes and told him, in substance, that he had 'cut up' my music, and I told him that he was not entitled to make those changes under the contract."

Neil then listed the changes he asserted he had not approved. Among them was the addition of Lee Holdridge's "Other World" cue to the score, which, Neil wrote, "significantly impairs the integrity of my concept for the musical integrity of the picture," and the "substantial deletions from and rearrangements" of his songs and the score, which, he claimed, constituted "musical butchery" on Bartlett's part.

Neil went on to take exception to the shared credit on the score with Holdridge, stating, "In the entertainment field, credits are an essential and vital right of creative talent. An incorrect credit . . . materially affects the ability of the creative talent to secure other employment and assignments in the entertainment industry." He then ended his ten-page statement by calling for either the restoration of the sound track as he submitted it to Bartlett, or its replacement with another score.

Two days later, Bartlett filed papers opposing both Diamond's and Bach's applications for preliminary injunctions. Among those submitting declarations on Bartlett's behalf was none other than Lee Holdridge.

In his statement, Holdridge defended Bartlett's editing of the songs and music: "A great many of the alleged problems about which Neil is now complaining regarding the editing of the music of the picture were due to his lack of experience and understanding of the process of scoring a motion picture, his ignoring the warnings given to him by [music editor] Mr. Hammell and myself as to the problems that were arising because of his failure to deal with the timing requirements . . . and his lack of understanding and experience as to the nature of extended and serious composition, as opposed to the writing of popular songs."

As for Neil's objection to the shared credit on the score, Holdridge stated that it was the credit he had agreed to at their August meeting with Bartlett.

The most provocative assertion in Holdridge's declaration concerned the composing and adapting work he felt he did on the *Jonathan Livingston Seagull* score compared to Neil's work: "From the time we started working together, Neil gave me a total of about ninety-six measures of music. In my opinion, this is the amount of actual original music written by Neil Diamond. The final score written by Neil and myself consists of 797 measures . . . The difference between the 797 measures of music written by Neil is accounted for by my adaptations and variations of Neil's melodies and my addition, at Neil's request, of new melodies and themes.

"In my opinion," Holdridge continued, "Neil Diamond wrote, *at most,* twenty minutes of original music."

Bartlett seized upon that claim in his own declaration: "I now discover, for the first time, the enormity of the breach committed by Diamond."

(In a supplemental declaration, Neil claimed that two one-and-a-half-minute cues he authorized Holdridge to compose for *Jonathan Livingston Seagull* were "the only instances of his actual composition of material in my score not based upon my themes and melodies.")

On October 18, Neil Diamond and Richard Bach met again with Hall Bartlett, this time in court. After two days of arguments—punctuated during one break by Diamond's and Bach's game of penny-pitching in the hall—a temporary accommodation between the parties was reached at 9:15 P.M. on October 19.

Under the agreement, Judge Campbell M. Lucas delayed his ruling on the suits to give the sides time to work out a compromise. Also, the parties agreed that both the October 23 New York premiere, at the Sutton, as well as the October 30 Los Angeles premiere, at Mann's Village Theater, would go on as scheduled, and that a "precede" would be run before the picture in each engagement stating, "By agreement of the producer, the author of the book *Jonathan Livingston Seagull* and the composer of the music, certain changes are now being made in the dialog and music of the picture you are about to see."

By October 29, the date Lucas had requested that the parties return to court, no accord had been reached, however. Nearly a week of hearings followed, leading, finally, on November 5, to those accords and Lucas' issuance of separate preliminary court orders.

As for the Bach suit, Lucas called for a redubbing of twenty-four pages of dialogue, encompassing all of the agreed-upon changes. He also ruled that Bach's name be removed from the film's credits, which the author had insisted on.

Regarding the Diamond suit, the judge stipulated that a handful of changes be made in the score, including, most significantly, the replacement of some four minutes of Lee Holdridge's "Other World" cue from the "New World" segment of the picture, with Diamond's "Anthem" (the former "Sanctus"). Lucas also ordered that the following new music credit be run:

Card No. 1:

Music and Songs

by

Neil Diamond

Card No. 2:

Background Score Composed

and Adapted by

Neil Diamond

and

Lee Holdridge

Judge Lucas set the same deadline, November 20, in each order for these changes to be incorporated into *Jonathan Livingston Seagull*.

The next day, Bertram Fields, Bach's lawyer, said his client was pleased with the substantial "rewrite" of the dialogue. Neil, meanwhile, made no public comment at the time, although he would later declare to a group of reporters that he had "won" his suit. By Bartlett's reckoning, however, Bach and Diamond were the losers, in that *Jonathan* was never enjoined from being shown.

As for editor Jim Galloway, the changes Neil did secure in the score were important enough for him to conclude that the movie itself was the loser in the bitter fight.

Galloway was only beginning to form that opinion when Neil came in to screen the new version of *Jonathan*. Beforehand, the film editor said he collared Diamond and remarked: "I don't know what damage you might have done . . ." His response, Galloway added, was "quite cold rejection of any possibility that anything he had done might be wrong."

The new version of *Jonathan Livingston Seagull* was completed and premiered on schedule. The irony was that not many people cared at that point: The movie was already in a downward spiral at the box office, buffeted by a gust of contemptuous reviews, such as *Time's* judgment, headlined "Bird Droppings."

Neil's own musicians were not much kinder. Said Emory Gordy Jr.: "We later named it 'Jonathan Livingston Seaturkey.'" The only fun memory he had of the entire recording experience, he added, was the day at Warner Brothers' Studio One when, after hours of being parked under a seagull-crowded movie screen, jokester Hal Blaine bellowed, "Hey, what's all this pigeon shit doing on my drums?!"

(Neil would later pan the movie himself: "The film did not come together for some reason. I think it was an impossible film to make to begin with, much too ethereal.")

Jonathan did, however, enjoy its moments in the sun, thanks to Columbia Records. In July, Neil primed the Columbia team for the soundtrack LP by screening a thirteen-minute clip from the movie at the company's annual convention. (As for rejoining the CBS Records family, he quipped: "I've been waiting for this moment since the first time Columbia dropped me, about ten years ago.") Determined that Diamond's first release on Columbia be a smash, the label wound up lavishing one of the most comprehensive merchandising campaigns in its history on the album. Directed by Columbia's marketing vice-president, Bruce Lundvall, the campaign included radio and television commercials, print ads, and record store displays.

The investment in money and energy paid handsome dividends: "Jonathan Livingston Seagull," the album, soared to number two on *Billboard*'s chart, the best showing of any Diamond LP yet. Making the achievement all the more spectacular was the fact that there was no smash-hit single to stimulate sales, "Be" failing to crack the Top 30.

Having distanced himself in the eyes of the public, from Hall Bartlett and *Jonathan,* the movie, by virtue of his lawsuit, and having scored a hit album, Neil had, to all outward appearances, come out of *Seagull* smelling like a rose.

The bloom on Neil's "Jonathan Livingston Seagull" LP triumph, however, faded somewhat the following February when the National Academy of Motion Picture Arts and Sciences announced its list of Oscar nominees. The music branch of the Academy had earlier declared all five of Diamond's *Jonathan* songs eligible in the Best Song category, but none made it as nominees in the vote by music branch members, while such obscure songs as "Nice to Be Around," from *Cinderella Liberty,* and "Love," from *Robin Hood,* did. *Jonathan,* too, had been declared eligible in the Best Scoring: Adaptation and Original Score category, but it didn't make the finalist stage in the voting either, even though only three nominees were announced in that category: *Jesus Christ Superstar, The Sting,* and *Tom Sawyer.* Making the omission of *Jonathan Livingston Seagull* from the two lists of nominees even more curious was Neil's copping of a Best Original Score Grammy for *JLS* that month from the National Academy of Recording Arts and Sciences.

There seemed only one conclusion to draw: By his insistence that he had been the sole composer of the *Jonathan* score, Neil Diamond had alienated some music members of the Academy. "I've got to tell you, he cut off his nose to spite his face," said Lee Holdridge, who received $20,000 from Diamond for his work on *Jonathan*. "If he had been a little bit smarter and a little bit more magnanimous, he might have had an Academy Award . . . But because he acted the way he did, he lost it all.

"Neil is one of those persons who doesn't understand that it's the combination of people that makes something happen," he continued. "It's a very spiritual thing, when you think about it: a group of people accomplishing something. But he had this thing of thinking that he did it all by himself, that he alone was the genius and everybody else around him were just slaves and handmaidens . . .

"If I was a smarter person, I would have known about Diamond the day he walked out of the studio when we recorded the strings to 'Holly Holy.' Rather than have the graciousness of saying, 'Gosh, I loved what you did for my record—thank you very much,' all I got was a solemn, stony face. He didn't know what to say. He wasn't able to say *anything!*"

·16·
"SABBATICAL"

As the furor over *Jonathan Livingston Seagull* reached ebb tide in early 1974, Neil could be found holed up in Malibu.

According to him, he was finally airing out from *JLS* ("I never realized the agonies of composing for the screen"), as well as his all-consuming drive to superstardom.

Shortly before the scoring project had captured his fancy, Neil had admitted that he had another reason than his previously stated desires to study composing and arranging and to write "a great symphony" for going on a performance "sabbatical." He said he needed to cool it. But even in confessing that "I can't run the race every day," he didn't tell the whole story. The truth of the matter was that both his wife and son were hurting and they needed him home.

As for Marcia, she remained Neil's number-one confidante. "He bounced *everything* off of her," then–executive assistant Totty Ames said, while former Diamond guitarist Carol Hunter recalled her as being "always supportive and always loving and very perceptive"—as well as outspoken. "You know you were a little hostile to that audience," Marcia reportedly told him backstage one night, to which he replied in a soft, accepting voice, "Oh, was I, really?"

Set designer Jim Newton, meanwhile, observed Neil take on "looser," more adolescent qualities when Marcia was around: "She seemed older than he, more adult. And when she was busy being maternal, he would become a little boy." This pose stood in stark contrast to the chauvinistic attitude he was said to foster around members of the opposite sex in general. Complained one woman who dealt with him: "He doesn't treat women well. And I had a lot of trouble getting information out of him or getting to him, because all he wants to do is treat women like objects. And you'll be talking to him, and he will lean over and kiss you . . . It was just amazing."

And yet, important as she was to Neil, Marcia couldn't help but feel severely stressed by his sudden superstar celebrity. "She figured every time he went out the door on the road that might be the last time she'd ever see him again," Ames said. "*Very* insecure lady . . . And, of course, he was fair game for every female in the world."

The fact that Neil was bringing home his own pressures didn't help matters. "Everything could be just absolutely lovey-dovey perfect [one day], and the day after tomorrow they're not talking," the former executive assistant of Diamond's commented.

Marcia's unhappiness showed. She tended to overeat and smoke heavily. No more of a hobbyist than her workaholic husband, she was also prone to spend her time, by Ames' account, "idly." "She'd go shopping and never wear it," she added. "Twenty-two pairs of pants, all in different colors, that kind of thing. Just didn't wear them." (How Marcia made use of her time reportedly became a source of sparks between her and Neil in 1973, when, one source claimed, Neil enlisted the services of a time-management specialist to counsel her. Marcia, the source added, was furious with him for not consulting her first.)

Increasing Marcia Diamond's stress load were the demands of motherhood. Ames: "She wasn't very large with children at all, and Jesse was just an *absolute* handful."

Jesse Diamond's troubled state, meanwhile, seemed the most poignant indication of the heavy personal price Neil had paid for his relentless pursuit of fame and fortune. "He'd bite your leg, whack you, kick you," Ames recalled.

One night at the Greek Theatre, however, Jesse seemed like nothing more than a frightened, confused two-year-old. As his father stood on stage only a few feet away, he was seen screaming, "Daddy don't sing! Daddy don't sing! Daddy don't sing!"

The family's rental of a Malibu beach house following Neil's Winter Garden stand was designed to bring some serenity at last to the family. And, after Neil finally put *Jonathan Livingston Seagull* behind him, there were indications that they were beginning to achieve at least a measure of it—with the help of three psychiatrists, one for each of them.

The key, according to Neil himself, was changing over from rock 'n' roll time—sleep most of the day, work all night—to an approximation of Marcia and Jesse time, and then peppering his days with the kinds of activities he never seemed to have time for before: having breakfast with his wife, taking Jesse to school, picking Jesse up from school, drawing and playing music with Jesse, having dinner with Marcia and Jesse, putting Jesse to bed, telling Jesse bedtime stories.

A desire for simplicity, meanwhile, governed other aspects of their Malibu life style, including their eating habits. Confirmed noshers, they didn't even keep a cook around. A Diamond breakfast delicacy illustrated his down-home tastes: a plain old bagel smeared with cream cheese, and topped by a slice of American cheese, its drooping ends snipped off. Other staples: pretzels, Coca-Cola, McDonald's hamburgers, and grilled cheese, bacon and tomato, tuna salad, and chicken salad sandwiches.

Every bit the homebodies they were in Tarzana before they were married, they also kept a low profile socially when Neil wasn't working, despite their invitations to endless functions. The infrequent parties they did host were sizable affairs designed to rid themselves of the obligations they'd amassed. "If it was gonna be a party," Totty Ames recalled, "he'd say [grave voice], 'Totty we're gonna have a party on such and such a date. *Fix it.*'

"He hates to get dressed up," she continued. "*Hates* it. To him a tuxedo is a straitjacket." In Malibu, Neil reveled in walking around unshaven, and in T-shirt and jeans. "Sometimes when you'd go to his place, he would be looking very grubby, [and you'd go to yourself] 'Oh, god, Neil looks terrible,'" said Bruce Lundvall, who became president of CBS Records in 1975. "But he was hanging around the house . . .

"And he had a couple of dogs who were the worst-looking mutts I've ever seen—he could have had the most beautiful thoroughbreds. And there were never any pretensions about his home . . . For all the show business that surrounded him, he was very down to earth."

And yet, Neil would occasionally reveal a sudden—if sometimes only fleeting—interest in playing the jet-setter. One time, for example, feeling a sudden urge to visit Las Vegas, he rang up Totty Ames and requested a jet. Ames leapt into action, rousting a pilot from bed, and called him right back to tell him his plane would be ready at midnight— only to be informed by Marcia that he had decided in the intervening minutes to turn in for the night.

Lest Diamond's retreat to Malibu give the impression that he had turned over a new leaf—as, in fact, he would later contend in interviews—he remained his driven, authoritative self when he wasn't hanging loose at the beach. One of the first decisions he made in the wake of *JLS,* for example, was to go manager-less for the time being. That meant canning Ken Fritz.

By then, Neil's dim view of managers was common knowledge. Invoking the name of a superstar with a poles-apart attitude toward managers, songwriter/producer Al Kasha said, "Elvis feared [manager] Col. Tom Parker. Neil Diamond doesn't fear these people; he *resents* them. It's like, 'How dare they take 10 percent or 20 percent of me— I'm the one who made them successful.'"

According to Neil, his low opinion of managers was shaped by a disastrous deal he claimed he made with his "first manager" at eighteen—a seven-year arrangement in which he supposedly forked over 50 percent of his income. A year after signing, after realizing "I didn't want to spend my life working in a combo in the Catskills," he maintained that he bought his way out of the contract, with his father springing for the required $750. "I got taken for that ride because I wanted to be a writer and a singer and I wanted it very badly," he would say. "In this business, youth, immaturity, and desire can only spell 'getting taken.'" He vowed to heed a piece of homespun advice from dad: Keep your eye on the doughnut, not the hole.

Inclined to manager-bashing as he was, the abrupt manner in which he severed ties with the well-respected Fritz—as if he were flicking away so many doughnut crumbs—still gave people around him pause. "It was *the end,*" commented one well-placed source. "No speaking. Cut off. Like Neil didn't even know him." Fritz' transgression, the source guessed, was his decision to re-sign his longtime clients the Smothers Brothers, Neil perhaps deciding, in a fit of pique, that Fritz' office wasn't big enough for both clients.

Not long after Fritz' firing, Diamond's longtime engineer, Armin Steiner, twirled his last knobs on a Diamond project. The album was "Serenade," and the experience, according to Steiner, was a tortuous one.

"Nine months in the studio," he said. "As far as I was concerned, the album was a joke . . . just self-indulgence. I think we went through a hundred rolls of two-inch tape [where the average is] twenty or thirty reels. We kept doing the songs over so many times." Compounding matters, in the engineer's view, was the proclivity of Diamond to show up at the studio "blasted out of his brain" on pot, adding "How can you function that way?" Steiner also didn't approve of Neil's decision to record with several members of his band rather than with top-notch studio players like Hal Blaine, Larry Knechtel and Joe Osborn: "I always felt that that was a disaster because they were yes men to Neil. Everything is wonderful today, and then tomorrow we have to recut the track."

In sum, Steiner claimed that in Neil "I saw a guy who had everything and nothing. Certainly he had the stardom . . . but he wasn't satisfied . . . A painter paints a great painting—how does he know the next one is going to be great?" He added: "I don't think Neil knows what it is to be happy. That is a very strong statement to make, but I don't think he knows what happiness is. I don't think he will ever know what happiness is."

As it turned out, "Serenade," released that October, was an artistic wash.

It seemed obvious from the album's sweep and reach that Neil intended to continue from where he left off on "Jonathan Livingston Seagull" (one of his "Serenade" songs, "I've Been This Way Before," an ode to reincarnation, had, in fact, originally been written for *JLS*). But the sense of grating self-importance that imbued many of the grandiose arrangements, his elliptical lyrics, and overdone vocals—including his pretentious new habit of booming out words like a Shakespearean actor—made one long for the days of "Gitchy Goomy," when he seemed, at least, to be having a little fun.

Still, Neil was one of the hottest recording artists in the world now, and his single, "Longfellow Serenade," which he described as being about a young man who "seeks to woo and win his lady through a devious use of poetry," was a Top 10 hit, as was "Serenade," the album.

Promotionally minded as Neil was, he wasn't about to sit out the "Serenade" dance in Malibu, "sabbatical" or not. In November of 1974 he embarked on a Columbia-paid three-week promotional tour of Europe, which included appearances on television shows in Spain, West Germany, and England.

Along for the ride was film executive Jerry Paonessa, husband of Marcia's old friend Jody Paonessa. Cycling back once again to thoughts of starring in and/or producing movies, Neil had only a few days earlier hired Paonessa to help him find feature film material.

It was some ride for Paonessa, who was not aware at the time that Neil was a certified international superstar.

The red-carpet treatment accorded Diamond in Spain, their first and longest stop, gave him a big clue. Among the celebrations during their ten-day stay was an elegant Madrid dinner hosted by the head of CBS Records in Spain, Tomas Munoz, that was attended by such members of the Spanish aristocracy as the Duchess of Elba. Another highlight was an evening celebration in Segovia, where, with ancient aqueducts lit in his honor, Neil feasted on roast suckling pig.

This high-level hoopla, Paonessa confessed, left him agog. However, he noted that Neil took it all perfectly in stride.

In West Germany, the VIP treatment continued when Diamond was granted an audience with President Walter Scheel in Bonn. The two had something in common in Europe: hit records. The president, an amateur tenor, had cut a traditional German folk song, "Hoch Auf Dem Gelben Wagen" ("High on the Yellow Wagon"), earlier in the year. At the meeting, Neil, adopting a pose of easy familiarity, broke Scheel up when he cracked, words to the effect, "Look, Mr. President, I won't tell you how to run Germany if you'll only stop recording songs."

Los Angeles arranger Jimmie Haskell, who joined Neil in London for his final appearance of the tour, a guest slot on the "Shirley Bassey Show," saw the same royally self-confident Diamond when Haskell and his wife dined with Neil and entourage at the Inn of the Park:

"Between Neil and the other people around the table, I felt that I was seated at the Knights of the Round Table with King Arthur . . . And they began telling stories of their tour through Europe. Evidently they had been with royalty . . .

"They spoke very highly of this one princess or queen—how someone had spilled wine on her dress when she was seated right next to Neil Diamond, and how her manner was so amazingly good because she had worn the dress especially for the occasion . . .

"I was impressed with the humor and the wonderful descriptions. It was the most I'd ever heard Neil talk . . . He managed to describe things in such a way that the events were still grandiose but they had their humor to them. He had an interesting way of putting down certain people who evidently were not the top royalty but who thought they were . . . I think in one case a person actually did fall over their own feet—little incidents of that type . . . Neil also described certain ways that they had of leaving a place a little early when they had to. But it wasn't so much that he was explaining any of this to me and Barbara, it was that they were laughing amongst themselves . . . at some of the things they created in these social atmospheres."

Neil returned to Los Angeles in time for the holidays. After the first of the year, he put on his businessman's face once again, this time in plush new office digs on Melrose Place next door to his first office.

The previous October, he had leased the larger quarters—actually a U-shaped two-bedroom bungalow with a small pool in the middle— from Lee Lacy, a television commercials producer. Since then, the former home had been remodeled and refurnished.

Giving Neil's portion of "command central," the former living room and dining room area, a suitably posh look was designer Peter Shorr. Shorr relied on muted colors and understated furnishings, while turning up two stunning pieces: a beautiful antique tortoise-shell desk and chair set, and a huge tapestry featuring a woodsy animal scene that hung over one of the beige couches.

Meanwhile, Totty Ames went about the task of finding furniture for the rest of the bungalow. She also supervised the removal of mounds of memorabilia from boxes—Neil, it turned out, had been an inveterate collector of his press notices and other career keepsakes—and cataloguing and filing them.

Neil immediately felt right at home in his new sanctuary. Ames: "He would stretch out on the couch with his yellow legal pad . . . On weekends, when it was totally quiet—no ringing phones, no voices—he would be there until three or four in the morning."

Neil alternated between Malibu and his office in the early part of 1975. In the office, he was the focused career planner, scheming on when and how to bust out of his "sabbatical." Among the regular visitors to his inner sanctum were attorney David Braun, and his William Morris agent, Tony Fantozzi.

The upshot of those meetings was that Neil decided to delay his return to concert action another year. The only project that was a definite go for 1975 was the recording of a new studio album that fall. He wanted soap to sell when he returned to the concert trail.

That left him with some time on his hands in the first half of 1975. If he was going to keep true to his pre-"sabbatical" pledge to study composition and arranging, and to begin work on that "great symphony," that string quartet and that ballet, now seemed the perfect time to get to it.

Instead, he wound up taking care of more business, this time with the likes of Ellie Greenwich and Jeff Barry.

Neil had made his first attempt at renewing contact with Greenwich in 1972, when he invited her to one of his Winter Garden performances. Having been embroiled in the still-pending WEB IV–Tallyrand suit for more than four years at that point, Ellie had strong misgivings about accepting the invitation: "Once all this litigation happened, I had as much interest in Neil Diamond as the man in the moon . . . I was hurt by him, you know."

But she eventually decided to go, and was wowed. "Neil walked out more self-assured than he's ever been in his life," she recalled, "and he did it all the way, with the sequins and the quadraphonic sound, and a big band. I was really happy for him, he had really come a long way, he was definitely a superstar, and I'm going, 'I remember him from Massapequa Park, Long Island. Neil Leslie Diamond, I remember it so well.'"

But her ambivalent feelings for the man remained, even as she made her way backstage to talk to Neil.

"I wanted to hug him, I wanted to punch him," she admitted. "A gamut of so much . . . And it was [Neil:] 'Do you want to have coffee?' 'Nope, we mustn't have coffee.' 'How ya doin', OK?' 'Who cares? I love you, I hate you.'"

The next year, Greenwich and Jeff Barry gave Neil something more to think about than just his *Jonathan* score when they filed their own breach of contract suit against Diamond and MCA, Inc. in Manhattan Supreme Court. They asked for damages totaling $37,000,000.

Despite the filing of the suit—or perhaps because of it—Neil persevered in his attempt to reestablish contact with Ellie. In November of 1974, he invited her to accompany him to Elton John's Madison Square Garden concert. This time, Ellie, who had decided that despite her hurt and anger she still *liked* Neil, took him up on his offer.

That night she got her first insight into just how seriously he was wearing the mantle of star.

"Neil and I were sitting there—I was on the aisle and he was next to me," Greenwich recalled. "And people were looking around— 'That's Neil Diamond.' So a bunch of girls come over, and they sit down on the steps, and one turns to say, 'Is that Neil Diamond?' and I go, 'No, his name is Harvey Kornbloom.' And Neil looks at me. And I say, 'Looks like Neil, sounds like Neil, expression is like Neil, but it's Harvey

Kornbloom. Isn't that amazing?' And Neil started to laugh.'' But it wasn't the guffaw that the compulsive card expected from the man she remembered as having a terrific sense of humor, which made her think her kidding wasn't "so cool . . . I'm sure he wanted them to think he was Neil Diamond.'' When the fans finally decided he was Diamond and asked him if they could snap his picture, Greenwich noted that he was very quick to allow it.

A few months later, Ellie saw Neil step, literally, into his star persona during another of his visits to New York. The scene was Broadway's Minskoff Theater, where he had taken her to see Bette Midler's "Clams on the Half Shell'' revue. In the lobby before the show, she was surprised when he excused himself. "He found a spot where no one else was standing,'' said Greenwich, "and stood there, and had his cigarette, to make sure everybody saw him.'' When a bell announced the impending start of the show, Greenwich tried to coax him into the theater, but Neil would have none of it. "We were the last ones to enter,'' Greenwich said. "And we were front row center.'' She confessed that she enjoyed that portion of Neil's star trip: "Hey, I pretended I was Marilyn Monroe! Blond hair on black—everybody was going 'Who is she?' Because I had to be somebody to be with Neil Diamond.''

That night after the show, Neil finagled an invite to Greenwich's apartment. "He said, 'I'd love to hear some of the stuff you've been doing.''' She recalled. "I said, 'Well, come on back; I'll make you some coffee.' He said, 'No, do you have any Yankee Doodles?' So we stopped at the deli near my apartment, picked up some Yankee Doodles, and went back to my place.''

At first Neil was guarded. Ellie: "I'd play him songs I was doing and he'd say [formally], 'Well, I think—well, do you think this is really one of the—' 'Say you don't like it!' [Gravely:] 'Ellie, I don't like that.' He went into this whole thing to get his point across, beating around the bush.''

As the conversation moved to other areas, however, Neil gradually began to loosen up, enough, in fact, for Greenwich to remark, "Neil, I've never seen you so—open.'' "And he goes, 'Yeah, well it's kinda hard sometimes,''' Greenwich continued. "And I go, 'Yeah, except I'm pretty much an open book. But you're hard to read sometimes, you really are.'

"And I say, 'How often are you yourself?' And he goes, 'Well, more so now than I've ever been. God, back then you would never, if you knew what I was like . . .' 'What, what? Give me a for instance.' Then he started in about Jeff and I: 'I gotta tell ya—I was so scared of you and Jeff! I was in awe.''' The admission stunned Ellie at first. "Neil is very bright and Neil is very opinionated,'' she explained, "and he always allowed that side to show and work for him. He never showed fear, he never showed uncomfortableness.''

With the semblance of a confessional tone now established, Ellie took the initiative. "I say, 'Wow, Neil, you have the world by the balls. You have money, you have fame, you have a wife, you have a family. You really got the whole thing. You have to be ecstatic.'

"I didn't get a response. He goes, 'Well . . .' I say, 'Well, *what?* Neil, aren't you happy?' And he says, 'No.' I say, 'You're not? That's terrible.' And you saw he was struggling so . . . He couldn't get everything together in his life."

It was then, Ellie said, that Neil made a confession that seemed to speak of the personal arithmetic he had been tackling in the peace and quiet of Malibu: "Neil told me . . . [that] he loves his wife and he loves his son . . . he kept telling me how important his son was, the Jewish heritage, the family name being carried on . . . and he loves his daughters, too. But the only thing he is one million percent sure of, his 'ultimate orgasm' in life, is when he walks out on that stage and has a love affair with everybody in that audience . . . Nothing comes close."

"Ohhhhh, wow, *really?*" Greenwich replied, unable to disguise the dismay in her voice.

"I felt very sorry for him," she explained. "My God, you can't have a very intimate relationship with these people, you know."

Thinking back on that talk, and her relationship with Diamond in general, Greenwich added: "I always had a knack for bringing certain things out in Neil; he would loosen up . . . [But] I've never seen Neil really *relax,* you know, just really come down and be himself, and not be so afraid to disrupt the image he set out to create for himself. He seems always *on,* always *on,* and I feel very badly for that, 'cause I think underneath it all there is a nice little Jewish boy from Brooklyn who's done extremely well and forgot how to have a good time."

With the lines of communication to Diamond open in 1975, Greenwich, exhausted by the years of litigation, decided to pursue a settlement of her and Jeff Barry's suit against him as their ticket out of the WEB IV–Tallyrand suit. So she flew to Los Angeles, where she proceeded to play the "little hostess" in a series of meetings in her hotel room with Diamond and Barry, who had moved to Los Angeles himself several years earlier.

Diamond, not surprisingly, had replaced his vulnerable face with that of the unsentimental businessman.

"He goes, 'Well, we'll make you happy,'" Ellie recalled. "I say, 'A million dollars, Neil. Gimme a million dollars, and we'll drop everything.'

"'What do you want me to do, close out a bank account?'

"'Close out *a* bank account? *A?* What are you saying to me?'"

Finally, after several weeks of hashing, the three hammered out the basics of a deal, after which they contacted their attorneys to draw up the papers.

Under the terms of the agreement, Greenwich and Barry dropped their suit against Diamond and sold their interest in Tallyrand Music to him, thus removing themselves as defendants in the WEB IV–Tallyrand suit. In return, Neil agreed to pay them, according to Ellie, "less than half a million dollars" apiece, not nearly as much as she claimed she had been hoping for.

It was a good deal for Neil. As the sole owner of Tallyrand Music, he was now free to seek a settlement with WEB IV. And, in the bargain, he had gained complete ownership of more than twenty of his treasured early songs—his "children"—at what seemed a bargain price.

While Neil was working out a settlement with his former partners in the summer of 1975, he began writing songs for his next LP. The project promised to be a notable one in at least one respect: He had broken up with Tom Catalano, his longtime champion and the last and most intimate of his key studio associates dating back to his first days in Los Angeles.

Their relationship had been going downhill ever since Catalano, enraged by the star attitude that he felt Neil was copping, walked out on him for a short time during his 1972 Broadway engagement. According to Lee Holdridge, who later talked to Catalano about his split with Neil, Neil's "royal we" attitude figured in their eventual split: "In a way, Neil acts a little bit like royalty . . . There's a feeling that you can't reach him. And I would imagine that Tom was the *only* person [who did] . . . But I think he could only take so much."

In a later interview with *Songwriter* magazine, Catalano, however, blamed his parting with Neil, ironically, on the success they had achieved together: "It is like a painful crisis because it's like two guys wearing the same pair of shoes at the same time. A love-hate relationship develops because . . . they know what you've given them and may likely not give you credit for. [And] they know what they've given you to help you to get to where you are . . ."

Catalano's departure came at a crossroads time in Neil's recording career, when he was still agitating over his image as an artist. "I think probably in his heart of hearts he knew that what he really was was a fine craftsman of songs and a fine, mature singer, but obviously was sensitive in not wanting to lose a young following," commented then–CBS Records president Bruce Lundvall. "I kept telling him, 'Look, Neil, you have made it as Neil Diamond, and you'll continue making it on that basis. There is no reason to put you in a category at all. You're your own category." Marcia Diamond, according to one source, put it even more bluntly, admonishing him on one occasion: "You'll never *be* Paul Simon or Bob Dylan. You're Neil Diamond, and that's good enough." (Coincidentally, Diamond and Dylan, a fellow Malibu resident, had become acquaintances, with Dylan attending the surprise party Marcia threw for Neil's thirty-fourth birthday in January.)

And yet Diamond persisted in setting his sights on nothing less than a musical masterpiece. He decided on his first semiautobiographical concept album.

The subject matter—his experiences as a young striver in Tin Pan Alley in the '60s—was dear to him. It had been the very topic of a tabled screenplay he had worked on some five years earlier. His producer friend Saul David considered the screenplay "damn good . . . It was full of sharply observed scenes, and pieces of dialogue which rang true."

Neil threw himself into the project in 1975 like a man possessed, making several clandestine fact-finding and atmosphere-sponging trips to New York City. The trips did him good in another respect, according to CBS' Lundvall: "He felt regenerated and revitalized being back in the New York environment . . . I think there was always a conflict with him about being an East Coast writer, coming from a very vibrant and vital place, then living in California in a much more comfortable life style without the same kind of pressures."

In his Plaza Hotel suite in New York City one night that summer, Neil took a big step forward in the project—with thanks to his older daughter, Marjorie, then nine. Listening to the sounds of the city outside the window as he strummed on a guitar in the living room, she suddenly said, "Oh, daddy, what a beautiful noise." Those words struck Neil, who replied, "Marjorie, some day I'm gonna write a song called 'Beautiful Noise.'" With his daughter's urging, he penned his first version of the tune celebrating noisy New York as a Naked City of songs that night.

With his concept down and title song finished, he began casting around for a new producer. He tentatively decided on Brooks Arthur, his Bang Records–era engineer.

Arthur was a logical choice. Not only did he share Neil's empathy for Tin Pan Alley as a '60s contemporary of his, he was also beginning to make a name for himself as a producer, having produced as well as engineered Janis Ian's recent hit album, "Between the Lines."

Arthur attended a couple of rehearsals with Diamond and his band in which he sang "Beautiful Noise" and one or two other new songs. "We started to map out some ideas," Arthur said. "I even talked to Neil about wetting down the backlot at 20th [Century Fox, for the album cover photograph]."

It came as a rude surprise to Arthur, then, when his manager received a note from Neil's attorney informing the producer-engineer that his services would not be needed, after all. "[At] this time in Neil's career they felt it would be more advisable for him to be involved with a producer of great reputation, as opposed to an engineer of great reputation," Arthur explained. He added: "This is probably the most painful time I ever had with Neil."

Neil then achieved the musical non sequitur of the year by hiring Robbie Robertson of The Band to produce "Beautiful Noise." Not only was there no Tin Pan Alley in the Canadian rocker's past, the singer/songwriter/guitarist/producer had come, by virtue of The Band's long association with Dylan and by its own string of critically acclaimed hits, to be regarded as the musical personification of hip by 1975. As such, he seemed poles apart from the ever-striving, but ever-commercial Neil Diamond.

Of course, one could appreciate why Neil would want to work with Robbie. One could see, at the same time, why the assignment would be attractive to Robertson: He had never worked with orchestrations before, and he had carved a career out of incorporating into his own music the sounds of specific geographic areas: New Orleans, Memphis, Detroit. Tin Pan Alley, circa the '60s, stood as a fresh challenge.

Neil had been on hi-how-are-you terms with Robertson for some time, and had visited with him the previous year during a date on The Band's tour with Dylan. Still, they probably wouldn't have teamed up if Robertson hadn't moved to Malibu, after which, Neil would say, "the relationship just grew."

That August, recording of the album's basic tracks began. Instead of motoring into Hollywood daily, Diamond and Robertson opted for The Band's studio a few miles up the coast in Zuma. Located in a converted house on a hill above the Pacific, the studio was called, appropriately, Shangri-La.

In contrast to the modus operandi on his last several studio albums, Neil finished writing the majority of his songs before entering the studio. Also, the hours he and Robertson kept at Shangri-La were not so much rock 'n' roll as the executive variety: ten to five Monday through Friday. Each morning, a friend of Totty Ames would deliver heaping platters of fruit and cheese. It was the most serene recording experience Neil had ever had.

"That was a different Neil entirely—he wasn't as uptight," confirmed keyboards player Larry Knechtel, the only member of the Catalano-Steiner-Holdridge-Blaine-Knechtel-Osborn recording nucleus to participate in the sessions. "He had written a couple songs on the piano, so naturally I wanted to see how he approached. it. But he wasn't the dictator he'd been on the other sessions . . . He wasn't calling the shots!"

The biggest problem that faced Knechtel, amazingly enough, was in getting too blissed out. He solved that by reluctantly drawing a curtain on the picture-window view of the Pacific. "Musicians are like Dracula—in the sunlight they can't perform," he laughed.

With the relaxed pace and good vibes, Diamond and Robertson gradually fell behind schedule with "Beautiful Noise." As 1976 dawned, the overdub recordings, including Neil's vocals, were still to be done, followed by the LP's mixing. As Robertson switched over to Village Recorders in Westwood, Neil temporarily took his leave from the studio.

The road was calling.

Having defined his priorities in life from "ultimate orgasm" on down, Neil had gone ahead and booked dozens of engagements for 1976, engagements that would announce in the grandest way possible that he was back. And the first batch of them was only days away.

·17·
RETURN

In interviews both during and after his "sabbatical," Neil rhapsodized on his new infatuation with performing. In the process he updated his 1972 statement "I see myself as another person onstage," noting: "I used to think I became another Neil Diamond onstage—but I psyched myself out of that. I realized it was part of what I did and that I was my own person."

Impressive as his claimed triumph of the will sounded, the truth was that he still had to screw up his courage to return to the stage in 1976. Jeff Barry, who had become friendly with him again, got a firsthand glimpse of just how antsy he was about performing one day in the summer of 1975 when they went motorcycle riding through Griffith Park. They wound up parking their bikes outside the Greek Theatre, walking inside the amphitheater, and sitting down on the stage.

"It was real quiet; we were the only two people there," Barry recalled. "We took our helmets off, and just listened to the wind a little while. It was kind of interesting, because I felt part of it all, and could feel that [returning to performing] was a real concern to him . . . You know, would they come to see him again? Did he stay away too long? And if someone had said, 'Look, there's a law against performing for another six months,' I bet he would have gone, 'Oh, OK, great—six more months to get ready for all this.'"

One indication that Neil was harboring worries about performing again was his decision to book his first full-fledged tour halfway around the world—in New Zealand and Australia. As he later explained, "I figured that if everyone hated me there, it would be far enough away so no one would have noticed."

However, the manner in which those countries reacted to the news of his first tour Down Under—particularly Australia, where the "Hot August Night" LP set had become the country's all-time best-seller—dashed the notion that his visit, be it artistic triumph or wash, would remain a secret. The $2 million in tickets that went on sale for his thirteen dates in Sydney, Melbourne, Adelaide, Perth, and Brisbane were snatched up virtually overnight. Increasing the Australia stakes was Neil's decision to have his final concert, at the Sydney Sports Ground, televised live around the country as a "thank you" to the Australian people.

With his Australia-New Zealand tour taking on the appearance of a major campaign in itself, Neil decided to prep for it with a handful of shows in Northern California and Utah.

The first dates were a January 30–31 stand at the 2,436-seat Sacramento Community Center. The day after the concerts were announced, the auditorium's box office manager arrived at work to find more than 30,000 ticket requests in the morning mail.

Neil arrived in town with a number of new people. Joining drummer-band manager Dennis St. John; keyboardist/synthesizer player Alan Lindgren; guitarist Richie Bennett; bassist Reinie Press, and percussionist King Errisson in the band were Tom Hensley, piano; Doug Rhone, guitar; and Press' wife, Linda, background vocals.

The new road manager was Patrick Stansfield. The new stage and lighting designer was New York's prestigious Imero Fiorentino & Associates, the associates in this case being George Honchar and Scott Johnson.

Also along were Josh White and his assistant, Kac Young, who had been hired to produce the live Australia concert broadcast. Their assignment in Sacramento: videotape the concerts so Diamond could review his performance afterward. Along to help with that task was drama coach Harry Master George, whom Diamond had taken lessons from in the late '60s.

Diamond and Master George had a retooled show to view. Neil had added a twenty-five-minute "Jonathan Livingston Seagull" segment encompassing the songs he had penned for the score. And he had worked into his two-hour-plus, no-intermission concert several recent creations: "Longfellow Serenade," "The Last Picasso," and, as his final encore, "I've Been This Way Before." However, the most significant change to his show dealt not with the song lineup, but with his stage stance. Having decided, evidently, that it was time to retire his Solitary Man persona, he had budgeted more time to kibitz with the audience, and to engage them, with "Song Sung Blue," in an extended sing-along segment—to portray, in short, the smooth, in-command superstar.

In Sacramento, this updated edition of Diamond was a hit. His nervousness, he claimed to the noisy, celebrative crowd, had dissipated backstage: "Back there I heard you, you know, excited. 'Oh this is gotta be a good one!'" In his rambling, playful greeting to the crowd, he chatted about his drinking goblet ("I said, 'Would you guys get me a goblet because generally they give you something very yucky to drink from"), and the lights ("I'm not accustomed to these lights . . . they're a little warm. But I love pain, so they're OK"). He also got a big laugh when he mentioned his new Elvis Presleyish stage clothes, which consisted that night of a white blousy shirt, glittery black vest, navy pants with a red stripe, and a wide, sparkly belt. "I feel like a kid who's coming to school for the first week," he cracked.

The next day, he granted his first post-sabbatical interview, to the *Los Angeles Times'* Robert Hilburn. "Either you control your goals or they control you," he declared. "I think I've gained control now."

After Utah concerts in Ogden and at Brigham Young University in Provo, Neil flew on to New Zealand with his fifty-three-member tour party. On February 13, he played his first date, at Auckland's Western Springs, a rugby field, before a record New Zealand crowd of 35,000.

It rained.

"We're all going to get dirty pants tonight," Neil announced after taking the stage. Later, alluding to the attendance, he crowed: "We beat Elton John; we beat John Denver; we beat BILLY GRAHAM!" "It's hard not to be amused by the ego of a person who'll compare himself in song to a frog who became a king," wrote one reviewer. "But his belief in his own material made last night's concert a success even for nonbelievers."

After another outdoor concert in New Zealand two days later, this one at windy Queen Elizabeth II Park in Christchurch before a crowd of 25,000, Neil and party flew to Sydney. The welcome he got there had to have exceeded his wildest expectations. An enamored Australia had done as a nation what pockets of European aristocracy had done on Neil's 1974 promotional trip: thrown out the red carpet, as if he were a visiting head of state. So caught up was the Australian public in his arrival that his February 17 Sydney press conference was televised live across the country.

"I knew I was going to come here when I stopped on Broadway," Diamond announced, as he sat behind a battery of microphones in the Boulevard Hotel. "Call it adventure, call it the fact that there's been so many good things coming from Australia toward me." Speaking on the personal progress he'd made during his time away from performing, he reflected, "I've read a lot, I've met more people, I've grown up. I was a mere child."

Two nights later, he inaugurated his Australia tour with the first of three shows at Festival Hall in Brisbane. "In a brilliant first night performance . . . [Diamond] more than justified the huge amount of money Brisbane audiences paid to see him," read one local review. "That the crowd thought so too showed at the end of the evening, when not a bottom remained on a chair."

From Brisbane, Neil returned to Sydney, where he performed three concerts at Hordern Pavilion. Then it was on to the Myer Bowl in soggy Melbourne, where Kac Young, line producer/associate director of the TV broadcast that Neil was planning of his final Australia concert, beheld a sight that symbolized the Aussies' utter devotion to Neil: "The lights were steaming, because of the rain hitting them. And through that steam was an audience soaked to the skin, and muted. The light bounced from the stage, and you could see the eyes of these people were more alive than I think they had ever been in most of their lives. They had come to drink from the fountain, and their god was there.

"He is a very powerful man in his music, in his sexuality, in his Diamondism—he is absolutely charismatic," Young continued. "My job was to be there to learn the concert, to know the light cues, and I would find myself mesmerized backstage every night at what he was able to do to an audience, and how his music affected him.

"I, at the time, thought Neil was the most egotistical person I ever met in my life. At other times he was the most generous. And I think it was the blending of the two [that accounted for his Diamondism]. This egotistical creature would walk on stage saying, 'Here I am, Neil Diamond.' And at the same time he would remember who he was: struggling songwriter from Tin Pan Alley, faced with the adoration of the crowd, humbled by it, moved and touched by it. And, therefore, he had to overcompensate for his feelings of 'Am I worthy of this?' So he would give like nobody else, to the max. And the more the crowd would respond to him, the more he would dig and give."

After concerts in Perth and Adelaide (where before his concert at Football Park he was spotted strolling the grounds in a T-shirt that read "I'm not Neil Diamond—I just look like him"), Neil returned to Sydney to begin final preparations for his March 9 "Thank You Australia . . ." TV concert from Sydney Sports Ground.

Priming Australia for the telecast was the broadcast, on March 7, of an hourlong TV interview Neil had granted to "A Current Affair," hosted by Mike Schildberger. The inverview was notable in that Schildberger managed to get his guest to spout off on a number of subjects that Neil didn't ordinarily discuss in public. Among them . . .

Politics: "I find very few real thinkers in American politics, people who really have an understanding of the future beyond when's the next time they come up for election."

God and religion: "I tend to be a very spiritual person . . . but I'm not religious . . . Organized religion is created by people who are fallible."

In the interview, Neil sounded a bullish tone for the most part. Asked by Schildberger, for example, if he considered life a bore, he responded, "Oh no. Life is ever-changing, ever-interesting, ever-expanding, ever-incomprehensible, ever-wondrous." Toward the end of the hour, however, he did add a sober, albeit dramatic, note when he talked of a lifelong "vision" of his: the premonition that he would not live a very long life. "And that was my main fear, a fear of death," he said. "I'm willing to accept whatever it is [now]."

"There may never be a night like this," television host David Frost, the copromoter of Diamond's Down Under tour, intoned from Sydney

Sports Ground as Neil's "Thank You" broadcast began two days later. After a few more minutes of banter, commentator Frost and the 38,000 in attendance quieted as a tape of "Missa" began. The television audience was treated to a backstage shot of a channeled Diamond—in canary yellow sequined shirt, black leather pants, and one of his wide, sparkly belts—waiting for his cue, the "Soolaimon" drum beat. When he heard it, he strode purposefully to the stage, strapped on his guitar, strode to the mike, and put on one of the shows of his life.

To his credit, he was able to project the same relaxed good-naturedness he had displayed at the comparatively tiny Sacramento Community Center a little more than a month earlier. He chatted at length with the crowd between inspired performances of his tunes, asking where everyone was from; joking about the huge white canopy he was performing under ("We have our own little inexpensive version of the Sydney Opera House"); wittily owning up to the fact that he had borrowed his "Song Sung Blue" melody from Mozart and then exhorting the audience to sing the song along with him: "We have a great opportunity here tonight, to create the largest choir in the history of man, the First Sydney Mixed Choir." He even read commercials live for the broadcast's two sponsors, Cadbury Chocolate and Pioneer Stereo—camping up the readings and, in the case of Pioneer, cheekily questioning the stereo maker's claim of being the world's sound leader. (Neil later apologized in writing to Pioneer, who did not share the audience's delight with his ad lib.)

When he left the stage after two-and-a-half hours, the Sydney audience gave Neil *their* thank-you: a standing ovation. His last words, delivered with misty eyes, "Thank you, Australia, it's been fantastic."

Having experienced Australia with him, TV producer/director Kac Young couldn't have agreed more with that sentiment. However, she also knew very well by then that the gregarious Diamond she had watched onstage was, offstage, the same old Solitary Star that others had been seeing for years, despite his new declarations to the contrary.

"He would come off the stage vulnerable, and the minute he would walk past his drummer, Dennis, whom he trusted and had a rapport with, the walls would go up," she said. "I could almost hear them. All of a sudden it was, 'Gosh, now there are people, now there are faces, now there are names that go with the faces. Now I have to deal with people one to one.' By the time he reached the stairs he was back to being Neil the untouchable."

There were only a couple of times during the tour, she added, where she saw Neil at ease. Once was on a Chinese junk that Levi, Strauss & Co. had loaned Diamond and party for a Sydney harbor cruise. The other time was on a late-night visit to a picturesque spot on the Sydney waterfront, where Neil, she said, for the first time seemed "at peace with himself and what was happening in that moment. And I don't think I will ever forget that because it was kind of a victory in the sense of finally being able to be a total person with this man, who very infrequently ever allowed that.

"I don't know what Neil is afraid of, but I was always curious to find out," she added. "I kept wanting to say to Neil, 'Neil, it's all right.'"

Back in Los Angeles, Diamond gave his final OK to what promised to be one of the most important U.S. engagements of his career: his first-ever Las Vegas stand. To give himself enough time to prepare, he canceled his planned June tour of Japan.

Neil had been pondering a Las Vegas engagement ever since he and Joe Sutton had caught Elvis Presley's Nevada showroom debut at the International Hotel in 1970. The International, as well as just about every other casino, also tendered offers to Diamond, but at the time Sutton said, "We decided it wasn't the right thing. Vegas was different back then. It was tuxedos and black ties, and Presley was Presley, with his jumpsuits, which were wonderful. And Neil was still not sophisticated enough in his show."

By 1974, however, superstar Diamond was flirting seriously once again with Vegas. That year he attended Frank Sinatra's opening at Caesar's Palace as his guest. (Sinatra had just recorded "Sweet Caroline.")

However, it took a new development in this performance mecca to finally persuade Neil that the time was right to play his Vegas card. That was the Aladdin Hotel's decision to build a $10 million, 7,000-seat, state-of-the-art theater, to be dubbed the Aladdin Theatre for the Performing Arts. The Aladdin people wanted him to inaugurate their concert series, and Neil, sensing a golden opportunity to one-up every artist who'd ever toiled in a Vegas showroom to the accompanying sounds of clinking cocktail glasses, gave a binding yes in March of 1976.

As the Aladdin Theatre's plans were formalized, Neil returned to the studio to help participate in the completion of his "Beautiful Noise" album.

Robbie Robertson and his recording team had been busy overdubbing and mixing the LP during his absence, and Neil had to be excited with what he heard.

Robertson had produced a collection of sparkling tracks, from the Dixielandish "Stargazer," to the bluesy "Lady-Oh," to the Caribbean-flavored "Don't Think . . . Feel" (a dead ringer melodically for the old Ernie Kovacs Nairobi Trio tune). Helping to give each track its own identity were a collection of special musical performances, among them Jerome Richardson's dancing flute on "Don't Think . . . Feel," Jim Keltner's military drumbeat on "Dry Your Eyes," a Diamond-Robertson collaboration that mourned the death of youthful idealism in the '60s, and Nick DeCaro's carnivallike accordion on the title song. (As for the melting-pot mix of sounds, Diamond would later quip: "I'm like the Will Rogers of pop. There isn't a musical form that I've heard that I haven't liked.")

Meanwhile, there were telling subtle touches. Among them was the building of a sound-effects montage at the beginning of "Beautiful Noise," the album's first cut. The montage, designed to simulate the bustle of Manhattan, consisted of various sounds Robertson had culled from effects records as well as a Nagra tape recording of Manhattan street noise. Bonding the sounds was the recording of a heartbeat, which, after a few seconds, gave way to Dennis St. John's bass drum.

But the single most important contribution Robertson made to "Beautiful Noise" was in helping Neil hone his increasingly ponderous lyrics. As the writer of such tasteful roots-flavored pop-rockers as The Band's "The Night They Drove Old Dixie Down," "The Weight," and "Up on Cripple Creek," Robertson was well suited for the task. Said Neil Brody, one of the album's engineers: "Robbie had a sense of how to separate the crap from the good. He really knew when to be schmaltzy without going over the line."

However, there was one area in which Robbie Robertson not only did not lift a finger to crimp Neil's style, he abetted him in his quest for grandiosity: the recording of his vocals. It was Robertson's idea to make arrangements with Capitol Records to use the label's legendary echo chambers, which, over the years, had enhanced the vocals of Bing Crosby, Frank Sinatra, and countless others. The echo, which through the wonders of technology was sent over the phone lines to Kendun Recorders in Burbank, where Neil and Robertson were working, gave Neil's already authoritative vocals a supremely important aura. Nowhere was that more evident than on "If You Know What I Mean." "It's almost like the voice of God," Neil Brody said, chuckling.

March came and went, but still, work on "Beautiful Noise" continued. While Robertson finished mixing, Neil hit the road in April for dates in the Southwest, Northwest, and Midwest.

After he returned home in early May, "If You Know What I Mean" was released as a single. Then early the next month, "Beautiful Noise" was finally released. At $450,000, an astounding figure for that time, it was far and away the most expensive LP that he had ever recorded.

(As for the album's inside photograph—a New York street scene featuring Diamond standing by himself in the doorway of a pool hall— there was a story behind his hostile expression. According to the photographer, Reid Miles, Neil showed up two hours late for the session, held on a 20th Century Fox backlot. "When he finally got there," Miles recalled, "[he] said, 'Oh, I'm sorry . . .' 'Sorry, my ass!' I said. '*How dare you be so late?* There's only one star on this set and that's me, because you're on my turf. And all you have to do is stand there and look at the camera, for Christ's sake, for a couple of minutes. You'd think you could whip yourself into shape.'" It was then that Miles snapped Diamond's picture.)

While "If You Know What I Mean" and the "Beautiful Noise" LP climbed the *Billboard* charts, peaking at number eleven and number six, respectively, Diamond made final preparations for Las Vegas. That he was treating his Aladdin stand as a Broadwaylike showcase was illustrated by his decision to plow back $300,000 of his $750,000 fee into the show. Included in that sum was a specially built thrust stage, another set design by Jim Newton, and the trucking in of Diamond's own lighting and sound systems, the latter manned by his resident sound man, Stan Miller.

Therein lay the one major problem Neil had with the Aladdin in the days before his engagement. Theater designer Joseph Locricchio, who was overseeing the around-the-clock construction of the Aladdin Theatre for the Performing Arts, felt that Diamond should use the Aladdin's brand-new sound and lighting systems.

Scott Johnson, Diamond's lighting director, was one of a handful of tour personnel who met with Locricchio in an effort to work out their differences. "It was a terrible, terrible meeting," he recalled. "There was a lot of animosity. As I remember, they couldn't accept the fact that Stanley wouldn't use their sound system because they had spent a zillion dollars on [it]. But it would have been crazy to use their system—you would have spent a week debugging it."

That, apparently, is the message that sound man Miller took back to Neil. Diamond, characteristically, stood tough: Either Miller moved in his sound system or the engagement was off.

He won out. In the process, however, he may have rubbed some people the wrong way. "There seemed to be a general impression that people in Las Vegas were not happy with Neil," Scott Johnson noted.

By June 30, the day before Neil's "preview" Aladdin gig, Marcia Diamond had arrived and was occupying their Aladdin suite; Totty Ames was operating out of another Alladin suite, which was doubling as the Diamond party's command central; and the band and staff were ensconced at the low-key Jockey Club. The only people missing were Neil, Jesse, and Jesse's governess, who were in Los Angeles, at the

Holmby Hills house that Neil, in a moment of levity years earlier, had dubbed the Solitary Manor.

Some solitary time was what Neil wanted on the eve of his engagement. Instead, he wound up playing host to fifty members of the Los Angeles police and sheriff's departments while a police helicopter hovered overhead.

The cops had gotten a hot tip that cocaine could be found at Diamond's address, and they had arrived with a search warrant.

Totty Ames learned about the raid early the next morning from Marcia, who had received a call from Neil. "Marcia came tearing into the suite . . . in hysterical tears," she recalled. The cops had combed every one of the rooms in the house. While they hadn't found any cocaine, they had come across a package containing less than an ounce of marijuana—enough to cite him for misdemeanor possession. Neil, who was stunned at first ("I don't know what you're looking for, but you're not going to find it," he told the police at the front door), had characteristically managed to keep his cool throughout the ordeal, even to the extent of handing out autographed copies of his albums.

The next afternoon, he arrived, as scheduled in Las Vegas. He had nothing to say about the raid to Ames, who wasn't surprised: "He was *very* quiet about anything that was private." Figuring he had been set up, possibly by a person or persons in Las Vegas—perhaps the same person or persons who had been phoning in anonymous death threats—he did, however, speak his concerns loudly in his actions. He remained secluded in his Aladdin Hotel suite rather than move into the house that Ames had rented for him and Marcia, and he beefed up his already-substantial personal security force.

Pot smokers in his band and road crew, meanwhile, took precautionary measures as well, including rounding up their stashes of grass and burying the pot in a vacant lot next to the Jockey Club. (In an absurd coda to the tale, the vacant lot was paved over the next morning, ruining any chance, short of jackhammers, of retrieving the stash. "People just stood at their windows and looked at this sad scene," recalled lighting director Scott Johnson.)

His flanks now covered, Diamond sat tight and waited to hit the stage.

To someone who hadn't seen Neil perform in Sydney and who didn't know he was operating under great stress at the Alladin, he probably seemed more outgoing and personable during his Las Vegas engagement than he'd ever been onstage.

However, contrasted to the genuinely relaxed, conversational style he displayed at the Sydney Sports Ground, his show at the Aladdin Theatre for the Performing Arts was marred by a swaggering attitude that seemed to reflect his agitated state. Having to live up to his billing, in the program, as "The World's Greatest Performer" couldn't have helped his nerves, either.*

Even in the fourth of his five concerts—his 11 P.M. July 4 Bicentennial show, the late show in which performers traditionally let their hair down—Neil was "on" to the point of being off-putting. After telling one fan he'd sign her banner backstage after the show, for example, he added in a jivey voice, "But that's all I'll be able to do after the show." "That's positively *lewwwwwwd*," he said in the same put-on voice when he spied a binocular-toting female fan in the first row. After his rendition of "Morningside," meanwhile, his first words were a supremely self-satisfied, "Yes, yes, yes, *yes*, yes, yes, *YES*."

His attitude, combined with his glitzy all-gold outfit, gave the impression that Neil, for these few nights in Nevada at least, had gone Vegas in the worst way.

When he returned to Los Angeles, Diamond had his office swept for bugs, and the locks changed. He also made another of his stunning firings, this time canning Totty Ames. To soften the blow, he awarded her a full year's salary as severance pay.

(Ames claimed that her firing had nothing to do with the drug raid, and that, further, she wanted to leave after a grueling four years on the job. She added that she felt no envy of Neil as she took her leave: "[Being around him] was a real clue to how instant riches can *screw up* your life.")

Meanwhile, displaying the same bulldog determination he had shown in going through with his Vegas dates, Neil resolved to maintain his driving pace for the rest of the year. That meant signing papers committing him to yet another Event engagement: a September stand at the Greek Theatre, scene of his greatest artistic triumph.

---

* The billing may have been Diamond's idea, judging by the copy that star album designer John Kosh (the Beatles' "Abbey Road," the Eagles' "Hotel California") observed him scribbling out for a trade ad he had hired Kosh to design around that time. Kosh: "It was going something like, 'Neil Diamond—The World's Greatest Entertainer.' And then he crossed it out and wrote, 'Neil Diamond—Living Legend.'" Kosh added that the sight of Diamond laboring over his own hype caused him to giggle—"I thought maybe he was joshing." It was his first and last mistake with Diamond: "Neil looked up and looked through me as if I was certainly not welcome. And then he just sort of motioned to his flunkies that I was to leave [his office]. And sure enough, someone walked over to me, touched me on the elbow, nodded to the door, and off I went."

·18·
BROADENING

The day in 1975 that Neil pondered his performing future at the empty Greek Theatre with Jeff Barry he knew that his return to the stage couldn't be a total triumph unless he played there again.

Yet, even though he'd put a hold on eight dates in September, he didn't sign the final contracts until after he'd negotiated his Las Vegas hurdle. During his second July 4 show he had his fans cheer him on into finally inking the Greek deal, asking, "Should we come back again this year?" The roar of approval, however, didn't seem to satisfy him. "It's kind of a problem, you know, this year," he fretted, "because the show—we did it on the record and people are expecting a lot.

"But we have enough time." Then he asked the crowd once again, "What do you think, guys?"

After he signed the contracts, Neil took steps to ensure that this Greek engagement, too, would be documented for posterity. He decided to do his "Hot August Night" stand one better, in fact, engaging not only "Beautiful Noise" engineer Neil Brody to record all but the first dates, but also TV producers Dwight Hemion and Gary Smith to videotape the final two shows. His tentative plan: to fashion from the videotape his first network TV special, and to support the special with the release of a second live LP set from the Greek—sales of which, in turn, could be sparked by the special. However, once again displaying a curious degree of caution, he refused to give the final OK to either project until after the engagement.

A surprising thing happened on his way to the Greek—Neil got a positive cover story in the September 23 issue of *Rolling Stone,* which hit the newsstands early that month.

Neil had taken a calculated risk when he allowed his PR man-to-the-stars Paul Wasserman (Bob Dylan, Paul Simon, Linda Ronstadt, the Rolling Stones) to pitch the magazine on a piece six months earlier. Over the years, the magazine had been prone to view him and his music with contempt.

With *Rolling Stone* still representing hipness and artistic integrity in 1976, and Diamond still seeking critical validation, he could, however, rationalize taking his chances with the magazine—as long as he got the cover.

Wasserman made his case for the cover treatment in a letter to senior editor Ben Fong-Torres, invoking the magical words "Robbie Robertson"—a darling of *Rolling Stone's* critics. The PR man also talked up Neil's desire to talk about life in the dying days of Tin Pan Alley in conjunction with the release of "Beautiful Noise"—including the times, the press agent tantalizingly wrote, when Neil walked around with a gun because he "defied the Mob." *Rolling Stone* editor Jann Wenner agreed to the cover stipulation.

Fong-Torres, who was assigned the piece, wound up interviewing Neil extensively. His thorough approach, as well as his desire to broaden the scope of the interview from "Beautiful Noise," apparently didn't sit well with the wary Diamond, who, for a while, resisted the editor's request for a final phone interview and photo session.

Whatever fears Neil was harboring about the treatment he was going to get dissipated when he saw the September 23 issue. Fong-Torres' piece turned out to be a sympathetic one, angled, like so many Diamond profiles before it, on this "consummate searcher's" confessional ruminations on his life and times. (One surprising rumination, especially considering he was talking to *Rolling Stone,* concerned his lack of hipness: "Hip was something frivolous people had time to be. I didn't have time to be hip and with it and groovy.") The article contained no critical words from former associates, no mention of the WEB IV suit or Diamond's suit against Hall Bartlett. The *Rolling Stone* verdict: "Neil Diamond, when he's not fencing with life, is just a nice Jewish *mensch.*"

A few days later, Ben Fong-Torres received a handwritten note from Neil. "You were more than fair," he wrote, adding, parenthetically, "I can breath [sic] again." As for the cover of the magazine featuring his convincingly wounded visage, Neil had it laminated and hung in his office.

Tickets for Neil's first Greek Theatre engagement in 1971 were still available from the box office during the stand. In 1972, after he sold out in advance, they were being hawked for up to $50 apiece. In the days before he began his sold-out 1976 engagement they had hit a new high on the scalp front: $100 each.

Fans weren't the only ones sweating out good seats. Gail Roberts, a Columbia Records PR staffer at the time, had made a $10,000 ticket buy for radio people, retailers, and the press, and she was dismayed to learn that none of her seats were any closer than the twenty-sixth row. After trying unsuccessfully to get better tickets through manager Jerry Weintraub's office, she called Diamond's office in desperation. She was surprised when Neil's new assistant, Marge Johnson, called back with Neil himself on the line. "Send over a list of who these heavies are," he told Roberts. She did, and later that day she received a new batch of tickets from Neil.

On stage at the Greek, Diamond took care of business as well. Appearing less affected in his manner than he'd been in Las Vegas, he opened the shows with a jolt of freshness: six songs from "Beautiful Noise." His sing-along on "Song Sung Blue" took on a Hollywood flavor on the nights the cameras rolled as he stuck a microphone in front of Henry Winkler, Helen Reddy, and Roger Miller. And his "Brother Love" encore was as electrifying as ever with the unveiling of a new set of mirrored panels that caught the audience's reflection, contributing to a revival-tent effect. Through it all, Diamond acted like he was having the time of his life.

Neil was satisfied enough with the engagement to give the green light to his TV special and sign with NBC. His one-hour date with the nation was set for February 21 at 9 P.M.

His decision on the matter of the live album was complicated, however, by the less-than-wholehearted support of CBS Records. According to Bruce Lundvall, CBS worried that he had not recorded enough new material since "Hot August Night" to justify another live album, and that "Hot August Night," with its whopping worldwide sales of eight million units, had saturated the market for another live LP.

But by 1976 no one told Neil what to do or not to do, and a second live Greek LP was what he wanted.

While Smith and Hemion went about the business of piecing together the videotape of the Greek dates, Neil imposed on Robbie Robertson to produce his live album.

It turned out to be an unorthodox production. Consumed at the time with finishing The Band's final studio album and preparing for the group's "Last Waltz" at San Francisco's Winterland on Thanksgiving night, Robertson didn't have any time to work in the studio on the Diamond tapes until they were ready to be mixed. Instead, he phoned in his instructions to engineer Brody from home.

Robertson did manage to formulate an interesting concept for the two-record package, deciding as Armin Steiner had with "Hot August Night" that there would be no studio overdubbing of vocal or instrumental parts. Instead, with seven recorded versions of each song available, they would cut from one night's take to another to achieve the desired results. Explained engineer Neil Brody: "We wanted it to be action, action, action." On "Song Sung Blue" alone, 100 cuts were made; in the process, ten minutes of the fourteen-minute-long track wound up on the floor. (Against his better judgment, however, Robertson retained Diamond's references to guest singers Helen Reddy and Henry Winkler as "bubby" and "bubula.")

Both Robertson and Diamond showed up for the mixing phase of the project, at Village Recorders, when it was decided to build the reels so that each song on a side segued into the next—another formidable undertaking, but one which promised to give the album cohesiveness.

To help pull off this trick, Robertson made his one concession to studio sweetening, directing Brody to make liberal use of a library of a dozen kinds of audience noise he had compiled. Anyway, "You don't do a Neil Diamond album without hearing the crowd go nuts," Brody said, chuckling, "and the idea was to make it sound like this was the coming of the New Age."

Meanwhile, Neil was his goading self as he stood over Brody's shoulder at Village, sternly exclaiming, "More vocal! More echo! More vocal! More echo!"

Dwight Hemion's and Gary Smith's job, meanwhile, entailed selecting, with Neil, the best of the two videotaped performances of each of the thirteen songs selected for broadcast in the hourlong special, and editing them down. The only extra videotaping they did was for the beginning of the show: an aerial view of Griffith Park and the empty Greek Theatre followed by a brief introduction from Neil in which he discoursed on performer-audience interplay from a seat in the amphitheater. "You're a man having a love affair with thousands of other people," he said. "And most of all, *best* of all, you're not alone anymore."

While progress was being made on both his album and special, Neil was receiving good news on other fronts. In November, Los Angeles Municipal Court Judge Louis Feder ruled that Neil, who had previously entered a not-guilty plea on his marijuana possession charge, could take a six-month drug rehabilitation course, the successful completion of which could free him of the charge. (Neil wound up taking the course, and the charge was dropped the following May.)

Also, Diamond had to be pleased with the imminent settlement of the bitter suit WEB IV had launched against him eight years earlier. The previous September, WEB IV attorney Bernard R. Diamond requested in a letter to Judge Sidney Asch of Manhattan Supreme Court that its suit against Tallyrand Music, Diamond and MCA, Inc. be marked "settled subject," signifying that the parties had begun serious talks. By November, those talks were well on their way to producing the eventual February 18 agreement, whereby WEB IV dropped its suit and Neil purchased his Bang Records recordings for what one knowledgeable source said was $1.2 million.

Even with all these good things happening, Neil claimed he was a nervous, sleepless wreck for the three months preceding the airing of his special.

His appearance at The Band's rock-superstar-studded "Last Waltz" on Thanksgiving did nothing to jar him out of his funk. Looking like a fish out of water amid the denim crowd in his blue suit and sunglasses, he gave an uncharacteristically understated performance of "Dry Your Eyes," his collaboration with Robbie Robertson. During the all-star finale, the Bob Dylan–led "I Shall Be Released," he could be spotted easing his way off the stage; by midsong, he had disappeared.

Still, Neil was not so consumed with his special that he wasn't beyond reacting to a cute stunt his effervescent assistant, Marge Johnson, whom he had nicknamed Sunshine, pulled that December: putting up a Christmas tree outside his office. "He laughed hysterically when he came in and saw this tree all lit up by the pool," a reliable source recalled. A tree henceforth became a holiday office tradition, even though Neil, as a Jew, did not celebrate Christmas. (Diamond's light-hearted response was a far cry from his reaction to another scene John-son staged a few months earlier, this one by accident: getting them stuck behind a locked door in a hallway underneath the Greek Theatre fol-lowing one of his "Love at the Greek" concerts. For the entire ten min-utes they stood there waiting for someone to come along and get them out, Diamond was said to have glared at his unnerved assistant without saying a word.)

"Love at the Greek" was released in January, and immediately surged up the charts. However, Neil could find no peace in having primed his fans for his NBC special. In an interview with the *Chicago Tribune* to hype his show, he hit his neurotic, paranoiac peak when the subject turned to rival network ABC. "They're having secret meetings about me, I know," he agonized. "Originally they had this movie, *How the West Was Won,* scheduled to run opposite me. Then I heard they were looking for another movie, something really monstrous, to try to flatten me with . . . The goal is to kill Neil Diamond on television. This is a *vendetta.*"

Presumably, Neil did not breathe his first sigh of relief until the ratings and the reviews were in, and he found he had done well on both scores—seventeenth place in the Nielsens and a rave from *Los Angeles Times* TV writer Lee Margulies: "a smashing bit of television."

Temporarily steeled by the success of his first foray into television, Neil decided in early 1977 that maybe the water was right at long last for his first dip into film as an actor and/or producer.

Diamond and the movies. Even with his failed attempts at landing a screen role in the '60s, and his foot-dragging on the movie front ever since, the match seemed more inevitable than ever in 1977, and not only because of his huge audience and his sex appeal. As he told the *Los Angeles Times* in 1973, "Because of the fickleness of public taste . . . you have to keep expanding in some way to survive in the entertainment business. They call it broadening your career."

The problem with "broadening" at that time, however, was the big stakes involved. Having dropped his public Solitary Man pose for that of a self-confidence-oozing "king" of pop, Diamond undoubtedly felt he couldn't afford to fail in any undertaking. Hence his anxiety dances lately even in the performance arena, the arena where he shined best.

As his assistant in charge of finding potential film properties, Jerry Paonessa had been in a perfect position to view his glacial pace toward a film commitment of some sort before he finally decided to get serious in 1977.

One of the first properties Paonessa talked up after taking an office in Neil's headquarters in early 1975 was a dark, offbeat novel by Harry Crews titled *The Gospel Singer,* about a Marjoe Gortner–type character who becomes a world-famous gospel singer, only to be killed by some of his followers after his tryst with a young woman early in his career is discovered. "The point is that we create our own idols," Paonessa enthused. It was, he said, "a fabulous, fabulous piece of material."

However, when Paonessa pitched the book to Diamond, his only response was "Hmmmmmmm."

Neil did react favorably to another project Paonessa approached him with, James Kirkwood's then-soon-to-be-published book *Some Kind of Hero.* About a Vietnam War vet's personal troubles upon his return home, the book seemed to have what Neil was looking for: relevance and great drama. "It was perfect," said Paonessa.

With Diamond's blessing, Paonessa flew to New York to meet with Kirkwood, then immersed in the final preparations for the debut of his new musical, *A Chorus Line,* at the Public Theater. Kirkwood declared his willingness to pen the *Hero* screenplay, and negotiations were begun back in Los Angeles.

Before the deal could be signed, however, Neil decided he didn't want to do the movie after all.

(Still convinced the book would make an excellent movie, Paonessa, with Neil's blessing, attempted to produce the movie on his own. He succeeded in bringing the project to Paramount, but left the company before the movie, starring Richard Pryor, was finally made in 1982.)

While Neil was putting the kibosh to various Paonessa film proposals, he was also nixing outside offers; among them, he later claimed, was the rock singer's role opposite fellow Erasmus Hall attendee Barbra Streisand in a remake of *A Star Is Born.* Diamond: "That character was a very destructive person. A loser. Not the kind of person I could ever identify with."

Neil, needless to say, had his own ideas about possible movie ventures. One of them was a film treatment of his critically applauded "Beautiful Noise" album. Paonessa vaguely recalled putting a list of prospective screenwriters together for that would-be project ("I was *always* putting together a list of writers"). Diamond also apprised Paonessa of his apparently still-strong interest in *Death at an Early Age,* the heavy dramatic property that he first talked of doing in 1971.

Regarding *Death,* Paonessa was the one this time going "Hmmmmm." After reading, at Neil's request, the screenplay that had been written, as well as Jonathan Kozol's original tome, Paonessa informed Neil that he thought the material was antiquated, and, at best, would make an "issue" TV movie. And yet, he noted, "It would keep coming up in conversation . . . so that you would know there was still interest [on his part]."

After a couple of years on the job, Paonessa came to conclude that, in Diamond's modus operandi, "Nothing is ever officially tabled, nothing is ever officially undertaken. Everything is sort of ongoing." Thus, Paonessa couldn't have been surprised when, early in 1977, Neil resumed talking about a potential project he had first considered a couple of years earlier: a second remake of the 1927 Al Jolson classic, *The Jazz Singer*.

There was a simple explanation for Neil's decision to move *Jazz Singer* from back burner to front burner: Tony Fantozzi.

By then the William Morris agent, who had been with Neil since 1973, had become his closest and most influential advisor. There were a couple of reasons for that, among them the fact that his devotion to Neil transcended usual agentry bounds. "If Tony had a fault it was only that he thought there was nothing in the world that Neil couldn't do," explained writer/producer Abby Mann, whom the agent approached unsuccessfully about finding a part for Neil in *King*, Mann's television drama on the life of Martin Luther King, Jr. "He just really adored Neil . . . He really would act far more as a manager than as an agent." (Fantozzi's presence on the scene may have been one of the reasons Neil went managerless for 1974 and most of 1975 before hiring Sherwin Bash as his fourth manager since Bang Records days late that year, and the high-powered Jerry Weintraub [Frank Sinatra, John Denver] as his fifth manager in 1976.)

Another reason Fantozzi had become so important to Diamond was his style. While other close associates chose to pussyfoot around Neil, the tall, mustachioed, cigar-smoking agent dared to speak his mind. "He was the one who said, 'Neil, it's bullshit they're telling you—the truth is this,'" said someone who knew them both.

By putting himself on the spot, of course, the self-styled Fantozzi had to deliver. And he did consistently, most recently with the "Neil Diamond Special," which he had lobbied for with Neil, made the deals for, and then stood proudly by as it was nominated for an Emmy.

It was at lunch in early 1977 with an old agent pal of his, Jerry Leider, that Fantozzi got the idea, courtesy of Leider, to sell Neil on the notion of *The Jazz Singer*. "Tony talked about Neil's position as he saw it in the music world," Leider recalled. He said that Fantozzi discussed Diamond in terms of a "Sinatra or Presley, the artist who can go from twenty-five to fifty and touch audiences all along, and who somehow has that magic that goes back as far as Jolson." The reference to Jolson immediately struck Leider, who was getting into movie producing at the time after having worked in Europe as Warner Brothers' executive vice president of foreign production. The two began talking about possible material, and "out of that conversation," Leider said, "came, 'Why don't we do *The Jazz Singer*?'

"Tony was all for it," he added. "I thought it was a good idea, too."

One could imagine why: Diamond's Brooklyn Jewish Roads, the promise of a Neil Diamond score, and the fact that there was musical remake fever in the air thanks to the box-office success of Streisand's *A Star is Born* made the project seem eminently bankable, if not exactly artistically inspired.

Neil obviously was intrigued. *Jazz Singer,* Jerry Paonessa noted, "would come up *constantly* in conversation."

Of course, before Neil would sign a deal to star in his first movie, let alone enter into serious negotiations, he had to see a script. And one couldn't be written until Leider secured the sequel rights to *Jazz Singer*. Because Warner Brothers and United Artists each claimed they owned the rights, those negotiations promised to be prolonged ones.

In the interim, Diamond turned to other matters, such as making the final arrangements for his third tour of Europe, from May 31 through July 2. It promised to be another of his newsmaking sojourns for two royal reasons: Princess Margaret's attendance at his opening-night performance at the London Palladium, and his tour-ending outdoor extravaganza at Woburn Abbey in Bedfordshire, residence of the Marquis and Marchioness of Tavistock.

As for the Abbey gig, while it may have seemed a natural for the "king" of pop, the fact was it never would have come about had it not been for the perseverance of Lord Robin Tavistock and his wife, Lady Henrietta, whose idea it was in the first place.

After deciding that hosting a pop concert would be a novel way of raising some extra money to help with taxes and the high upkeep costs of their castle and property, the Tavistocks had narrowed their list of desired artists to two: Diamond and Barbra Streisand. Opting for Neil, they had flown to Los Angeles to discuss their idea with Neil, who had agreed to see them.

In Los Angeles they checked into a hotel and waited for an appointment. And waited. Days and then weeks went by as Diamond sent word daily that he was busy and unable to meet. "I think Neil was intimidated," said one knowledgeable source. "In fact, I know he was."

Finally, Diamond did sit down with his thoroughly perplexed visitors. The wonder of the meeting is that he and the Tavistocks warmed up to one another right away. Neil then warmed up to the idea of Woburn Abbey.

As it turned out, Princess Margaret and Woburn Abbey weren't the only news connected with his Europe visit. Neil also planned to record there following his tour with his new producer, Bob Gaudio, of Four Seasons writing/producing fame. And, even more noteworthy, he planned to tape his second television special.

The hand of Tony Fantozzi could be seen in the surprising choice that Neil made for director of the special: Fantozzi client William Friedkin, the high-powered moviemaker whose credits included *The Exorcist* and *The French Connection*. While Friedkin was hardly a name in television music specials, he did have a thorough grounding in TV directing, having worked for Chicago's WGN and for documentary maker David Wolper.

It was clear by the saga that Neil had in mind for his special that Friedkin's documentary experience would come in handy. Among the ideas discussed were trips to Africa and Atlanta, to shoot "Soolaimon" and "Brother Love" segments, respectively. Jerry Paonessa, who attended many of the spring brainstorming sessions for the special in Diamond's office with Diamond, Friedkin, and actress Jeanne Moreau, the director's wife at the time, described Neil's TV vision:

"It was so ambitious I didn't know whether it could be done. It was going to be the visualization of how music was born . . . I'm talking a very lofty, brilliant idea. And it was going to be multifaceted. We were going to hire a crew of documentary filmmakers [and] follow Neil around, whenever he burped, whenever he was changing, whenever he was on the road. Part of it was going to be actual written dialogue that would be fictionalized drama. And the other part of it was going to be staged musical numbers."

(Casting a pall over the deliberations was the drowning death, in France, of the three-year-old daughter of a young French producer friend of Jeanne Moreau, who had been taking part in the discussions. When Diamond's assistant, Marge Johnson, was unable to book the producer on a commercial flight back to Paris, Neil instructed her to hire a private jet at his expense.)

Neil began his tour of Europe in regal style, via private German railroad car.

His three-car express (actually, the cars were pulled by various public trains) consisted of a second-class traveling car, a first-class dining car and—for Neil, his family, and VIP guests—a magnificent private car, all burled wood and brass and green velvet.

This one-of-a-kind car turned out to have an infamous history: It had been built and occupied at one time by Hermann Goering, Hitler's Gestapo chief. When the would-be Jazz Singer learned of that he cracked to reporters that he hoped Herr Goering was turning in his grave.

Diamond's first stop was the Ahoy Sports & Expo Complex in Rotterdam. "He turns out to be a first-class entertainer who manages to get the usually rather stiff Dutch audience swinging within fifteen minutes," read one local review.

His June 7 date at Paris' Palais des Sports as well as his "Love in Germany" dates in Hamburg, Berlin, Dartmund, and Munich drew raves, too. He ended the European continent portion of his tour with a June 19 concert at the venerable Stadhalle in Vienna.

From there, Diamond trekked to London for his five-show, four-night stand at the Palladium, which included his opening-night concert before Princess Margaret.

The princess had been a fan for some time, having attempted, in vain, to get Neil to headline the Royal Charity Show at Royal Albert Hall during his performance sabbatical (along with delivering his regrets, Neil sent a check to the Royal Crippled Children's Society). Now that he and the princess finally had a date, Diamond resolved that every aspect of his show pass royal inspection. Among his quality-control measures was to show up at the empty Palladium to watch his lighting designer, Scott Johnson, run through the show's lighting cues.

Johnson wished he hadn't: "It is a very futile thing to stare, in silence, at an empty stage with light cues going on—there is almost an incredible dullness. For a performer, I can only imagine that it would be incredibly depressing."

Sure enough, Johnson saw Neil "sinking into a funk" as he watched the lights. "At one point," he recalled, "Neil said to me [intense voice]: 'Scotty—*no yellow. We're not going to have any yellow in this show!*' It was almost a panicky directive." (Johnson, who took the order in good-humored stride, wound up downplaying but not eliminating yellow lights from the engagement; the color, after all, was a crucial element in his lighting palette.)

Diamond also girded mentally for opening night by flexing his ego. After being informed by one of Buckingham Palace's protocol people that the length of his post-show visit with Princess Margaret in the Royal Box would depend on her, that royalty always left the room first, he remarked to one aide, "It's going to be a hell of a long night in the Royal Box."

Onstage at the Palladium at last, Diamond, the picture of flash in his sequined peacock blue shirt, spangly oversized black belt and gray slacks, flaunted one royal no-no early in the show by addressing the princess. "I must apologize about the seats," he announced, alluding to the Royal Box's location next to a bank of speakers. "We have supplied some royal ear stoppers in case the sound is too strong."

Neil was his exacting self throughout the rest of the engagement, even delaying his appearance onstage one night until a few dead flowers he had spotted in a vase on the left side'of the stage were removed. He took his final Palladium bow June 26.

Suddenly, it was six days and counting before Woburn Abbey. Because of the bad weather—it had already been raining weeks in the London area—they had to be six of the more nerve-racking days in his career.

To the press, however, he exhibited his usual cool. "I know [the weather] is going to change dramatically," he told a BBC Radio reporter. "It is in my contract. I'm looking forward to a beautiful day."

He got it. "The clouds parted that particular day for the Neil Diamond concert at Woburn Abbey," guitarist Emory Gordy recalled, wonder in his voice. "It was unseasonably warm . . . probably one of the best days England ever had. And I told Neil, 'Listen, you must have a direct line with God.'"

Diamond's new recording engineer, Bill Schnee, there to record the concert, was awed by another sight as he stood by the Abbey, that of 55,000 Britons streaming toward him as the gates were opened that afternoon. "They were like ants in the distance—this big funnel of people running like lunatics," he recalled. Standing next to him at the time was the Abbey's proprietor, Lord Robin Tavistock, decked out in a black Diamond tour jacket embroidered with the words "Robin of Woburn." Tavistock had a "What-have-I-done?" look on his face as he watched the spectacle.

Meanwhile, Billy Friedkin filmed. The director, who had arrived in London several days earlier—about the time *Variety* noted that Diamond's ambitious special would feature such European stars as Brigitte Bardot, Catherine Deneuve, and Jean-Paul Belmondo—had pinned high hopes on Woburn. He had brought along six camera crews, and had already filmed the estate's wildlife and a fictional scene with actors in the Abbey itself in which, in a "Twilight Zone" touch, a handful of seventeenth-century lords and ladies are drawn to the windows by Diamond's musical ruckus outside.

The filming of the fans' stampeding entrance completed, Friedkin prepared for the shot of the day, Neil's entrance onstage.

Friedkin had a specific shot in mind. At precisely sunset, after the Corps of Drums of the Second Battalion Grenadier Guards had made its entrance, Diamond would take the stage, his spangly blue outfit catching the day's last rays of sunlight. All six of his cameras would be blazing, capturing every second of his most glorious stage entrance ever.

There was only one problem: Neil didn't want to start his concert until after dusk. "We're going to wait," he informed Friedkin.

The director did not take the rebuff well. Said his editor, Bud Smith, who was there with him, "You put someone in charge like Friedkin, who is a very dynamic director, and if he wants you to be out singing at sunset you better be out there singing at sunset." And, in fact, Friedkin was said to have replied, "If you wait, you'll see two Daimlers rolling up the hill"—one, presumably, carrying him and the other, his wife, Jeanne Moreau.

"Well, we're waiting," Diamond replied.

Sure enough, sunset came and went without Neil taking the stage, and two Daimlers were said to have been spotted rolling up the hill.

By then, Neil was concerned with one thing only, steadying his nerves. As he paced around backstage puffing on a cigarette he encountered his recording engineer, Bill Schnee. "Are you ready, Bill?" he said. After Schnee cheerfully reported that he was, Diamond dourly cracked, "That makes one of us." A few minutes later, he stretched out on the grass with his eyes closed, trying to calm himself.

He wasn't completely successful, despite the enormous standing, cheering reception he got as he raced onto the stage. But after the nervous delivery of his first several songs—punctuated by his bellows of *"Oh, yes!"*—he managed to settle into a groove. His biggest challenge from then on was not to overexert. A *Daily Express* reporter wrote: "The amplification effectively revealed to people many miles away that the young man was breathing hard."

Afterward, Lord Robin Tavistock was aglow, calling the performance, and the experience in general, "everything I wanted and more."

Back in London, Bud Smith met up with Billy Friedkin. At the director's suggestion, Smith had remained at Woburn Abbey with the six film crews and shot the performance. He screened the footage for Friedkin, and the director, pleased with what he saw, met with Neil in Paris in an attempt to get their project back on track.

According to Smith, the meeting went well, and Friedkin began once again plotting shots. "And then all of a sudden," Smith said, "Neil decided he didn't want to come out of his hotel room and be bothered."

At that point, Smith added, Friedkin threw up his hands and went home to his house in the French countryside.

Enter an on-the-spot Tony Fantozzi.

Among the deals the agent had made for the special was a sponsorship deal with Datsun, who was underwriting the special's approximate $1,500,000 cost. As part of the deal a firm November airdate was agreed upon, so that Datsun could use the special to hype its 1978 line of cars. That meant that the agent had to put the special back together again, or Neil would be in a sticky legal situation.

Fantozzi didn't have to look far to find the best candidate for finishing the European portion of filming, at least: Bud Smith. Smith was willing.

Instead of butting heads with the recalcitrant Diamond, however, the affable Smith tried the accommodating approach. He began his filming in Neil's Paris hotel room, capturing Neil in the act of writing a song and gazing out his window, Lord Byron style, at the Eiffel Tower. "He would just as soon spend all of his time in his hotel room," Smith chuckled. "He liked to be by himself from all that I observed."

After a while, however, Neil did agree to venture out into Paris, although his forays with Smith were hardly spur-of-the-moment affairs: "Everything would have to be perfect before he hit the streets—clothing, hair, everything." Smith eventually filmed Neil writing a song with French composer Gilbert Becaud at Becaud's apartment (the two had met backstage after Diamond's Paris concert the previous month); Neil playing chess with an old man in a park; Neil visiting the Pompidou Museum; Neil bicycling by Notre Dame; Neil fencing outside the Palace of Versailles. "I think we spent almost a month in Paris filming him," Smith said.

Smith came to like Neil, but as a subject he described a person who hardly seemed to be gearing up for his feature film debut: "He seemed to be stiff all the time."

When he returned to Los Angeles, Smith edited together his Paris material with the film of Woburn Abbey and some earlier tour footage shot by documentary filmmaker David Meyers. The show's writer, Wally Green, then viewed the approximately three-hour-long epic and made a recommendation: Hire a crackerjack TV director to shoot some studio performance sequences and intercut those sequences with the choicest European footage.

With the hiring of TV veteran Art Fisher, that suggestion became a reality. So much for Neil's grand "visualization of how music is born" concept.

For those performance sequences, Diamond had a new album's worth of songs to choose from, not to mention his catalogue of warhorses. During his London stay he had, as planned, gone into Scorpio Studio to lay down the basic tracks for his first LP with producer Bob Gaudio. The album, which marked his retreat from the ambitious concept approach of "Beautiful Noise," was finished in Los Angeles just in time for the special. So that no one would mistake the fact that they constituted a marketing package, the album and special were both dubbed "I'm Glad You're Here With Me Tonight," after the bland romantic ballad cowritten by Gaudio and Judy Parker.

As it turned out, the special was hardly the artistic triumph that the "Greek" special was, even though it did win Neil a second Emmy nomination. It did have its moments, however . . . Neil taking the stage at Woburn Abbey following the amusing fictional scene inside the Abbey . . . Neil crooning the classy "You Don't Bring Me Flowers," by far the best song off his tepid "I'm Glad . . ." LP, during a Los Angeles studio recording session (Diamond originally wrote the tune for Norman

Lear's short-lived TV series "All That Glitters" and then expanded it with the help of Alan and Marilyn Bergman) . . . and Neil performing for a welcome change without glitzy clothes in the extended soundstage performance segments.

There was a funny story behind his choice of relatively subdued threads. Originally intending to record the segments dressed in a spangly tuxedo that would have done the late Liberace proud, he was stopped in his tracks backstage by his glitz-loathing assistant, Marge Johnson, who, in a moment of daring candor, piped up, "It's ridiculous, Neil. You can't *possibly* wear that." Furious, Neil stormed back into his dressing room. When he stomped out of it, however, he was wearing a sedate dark blue suit.

The special was still very recent history when Diamond hit the road yet again in December for a string of U.S. dates. Joining him for several of them was a new face, screenwriter Jerome Kass.

There had been several developments on the *Jazz Singer* front while Neil had been occupied with his special: (1) Jerry Leider had finally secured sequel rights to the movie after a six-month effort; (2) MGM had taken the project under its wing; and (3) Leider had hired Kass, author of *Queen of the Stardust Ballroom,* to write the screenplay.

·19·
ALL THAT
"JAZZ"

There was a good reason why Jerry Kass wanted to accompany Diamond for a portion of his December tour: He was still looking to get inspired for the screenplay assignment.

The creative juices hadn't flowed when his agent, Bill Robinson, a Diamond fan, first pitched him on the project. "I didn't think the story of a cantor's son could work in 1978, and I protested doing it," Kass said.

Nor had they flowed when the then-forty-one-year-old screenwriter finally agreed to meet with Jerry Leider and read the fourteen-page story outline that was the fruit of the producer's attempt to contemporize *Jazz Singer*. Kass found the story, which featured the elimination of the mother character, the recasting of the father and son as Holocaust survivors, and the addition of a wife and a love interest, to be "filled with clichés. [They were] ideas and scenes that you have seen so many times that you can't believe that somebody is telling you that's what they want."

One aspect of the story had started his creative juices trickling, however: the curse the father puts on his son when the son turns his back on his cantor calling to seek a career in secular music. "I told Leider that I thought the only way I could make this work would be if I treated it as a kind of Jewish fable, in which the curse of the father pervades the man's life."

Leider, and then MGM, had been amenable to that approach, he added.

Kass then met Neil for the first time at his Malibu home. It was a disconcerting encounter for the screenwriter on a couple of scores, one of which was the presence of Robbie Robertson, who, with his wife, Dominique, had become friendly with Neil and Marcia.

"What Robbie was worried about for Neil was that it shouldn't be another *Star Is Born*," recalled Kass, who was also disconcerted to see Robertson do more of the talking than Neil. Kass explained that he was of the same mind; that, in fact, he had already cautioned Leider that he couldn't write a gritty, hard-edged musical like *Star*.

The meeting had gone vaguely downhill from there. "I knew what he was asking me not to do," said Kass, "and I had the feeling that he had an expectation of a certain kind of movie for Neil. [But] I didn't know what it was." What did come through loud and clear in both Robertson's and Diamond's "pussyfooting," however, was their skepticism about *Jazz Singer*. "And since I was skeptical, too, I found the whole meeting to be kind of strange. That's when I began to sense that Neil was nervous about doing his first movie and doing this as his first movie."

After sizing him up, Kass was worried for him. Like Saul David years earlier, he feared that Neil lacked the instincts of an actor: "I found him . . . self-conscious. I didn't know what he could project except 'nice guy, intense, serious.' That's not enough."

Still, after the meeting, Kass had gone ahead and signed a contract with MGM to produce a *Jazz Singer* screenplay. He had decided, in the end, that "there is something about a star that is exciting."

At Kansas City's Kemper Arena on December 12, the screenwriter expected to have his first opportunity on tour to tap into that excitement. Instead, he left the arena befuddled.

"There was one moment when Neil was onstage that I thought, 'Oh, I see, he's doing something which is theatrical.' That was at the end of 'Jonathan Livingston Seagull,' when he lifts his hands up in the cathedral lighting as if he's Christ on the cross, and the audience actually rose up with him. It was so outrageous that I thought it was great. But other than that, I thought he had no identity." Complicating matters for Kass was Neil's sparkly Las Vegas–style outfit, which left Kass "totally shocked . . . I thought he was much more sober onstage, understated . . . Now I really didn't know who he was."

In their conversations, Jerry Kass said he didn't get any closer to the real Neil. The one time he thought he stood a chance was on a plane ride, when Neil asked to have a chat. "He said to me, 'Do you mind if I ask you some questions?' I said, 'Not at all.' He said, 'When you write, do you use a typewriter or do you use a pen?' And I thought, 'Are you serious? This is how you ask a person who he is?'"

When it was Kass' turn to ask questions, the screenwriter found to his dismay that "either there was somebody else there or Neil didn't hear the question. There was a way in which he avoided me that made it almost impossible for me to know almost anything about him.

"I had the feeling that everywhere we went he was uncomfortable," Kass continued. "I never got the feeling he was totally relaxed, hanging loose. *Ever*. Even the one night we saw him at the Hospitality Suite, where we had dinner, I found him not to be with us . . . not relaxed.

"It may have been my presence that made him uptight . . . But I was there not to judge him, I was there to find him."

Asked if he had found Neil Diamond by the time he left the tour, Jerry Kass said, *"Unnnnhh-uh."* He added: "I don't think he's a man of great self-knowledge. Because people who know themselves give you more of themselves than he does. If you know yourself, what do you have to lose?"

Still, the screenwriter did return to Los Angeles with several revealing memories of Neil. One was of the time Neil allowed him in his dressing room as he received a before-show manicure from a woman he had flown in from Los Angeles. "And I thought, 'Now, *this* is absurd—you fly someone in for a manicure?' Well, it turns out that he bites his nails down to the nubs—he doesn't want anybody to know that. At the same time he wants his nails to look clean and nice, so he uses the same manicurist, which protects him from being found out as a nailbiter. I thought that was kind of fascinating. It revealed to me that he was vulnerable."

Kass also had a vivid recollection of a benefit screening of *Close Encounters of the Third Kind,* the hot new movie at the time, that Diamond, he, and the band attended incognito in Kansas City. Kass: "We waited until the lights went out and then they shepherded us in. And as we were going into this theater, Neil said to me, 'Save me a seat.' And I thought, 'This is *great*. This is like when you're fifteen and you go to the movies with your buddies and they say 'I want to sit next to you.' So I saved Neil a seat in the very back row, where they put us . . . he sits down and the movie begins.

"But the lights didn't go out [all the way]. And I say to Neil, 'The lights are still on.' And he says, 'Oh, does it bother you?' And I say, 'It's weird, a movie with lights on.' So he goes, 'Hey, Pat'—who's at the end of the row—'the lights.' So Pat [Stansfield] goes out, and the next thing I know the lights go out.

"Now the movie's just beginning, and I say to Neil, 'It's suffocating in here.' 'Oh. Pat—*air conditioning.*' Pat goes out and the air conditioning goes on. I was floored. This was the greatest power I had ever seen." At the same time, he added, he was thoroughly amused: "When I looked at Neil I saw somebody who was kind of needy and lost and could use a friend. But here he was in a position where he had to at least pretend he was together, in a position of power."

It was observations such as these that led the screenwriter to conclude that Diamond was "really a sweet guy basically." Not coincidentally, that's how Danny Rabin, the protagonist in *Jazz Singer,* turned out in Kass' screenplay, which was completed in January of 1978. "I kept it very simple," he explained. "A good Jewish boy who wouldn't hurt a soul but who had a passion for singing, and therefore had to fulfill this passion. It was quite old-fashioned in its temperament. There was none of that *A Star Is Born* sex all over the place."

Pleased with his script, Kass did "one of the gutsiest things in my life": He insisted on reading it aloud to Neil in his office, rather than allowing Neil to read it himself first. Kass made the request because "my instincts told me that Neil could not read a screenplay—it's a very special skill—and I wanted to make sure that he knew what I was trying to write."

To his delight, Jerry Leider and Jerry Paonessa were able to arrange the reading. In the process, Kass had to compromise a bit: Instead of a solo performance, he agreed to share the stage, so to speak, with Leider, who wound up reading the women's parts.

The reading exceeded the writer's hopes. Kass: "He loved it. I think he began to see himself [in the role]." The most glorious moment for Kass came when he read the climactic reunion scene between father and son, and Neil was moved to tears.

Afterward, Kass, who had earlier resigned himself to a short tenure on *Jazz Singer* because of Neil's ambivalent attitude, was moved to optimism: "I said to Jerry Paonessa, 'Gee, maybe I'll be the writer of this movie after all.'" Shortly thereafter, however, reality set in. MGM didn't like the script and wanted a complete rewrite.

Said Kass, who discussed the matter with MGM executive Ray Wagner: "They wanted something that was much more hard-edged. They wanted a sense of the streets. They didn't want this sweetness."

What they wanted, Jerry Kass was told in short, was another *A Star Is Born.*

Kass hoped that Neil would stand up for the script, but he didn't. "He was needing the support from the studio rather than being able to provide it," he hypothesized. Jerry Leider, he found, had a similarly acquiescent reaction. (In February, as Neil hung out at home with a new Diamond, Micah Joseph, born on Valentine's Day, he wrote to Kass: "I don't think they'll get it better than your version, but that's the insanity of this business.")

There was nothing the frustrated Kass felt he could do under the circumstances but quit the project, without offering a rewrite. His parting words to Leider came in the form of a prediction: "This movie is not going to get made."

Leider, Kass added, was unflappable: "Oh yes it will—I tell ya I want to make this movie. And Neil wants to make this movie."

Six months later, Leider got a chance to show his stuff as a project salvager when MGM put *Jazz Singer* into turnaround.

The studio's decision came after executives tested the title and concept in a study group and read a second *Jazz Singer* script, this one turned in by Stephen H. Foreman, a thirty-seven-year-old writer whose biggest credit at the time was an Obie-winning play, *The Reliquary of Mr. and Mrs. Porterfield.* The test results revealed, in Leider's words, that the project "was not immediately identifiable as a contemporary movie," and the MGM hierarchy didn't like Foreman's script, which featured a glibber, stronger protagonist—now named Jess Robin—but adhered to the same basic story line. "The major criticism was that the script was too Jewish," recalled an amazed Foreman, who attended a meeting with the MGM brass. "And of course my response was 'Isn't *Godfather* too Italian? It's the story of an orthodox cantor and his son.'"

Instead of losing his cool over the setback, Leider adopted the pose of the tiger agent he once was and took to the phone in search of another studio. Within twenty-four hours, he had a handshake deal with EMI chairman Bernard Delfont. Playing a crucial role in the development was Tony Fantozzi, who not only arranged Leider's meeting with Delfont, but also made the deal an irresistible one for the EMI head by stating that Capitol Records, an EMI company, could have the soundtrack album.

One trick Leider couldn't pull out of his hat, however, was keeping to the planned fall shooting schedule for *Jazz Singer.* He resigned himself instead to an early 1979 start.

As Leider, Fantozzi, and Delfont negotiated the turnaround in the summer of 1978, Neil, whose doubts about *Jazz Singer* couldn't have been quelled by MGM's abrupt pullout from the project, stuck to familiar turf, the recording studio.

He happened to have another ambitious album project on the drawing boards: a two-record set to be called "The American Popular Song." The album, which would include a mix of original and cover recordings, was to be his tribute to great pop tunesmiths.

Neil had spent the month of June laying down tracks for the LP at Sunset Sound in Hollywood. It had been a productive time; no fewer than thirty tunes had been recorded, including Bob Dylan's "Lay Lady Lay," Bacharach-David's "Do You Know the Way to San Jose," and Elton John's "Rocket Man" (so much for the "American" angle).

Neil's enthusiasm for the LP was obvious as he animatedly described it to CBS President Bruce Lundvall at a CBS Records convention at Los Angeles' Century Plaza Hotel in July.

Lundvall, however, didn't quite share his excitement: "I said, 'You know, Barry Manilow has had a two-record set, and that queered him on the whole idea of two-record sets. Don't count on this as being one of your biggest sellers just because it's two records of Neil Diamond.'" The CBS president then renewed a pitch he had made weeks earlier to Diamond's manager, Jerry Weintraub, a plea for Neil to do in the studio what a Louisville deejay by the name of Gary Guthrie had done electronically on the air several months earlier: team Neil and Barbra Streisand on the ballad "You Don't Bring Me Flowers," which Streisand had recorded herself that spring. "An *event* is you and Barbra Streisand doing 'You Don't Bring Me Flowers,'" he argued to Diamond. "Everyone understands what that is. That's two of the biggest stars in America—in the world for that matter—singing together for the first time on a record, a great song. And it's your song."

At first, Lundvall recalled, Neil was noncommittal, responding, "Oh, I don't know. I don't know." But as the CBS president persisted in promoting the idea, Neil evinced tentative interest: "You really think this thing with Streisand is a good idea?" "Neil, it's an absolute number-one record," Lundvall replied.

That did it. "I think I'm willing to do it, if Barbra wants to do it," Neil announced. He added that the recording could go on "American Popular Song."

As it turned out, Neil's Malibu neighbor was more than willing. The recording took place at Hollywood's Cherokee Studio on the evening of October 17.

"You knew it was a big date because all of the employees were hanging out in the room, sticking their heads in the doors," said Ron Hitchcock, who engineered the session. "There was magic in the air, absolutely a feeling of something real special going on.

"All of a sudden, Jon Peters [Streisand's boyfriend-manager] and Jerry Weintraub arrive. And Barbra shows up, and Neil and Alan Lindgren and Bob Gaudio. They went into the studio and started playing for key and tempo. They tried a couple of keys, and pretty quickly established where they wanted to be—Neil can't sing in just any key, he's got a really deep voice. Barbra hit a couple of high notes, and it was fine . . .

"Then they started running through it for structure, working with Gaudio to find out who was going to sing which line. All of a sudden the Bergmans appeared. They were rewriting. Not rewriting the whole idea of the song, [but] making a duet happen, [changing] an 'and' to a 'but,' a 'you' to an 'I.' They were in the control room with Gaudio listening, and Barbra and Neil were in the studio.

"All in all, Neil and Barbra experimented for forty-five minutes . . . 'Let's both sing this line,' 'No, maybe I should take this line.' It was *really* magical.

"They sang the song seven times, and made changes in it . . . 'You sing the intro this time.' A couple of takes they broke up each other . . . so it wasn't an uptight session, they were having fun."

Hitchcock added that he knew Barbra, at least, was pleased with the recorded results: "The only thing she said to me was 'Sounds great.'" However, that was two words more than Hitchcock heard from Neil. Still, he said, "Everyone knew this was a number-one record by the time they walked out the door."

Tapes of the seven takes were given to both Neil and Barbra. "Where they both liked what they sang, that's what we chose from," Hitchcock explained. In the end, portions of each of the takes were used.

After the vocals were pieced together, a cassette was given to keyboards player Lindgren, the only musician on the date. Lindgren orchestrated the song and, two days later at Cherokee, his work was performed by thirty-five string players. Hitchcock: "At the end of that string date, that was the finished record." Within several days, Columbia was distributing test pressings of "You Don't Bring Me Flowers."

"Flowers" shot up the charts. So, too, to Neil's chagrin, did "Barbra Streisand's Greatest Hits, Vol. II," which included the track. At the time the Streisand album was released, Neil was still putting the finishing touches on his "American Popular Song" LP, now a one-record set, which also included the track. "Jesus Christ, I'm working on a studio album, and the Streisand greatest hits album comes out first," he fumed to Bruce Lundvall.

It was not the most ideal time for the CBS Records president to recommend to Neil that he repackage his album to take advantage of his biggest hit in eight years, delaying its release further, but he did so anyway. Alluding to the cover that Neil was planning to use for "American Popular Song"—a photo of a lit-up Wurlitzer jukebox against a black background—Lundvall reasoned: "First of all, you've got a hit single record—it's not on the cover. Secondly, you don't have your picture on the cover, and you're rather a major selling point visually for your records."

Lundvall chuckled in recalling his appeal: "You know, it's funny, because Neil did not like to have his mind changed on things very often; he had very strong views. But if I could really rationalize with him the reasons why, he would listen. He would always listen. He was always a total gentleman. And he would labor over things endlessly."

Finally, at 4 A.M. one day in November, presumably after some marathon mulling, Neil decided Lundvall was right: The album should be called "You Don't Bring Me Flowers." He phoned his personal album designer, David Kirshner, and set up a 7 A.M. meeting that day, and then called Columbia to stop the presses on the production of the expensive "American Popular Song" packaging.

In the end, he decided to scrap all the album art (including the single best piece ever produced for a Diamond album: an airbrush painting of a teen-age Diamond playing guitar in front of the bathroom mirror revealing his modern-day reflection, surrounded by such evocative accoutrements as a Zenith portable phonograph, an Everly Brothers LP, and a squished tube of Brylcream). In its place, he opted for a starkly simple look: on the cover, just his name and album title in script, and another in his long series of unsmiling portraits; on the back the song titles, in script as well. Further disguising the fact that the album was originally intended as his tribute to popular song was his decision to remove such cover tunes as "Lay Lady Lay," "The Sun Ain't Gonna Shine Anymore," "Teach Me Tonight," and "Rocket Man," which were replaced with originals.

For his efforts, Neil was rewarded with his longest-charting Top 40

LP since "Jonathan Livingston Seagull." The LP peaked at number four on *Billboard's* chart, only several slots lower than "Flowers" the single, which fulfilled Bruce Lundvall's prophecy, becoming the third number-one hit for Neil Diamond the recording artist.

(A second Grammy award, however, proved beyond his reach, with the Doobie Brothers nabbing Best Record of the Year honors for "What a Fool Believes" at the twenty-second annual awards ceremony in February of 1980. But he and Barbra were hands-down winners in the unofficial most electrifying appearance category, walking onstage unannounced, and then singing the Grammy-nominated "Flowers" face to face amid screams from the audience.)

Neil's continued high profile on the charts a dozen years after "Solitary Man" served as another reminder to all those involved in *Jazz Singer* in late 1978 that he was the single most important reason the movie was being made.

One person thoroughly impressed with that fact was a new principal in the unfolding *Jazz Singer* drama, director Sidney J. Furie, whom Jerry Leider hired in December, several months after finalizing his deal with EMI.

Furie had not been Leider's first choice; as Burt Nodella, an executive with his production company put it, "Any project you're doing you go for John Schlesinger, you go for Sydney Pollack." Still, the Canadian-born Furie was a respected pro who had something important going for him: his proven ability to draw performances out of beginning actors. Among the first-timers he had guided along were Barry Newman in *The Lawyer,* Michael Caine in *The Ipcress File,* and, most recently, a pop-singer-turned-actress by the name of Diana Ross in *Lady Sings the Blues.*

It was easy to see why Furie worked well with nervous neophytes. "There's a Yiddish word for Sidney—'*hamish,*'" said Nodella. "Very like family, easy to talk to. He wouldn't come in and talk business right away: 'How's your father feeling?' 'How's everything going?'" Said assistant director Robert Webb, who had worked with Furie on several features, and who was destined to be his first assistant director on *Jazz Singer*: "If you've got a problem, it's his problem."

In his talks with Jerry Leider, Furie seemed up to the challenge of helping Neil work out all of his problems vis à vis *The Jazz Singer.* "He was very excited about doing the movie," the producer said.

One of the first people to work directly with Furie on the project was screenwriter Steve Foreman. At their first meeting, which took place before Furie had spent much time with either Diamond or Tony Fantozzi, Furie announced to Foreman that, at most, his already-rewritten script would require a 10 percent rewrite. When the two of them sat down in December in front of a typewriter and Foreman's box of cigars in a rented bungalow at Sunset Gower Studios in Hollywood, however, the screenwriter learned to his shock that Furie had decided differently. "From day one Sidney completely disregarded the script," Foreman claimed. *"Completely. . .*

"His approach was 'Let's explore . . . let's get into background . . . let's see what happens if . . . ,'" he continued. "On one level it sounds quite valid, but we already had a script, and that was the script that, as far as I knew, had been approved. He was dispensing with it."

In the weeks that followed, not only did Foreman's cigars disappear ("He was chain-smoking my goddamn cigars!"), so did his cool. Far from Furie acting *hamish,* the screenwriter found the director to be an "incredibly . . . mercurial individual . . . Sidney would literally say things like, 'Take this down.' Or I would write a scene and he would come back into the office and say, 'Now let's talk about the scene I just wrote'— referring to him, not me."

Foreman didn't think much of some of the director's ideas, either, including Furie's decree that they write in a scene where the Diamond character, in a sly reference to Jolson, disguises himself in blackface to perform in a black club. "I think he thought it was good entertainment," said Foreman, who had been a civil rights worker in the '60s. "But I said, 'No way am I gonna write that scene. In the first place, it's racist, in the second place it's bullshit.'"

Steve Foreman said he couldn't recall Furie ever explaining to him why he had decided to fashion a new *Jazz Singer* script. But Foreman could hazard a guess why after watching him react to Diamond at meetings: "Every once in a while Neil would make a suggestion that I thought was absolutely invalid, and Sidney would take it as gospel."

As comforting as Furie's solicitous attitude may have been at the time to Neil—who Foreman, like Jerry Kass, saw as "very noncommittal; he was difficult to pin down on anything"—Foreman could survey the ruins of his script and argue that Furie was going too far: "To give somebody who knows nothing about movies, and who's nervous anyway, decision-making power or asking their advice all along seems wrong to me."

It also seemed wrong to Foreman that producer Leider wasn't doing anything about it. "Jerry Leider did everything he could to make me feel like I was really an important part of the team, except for one thing: He did not control Sidney Furie.

"But Jerry was hungry to get a movie done. Who isn't? So I think he was willing to do anything he thought was necessary."

It was with these mixed feelings about *Jazz Singer* that Foreman, barely halfway into the third draft of his screenplay, left the project in February to take on another assignment.

As it turned out, finding a third *Jazz Singer* writer was the least of

Jerry Leider's problems at the time. In March he learned that Neil—who had been talking to the press about costarring with Streisand in a movie version of "You Don't Bring Me Flowers"—might pull out of the project himself. But not because of "Flowers" . . . because a tumor had been found crushing his spinal cord.

Neil had noticed a loss of feeling in his right leg for years, but he hadn't had it checked out. Even in February it was business as usual for him, as he toured the West Coast. But at one of his three end-of-the-month concerts at the Cow Palace in San Francisco, he knew he couldn't ignore the numbness any longer when he slipped onstage and had difficulty getting back up.

Two weeks later, on March 12, Neil checked into Los Angeles' Cedars-Sinai Medical Center for, as a hospital bulletin put it, "routine tests involving an old back problem." Those tests revealed the presence of the benign tumor. Surgery to remove it was scheduled for March 17.

The prospect of undergoing a delicate operation at the age of thirty-seven—"It was really a life-and-death situation," he later asserted—had to give Neil pause for the "vision" of his early demise that he had confessed to his Australian interviewer two years earlier. Indeed, on the night before he was scheduled to go under the knife he claimed he wrote "last letters" to friends and family members, shades of a fatalistic policy he had adhered to years earlier with Tom Catalano and Armin Steiner. Then, before hitting the tour trail, he would leave behind "last" mixing instructions on recordings in progress just in case his plane crashed.

As it turned out, Diamond's nine-hour surgery, performed by Drs. Charles A. Carton and Marshall L. Grode, was a success. That he spent a few extra days in the well-guarded Intensive Care Unit than is usual was not because of any health complications, but because he was safer there from inquisitive fans and hospital employees.

By contrast, the prognosis for *Jazz Singer* was bleak. "We were dead in the water," Jerry Leider said, as he awaited word on whether or not Neil would now choose to, or be physically able to, continue with the project.

A couple of weeks later, the producer got the news he was hoping for. With the aid of a cane, Neil was back on his feet and doing well in physical therapy sessions; mentally, he was his old ambitious, bold self. Leider: "He says, 'Yes, I do want to do the movie; I am serious about it. Let's get the script right.'"

That's all Leider and EMI had to hear. A fall shooting schedule was penciled in, and Leider hired a new writer, Herbert Baker.

The journeyman writer was both a strange and shrewd choice. The son of the late Yiddish singing star, Adele Baker, he had spent a long career specializing in TV melodrama and comedy—in a word, shtick, which hardly seemed to qualify him for modernizing a dated vehicle like *Jazz Singer.* But, the old pro had something that such contemporary whippersnappers as Jerry Kass and Steve Foreman didn't have: malleability.

"He was one of the nicest men in the whole world," said Leider Company executive Burt Nodella. "He'll make nice for everybody: 'Neil, you want this? OK, you got it.' 'Jerry, you want—sure.' 'Sidney, you want this? I'll do it.' I'm not saying he didn't have his own integrity, but he was a pleasant, lovely, very pliable man."

Unlike Steve Foreman, who insisted on writing his own script from scratch when he took the job, Herbie Baker was content to work over Foreman's last draft and pick up the threads from where he and Sid Furie had left off.

He was fast about it, too. By April 30, he had a finished script. Jerry Leider: "Diamond reads it, and the contracts are ready to be signed."

Breathing easier than he had in months about *Jazz Singer,* the producer met for lunch at La Scala in early May with his pal Fantozzi. "We were celebrating the fact that Diamond was coming into [David] Braun's office to sign the contract," he explained.

During the meal, however, Fantozzi received a call from Neil's attorney that suddenly soured their appetites: Neil had done a last-second turnaround and had refused to sign the contract.

"I couldn't understand it, I was confused," Leider said, recalling his immediate reaction to the confounding news. "I had heard these reports that maybe his back was causing him more problems than what was known . . . I just thought that maybe there was some physical or medical reason that he wasn't going to do it."

With Neil seemingly out of the picture once and for all, and another $150,000 due soon to extend his *Jazz Singer* option another year, Leider began weighing the previously unthinkable, pitching *Jazz Singer* to another star. As he rationalized to Fantozzi at the restaurant, "Well, the script is ready, we've got a director." Further emboldening Leider was EMI's immediate vow to carry on with the project.

Within a few days, he phoned International Creative Management agent Joel Dean, who happened to represent another Jewish, Brooklyn-born pop superstar: Barry Manilow.

Leider and Dean had talked several months earlier. Hearing through the grapevine of Neil's ambivalence toward *Jazz Singer,* Dean had asked Leider to see the script, commenting afterward that it seemed an ideal vehicle for Manilow. Learning that Manilow was still interested in the project, Leider decided to talk him up to EMI executives Barry Spikings and John Kohn at the Cannes Film Festival later that month.

After screening in Cannes a cassette of Manilow's performances that Leider had brought along, Spikings and Kohn pronounced themselves as impressed with the pop star as the producer. Leider returned to Los Angeles and made a firm offer to Manilow through Dean. That night, Rona Barrett reported the development on television.

Satisfied that he had weathered his last *Jazz Singer* storm for a while, Leider resolved to have a relaxing weekend at home with friends. On Sunday, however, a long-distance phone call changed that.

On the other end of the line was Tony Fantozzi. He informed the startled producer that the day before, Neil—whose back, apparently, was just fine—had had yet *another* change of heart about *Jazz Singer* and had decided suddenly to jet to London to talk contract personally with EMI chairman Bernie Delfont. The talks had gone so well, moreover, that Neil had committed his signature to a *Jazz Singer* contract!

The next day, Leider had the extremely embarrassing task of withdrawing his offer to Barry Manilow.

"It was a very hysterical situation," he said.

·20·
ACTION

With Tony Fantozzi and David Braun's help, Neil cut a very good deal for himself with Bernie Delfont. For starring in *Jazz Singer,* which he agreed to begin filming no later than January 1, 1980, pending his final approval of the costars and script, he was to receive $1 million, against 10 percent of the movie's gross. For recording his soundtrack album for Capitol, he was to get a cool $3 million guarantee.

Even though Diamond had embarrassed Jerry Leider by barging back into the *Jazz Singer* picture, the producer claimed to be happy about the end result: "I finally got what I wanted—Neil Diamond."

In the fall, Diamond, Furie, Leider and Leider's assistant, Joel Morwood, had a series of brainstorming meetings. At a Sunday meeting hosted by Neil in his Malibu home, he premiered two of the tunes he'd written for the movie, the anthemlike rocker "America," and the ballad "Love on the Rocks," the latter penned with Gilbert Becaud. At the meetings, Neil proved to be a fount of script ideas, including the suggestion that a Mafia angle be written in, giving the impression that his final OK of the script wasn't yet imminent. Furie and Herb Baker continued rewriting.

In the costar discussions, Neil had no argument from Leider and Furie on his choice for the actor to play Jess Robin's father, Cantor Rabinovitch: Laurence Olivier. "The idea of Olivier was something that we all talked about as being the ideal," Leider explained. After EMI president Barry Spikings agreed to spend the extra money, Leider, who had been discussing the role with the lower-priced likes of Herschel Bernardi and José Ferrer, made the pitch to Olivier. By the end of November, Olivier had accepted, for $1 million, the same salary as Neil.

The type of actress best suited to play Molly, Jess Robin's *shiksa* (non-Jewish) agent/love interest, was a matter of debate between Diamond and Furie, however. "Sidney wanted Lucie Arnaz to play the part," claimed Joyce Webb, Furie's script supervisor. "Neil wanted somebody prettier. Sidney said, 'But you shouldn't have a beautiful face. You should have somebody interesting and cute, somebody who is real and warm . . . Also it looks bad if you have a very plain wife and you go and fall for the pretty face. It has a different connotation to falling for somebody who you have this warm, interesting relationship with. It makes for a much better story flow. You're going to have more sympathy for your character.'"

Diamond, however, apparently won out; Jerry Leider began talking to several other actresses, including Jacqueline Bisset.

In November, Neil got his way on another key request: that he sing—and his band play, for triple scale—all his *Jazz Singer* songs live during filming, rather than lip-synching to a playback, a movie custom. Sid Furie realized the wisdom of this request when he tested Neil at an MGM soundstage, where he was rehearsing with his band for a handful of December concerts. "He loses about 30 percent of his energy if he is not putting the song out," commented assistant director Bob Webb, who observed Diamond.

Even with this progress being made toward an end-of-the-year start on *Jazz Singer,* by mid-December it was white-knuckle time yet again. The reason: Neil had still not given his final OK to the script. Further serving to cloud his intentions concerning *The Jazz Singer* was the release of his new album, "September Morn." Diamond had originally intended to use at least two of the LP's songs, including the title tune, in the movie.

Feeling that decisive action was needed to prevent Neil from walking out on the project once and for all, Leider recommended to EMI in mid-December that Sid Furie be replaced. It was he, the producer had decided, who had to shoulder the blame for the script fiasco. But EMI elected to stand by Furie, no doubt influenced by other persuasive considerations—his apparent rapport with Neil, for example, as well as the chaos that would result from replacing such a key figure at such a key moment in the project.

Leider felt, however, something had to be done to propel Neil to the *Jazz Singer* starting blocks. So a few days before Christmas, the producer, with the blessing of the studio, hired screenwriter Arthur Laurents, of *West Side Story* fame, to work his magic on the script—at the superstar salary of $50,000 a week. Leider: "It was a matter of taking the existing screenplay and seeing if it could be simplified, made more linear, more depth put into it, clarity."

Coming in cold to the project, Laurents, however, turned in a rewrite in early January that left Leider and everyone else on the project cold. It was scrapped.

By then, however, Neil, at the absolute point of no return, had decided, once and for all, to plow ahead with *Jazz Singer,* even with an unfinished script. "Furie said the writer is going to be on this picture, that 'We're going to rewrite the picture every day,'" recalled E. Darrell Hallenbeck, the executive production manager.

Jazz Singer began filming on Monday, January 7, in Maricopa, a two-hour drive north of Los Angeles.

That morning, Jerry Leider arrived at Diamond's Beverly Hills house in a limo. The producer's solicitousness didn't end when they got out of the car in Maricopa, however. After laying his eyes on a shooting schedule production manager Hallenbeck had put out for the first three weeks, Leider panicked: *"What happens if Neil sees that?"* "So we had to run down to the set and bring back all the schedules and tear 'em up," Hallenbeck recalled.

Director Furie took a similarly coddling approach with Neil when it came time to shoot one of the scenes that had brought them to the small town—Jess Robin's audition for a country music club proprietor, which takes place after he walks out on his girlfriend and career. While Neil chose to improvise the dialogue with actor Hugh Gillin, Furie let the cameras roll. Out of that came the addition to the *Jazz Singer* sound track of "You Are My Sunshine," which Gillin suggested, ad lib, that Neil perform. (As it turned out, Neil didn't know all the words to the song, and the improvised scene had to be reshot.)

Diamond had to be pleased when he viewed his first dailies the next night. "It was wonderful; the music was up," said assistant editor Eric Sears. Lest, however, Sears get the impression that Neil was anything but a film neophyte, Neil revealed his naiveté by asking, "What is that little board doing at the beginning of every shot?" So Sears and his boss, supervising film editor Frank Urioste, had to explain that the "little board," the clapper stick, was a film editor's synchronization and cataloguing tool. "Ohhhhhh," Neil said.

Diamond kept firing questions as filming continued in Los Angeles later that week. "By the end of the first week he knew every person's job on the set, and their level of responsibility, and he could address them on that level," recalled Bob Webb. The veteran assistant director was thoroughly impressed: "There are actors of twenty years that don't know as much as Neil knew the first week about a film company."

One of the questions Neil asked of Sid Furie at the running of dailies was fated to have a major impact on the production. After watching how difficult it was for him, an undisciplined actor, to "match"—that is, to maintain the same tone of voice and the same expression from shot to shot in a given scene—he asked, "Sidney, is there any way that you can get every cut you need from one take?"

Furie replied that there was: the use of multiple cameras, simultaneously rolling from various angles. Although the multiple-camera approach was used almost exclusively for musical or big production numbers because of its high cost, the time and difficulty involved in setting up the cameras, and the havoc it caused the lighting people, the apparently eager-to-appease director offered to implement the method immediately for Neil's benefit. Recalled a dismayed Darrell Hallenbeck: "We would have a shot of Neil and Olivier walking down a corridor—

we'd have five cameras lined up. What are they shooting? Two people walking from here to there!

"Sidney would laugh about it. He thought it was very funny."

Even assistant director Bob Webb, who approved of the multiple-camera method under the circumstances, allowed that it was an "absolute departure" from normal filming.

Soon afterward, those words would serve as an apt description of the *Jazz Singer* experience as a whole.

The first major controversy on the set came with the abrupt and stunning dismissal of Diamond's leading lady, Deborah Raffin, a week into the production, before she had even had a chance to face the cameras.

The way script supervisor Joyce Webb saw it, the blond, attractive actress, who had received good notices for her role as a truck driver in the Jerry Leider–produced TV movie *Willin'*, got lost in the *Jazz Singer* script shuffle:

"Deborah, all done up in her makeup and all ready to go, comes in for the first rehearsal. And Neil and the two or three guys in the black group are there—it's a backstage scene—and everybody's ad-libbing . . . 'Hey, Molly!' And she froze because she was waiting for her cue to say the lines she had learned . . . 'He's not supposed to say, "Hey, Molly," he's supposed to say "Hi there, Sweetheart."'"

"And they kept trying, but she couldn't work that way and didn't want to work that way."

Neil, Webb added, didn't speak his dissatisfaction, "but it was readily apparent he was not pleased with what he was seeing."

Raffin got the message. Said property master Vincent "Bud" Shelton, who had outfitted the actress with various personal effects before the ill-fated rehearsal: "She came walking by me, she laid the watch and ring in my hand and said, 'That's the end of me, Buddy.'"

A few minutes later, the property master claimed he encountered an addled Sid Furie, who said, "He [Neil] doesn't like her. I told you this was going to happen . . . I should have cast Lucie in the beginning."

The January 17 issue of *Daily Variety* carried word of Raffin's departure, and the report that she would be paid her entire $250,000 salary. "Evolving conceptual changes" in the script, Leider and Furie were quoted as saying, led Raffin to "relinquish" her role. The article went on to report that the search was now on for a singing costar, with Liza Minnelli among the candidates.

Several days later, nonsinging Lucie Arnaz was signed to play Molly. "Welcome to the *mishpuchah* [family]," Neil wrote her in a note accompanying a bouquet of flowers. "Nobody is more thrilled than I am."

The hiring of Lucie Arnaz promised to be an expensive proposition. Because she was now contracted to appear in the Broadway musical *They're Playing Our Song* through February, Jerry Leider and the EMI brass had no choice but to take the seventy-person production to her for a couple of weeks. It was a decision that astonished production manager Hallenbeck: "You . . . never move a company across the country and back . . . That was insanity, I thought."

While preparations began for the move, filming continued in Los Angeles, still minus a completed screenplay.

"There were days when I did not even know where we were shooting tomorrow," recalled assistant director Bob Webb, who was in charge of posting the next day's crew call. "A lot of times, it went out TBA: To Be Announced."

"There are rewrites on every script," said script supervisor Joyce Webb, the first assistant director's wife. "But nothing that was written in the *Jazz Singer* script was being shot; it was all new."

Even Herbie Baker's rewrites, which came down from the office every morning, Joyce Webb explained, were seldom touched: "Neil would look at it and Sidney would look at it, and then they'd totally rewrite it . . . in the dressing room or maybe in the corner of the set." When they were finished, sometimes not until 3 P.M., Neil would personally hand her their rewrite—sometimes scribbled in his hand on the back of the script pages—and Webb would have the material typed up and distributed.

Even after this tortuous road to his daily late-afternoon date before the cameras, Neil was not above scrapping his rewrite of the rewrite at the last second, and improvising the scene instead.

This chaotic method of working, not surprisingly, kept producer Leider and the EMI brass in a high state of anxiety. Recalled Dennis Brown, EMI's then-senior production executive: "The concern was there really wasn't a script . . . [So, while] the film was being shot, and people were going to work every day, it wasn't possible to say, 'All right, we shot two pages today, and we've got a hundred more pages to finish the film.'"

Furie, Brown said, was always unflappable when confronted with questions about his progress, or lack of progress, on the script, and, thus, on the film's production: "He kept saying, 'I have it in my head. I have it in my head.'"

Amid the ever-shifting sands of the *Jazz Singer* script, there were a few scenes that were shot pretty much as they had been written by Herb

Baker. It wasn't a coincidence that Laurence Olivier was featured in each of them. Neil was as deferring to his costar, whom he would later say "became like a grandfather to me, a *zeide*" on the production, as Leider, Furie & Company were to him. (Diamond demonstrated *his* solicitousness toward Olivier not only in refraining from tampering with the dialogue, but also in requesting that his and Olivier's motor homes on the MGM lot be switched so that the ailing actor, who was having difficulty walking, would have thirty fewer feet to navigate to the set.)

Still, ad-libbing of a sort did go on in at least one of the Diamond-Olivier scenes—the important deathbed reconciliation between Jess Robin and his father, later scrapped, that Furie intended for the end of the movie. Neil was so nervous speaking his lines to Olivier that Furie had to redo his closeup. This time, instead of looking at his venerable costar, Neil gazed at the pillow on which his dialogue had been pasted.

In mid-February, the move to New York was made. The change of scenery didn't help; trouble continued to stalk the production.

On the planned first day of shooting, at a fifth-floor Manhattan recording studio that, ironically, had been rented for the Los Angeles "Love on the Rocks" studio scene, a gaffer made the mistake of hooking up some lights too close to the automatic sprinklers. Before they could be turned off, members of Neil's band, still holding their instruments, were standing in four inches of water.

"It was one of the biggest screw-ups I have ever been associated with," said assistant director Bob Webb, shuddering at the memory of the episode. "We have our hot boxes where we plug in our lights. Everything's hot. And they're standing in there. They could have been electrocuted."

Webb yelled frantically for the musicians to get out of the water. Meanwhile, "The director saw me yelling at the musicians and thought I was losing control of the set." One heated word led to another and, before long, Webb found himself fired.

As he was collecting himself over lunch downstairs, Webb was visited by Diamond, who had been standing in safety in the control room when the sprinklers opened up. "Nobody leaves this show—they'll have to go ten rounds with me," said Neil, suddenly sounding like John Wayne.

According to prop master Buddy Shelton, sitting at another table with Lucie Arnaz, Diamond delivered the same message to him. Shelton added: "Lucie's saying, 'Jesus, what a bunch of fruitcakes this is turning out to be!'"

A few days later, it was Neil's turn to take a walk. The setting was Trax, a subterranean Manhattan club in which Furie was planning to shoot a Jess Robin Los Angeles performance scene. Bob Webb: "We were ready to shoot. Neil came in, about twelve. He finds the extras are there, he rehearses a little bit, and he doesn't like the acoustics."

During the break that followed, Webb continued, Neil came up to him and said "I'll be right back." Then, still in wardrobe, he led his band onto his bus, which had been parked in front of the club, and drove off.

He was not seen the rest of the day.

"And what happened after that was the beginning of the end [for Furie]," Bob Webb said, referring to the suddenly ominous presence on the set of EMI, in the persons of John Kohn, Dennis Brown, and, from London, company president Barry Spikings.

EMI had cast a shadow on the production once before, in the early days of the shooting. Neil, who was having a hard enough time reining in his own anxieties, didn't want to deal with theirs. Bob Webb: "[Neil's] comment was, 'Back off and let Sidney and me make the film' . . . And I want to tell you," Webb added, "EMI disappeared."

The executives continued their hand-wringing, however—they were just quieter about it. One of them, John Kohn, a writer, even joined the jittery producer, nonwriter Jerry Leider, in discreetly helping Herbie Baker rewrite his script.

Meanwhile, senior production executive Dennis Brown did what he could to chart the progress of the production without a finished shooting script. What he found out wasn't very comforting: "The film that was being shot . . . was not coming up very long. So we knew, as an example, after two weeks of shooting we only had x number of minutes of film, and it should have been quite a bit more."

Still, even with the haunting thought that Sid Furie wasn't going to get *Jazz Singer* to the celluloid temple on time, with millions of dollars of advance bookings at stake, EMI kept its collective mouth shut. Until New York, when Spikings joined the party.

Spikings' first order of business was finding out where they stood with *Jazz Singer*. That meant getting a copy of the script, what there was of it. The road led past the production office and copies of the decimated Herb Baker script and eventually to script supervisor Joyce Webb. "The production manager called me—it was like nine o'clock one night," she recalled. "And he said, 'We're just realizing that you have the only copy of the scenes that have been shot. Where is it?'" Webb turned it over.

Spikings then met with the other EMI executives and production manager Darrell Hallenbeck. "We had half a script," Hallenbeck recalled. "And we had to guess how many days it was going to take to finish it, and then multiply it by $50,000 a day, whatever the figure was, to see where we were budget-wise." The exercise revealed that *Jazz*

Singer, originally budgeted at $8 million, was going to cost $5 million more, at least.

Barry Spikings then did the shrewd thing: He met one-on-one with Diamond, who was suffering through a bad cold, at his Plaza Hotel suite. Dennis Brown: "It was to make him aware of the situation and of our concern." Joyce Webb heard that the Englishman pulled no punches as he buttonholed the bottom-line businessman in Neil: "[He] laid down the law to him—he and Sidney either got a script and finished it by a certain date or he wasn't going to have a picture."

Confident that Neil would be spouting no more back-off dictums, Spikings confronted Sid Furie and requested a completed script. Furie delivered one on February 29, just after finishing the two weeks of New York filming. "You ought to be thrilled that you have it," he was said to have told Spikings in a phone conversation.

According to Bob Webb, who later discussed the call with Furie, Spikings then gave the director a "choice": He could either agree to finish *The Jazz Singer* in five weeks, or he could leave the project. According to several accounts, the conversation ended abruptly with an angry exchange of words.

The next day, Saturday, March 1, Sid Furie looked back and didn't see Neil behind him any more. That's when he was informed, via another phone call, that he was being relieved of his directorial duties. "They had me call," said Jerry Leider.

"I think Neil was relieved," the producer continued. "I think he obviously felt that the situation could not continue. There was so much tension, there was so much uncertainty . . . there was so much shifting around."

For his part, Sid Furie was said to be disappointed—in Diamond. "He felt that, perhaps, Neil could have stood a little stronger," Joyce Webb said. "Sidney knew where he was going. He wasn't in a mess . . . And he would say . . . 'I'm trying to keep Neil happy and get a story that he likes, and something that I can live with as a product.'"

Sid Furie's firing was announced to the press that weekend. Not surprisingly, Hollywood columnist Marilyn Beck saw fit to write about it.

By then, Beck had become a serious thorn in the side of the production with her *Singer* zingers. Among them: the news of Deborah Raffin's exit; the report of a tiff between actress Catlin Adams (Rifka, Jess Robin's wife) and Sid Furie; and the titillating report that Diamond was spending much of his time on the set speaking to Barbra Streisand over the phone, presumably in a quest for advice. The items greatly upset Diamond and infuriated Furie, and led to the removal of one crew member suspecting of leaking information.

Beck's March 6 item was the juiciest yet: "There's a chance Neil Diamond's *The Jazz Singer* will never see release or completion." The columnist went on to report that while a search was being made for a new director, Neil was talking about starting up the project from scratch, EMI was talking about aborting it, and Jerry Leider was investigating the possibility of getting a Screen Actors Guild waiver which would allow him to suspend paychecks until a decision was made on *Jazz Singer*'s fate.

The ball was in the EMI-Leider-Diamond court, and the next day, Barry Spikings fired it back in a press release: "The entire production crew of more than fifty people, as well as the cast, will remain on full salary during our brief hiatus. Filming will resume immediately upon the appointment of a new director, which will be announced shortly by producer Jerry Leider.

"My enthusiasm, and that of my company, for the movie continues unabated. Neil Diamond will emerge as a major motion picture star. During the hiatus, Neil is rehearsing and prerecording new numbers for the second half of the picture.

"*The Jazz Singer* is our major Christmas release in 1980. It has a prestigious opening at the Ziegfeld Theatre in New York, the Cinerama Dome in Los Angeles, and over fifty other major cities throughout the United States and Canada starting December 19."

Several days later, another press release went out announcing that Richard Fleischer had been hired as the new *Jazz Singer* director.

Jazz Singer was not the first picture that the sixty-three-year-old Fleischer, whose credits included 1954's *20,000 Leagues Under the Sea* and 1967's *Dr. Doolittle,* had been asked to salvage. In 1971 he replaced John Huston on the George C. Scott starrer, *The Last Run,* and just a few months earlier, he stepped into *Ashanti* after Richard Serafian was fired.

These rescues had helped earn the son of animator Max Fleischer a reputation as a movie doctor of sorts. Indeed, he had a prescription for taking over a film in midstream: "You get in there and you have to be absolutely dead certain what you're going to do, and you restore everyone's confidence that this ship is going to sail without hitting the rocks and reefs, and it's going to go at full speed."

Going with the nautical imagery a little further, Fleischer (who, coincidentally, was a codirector of the naval epic *Tora! Tora! Tora!*) could see the *Jazz Singer* battleship listing badly as he reviewed the film Sidney Furie had shot. Nowhere were the movie's problems more evident to him than in the performances of Diamond and Olivier.

"The problem was that Olivier, being a very experienced actor, would naturally react very differently than a completely inexperienced actor when they're faced with the same situation of a director who isn't having contact with them," Fleischer said. "What happens is the experienced actor will go way overboard, because he's on his own and he's doing something to help himself . . . milk all the drama . . .

"And the inexperienced actor will go in the opposite direction and say, 'Well, I don't know how to get the drama out of this scene, so the best thing to do is to become as inconspicuous as possible.' And you could see Neil playing under, way under, down, down, down, down, all the time, until, finally, toward the last few days' dailies, you could hardly hear him speak, he was underplaying so much. It was just a mumble."

At Fleischer's first meeting with Neil, Neil confirmed what the director had suspected: "He felt a lack of contact with the director. He felt the director really wasn't talking to him." In turn, Fleischer explained to Neil what he had seen in his and Olivier's performances, vowing that it was a situation he intended to correct.

"It was love at first sight," Fleischer said of the get-acquainted session. "We saw eye to eye on everything."

Meanwhile, Fleischer saw eye to eye on the still-sorry script with EMI's Kohn and producer Leider, who had become full-time writers without portfolio on the project in the wake of Herb Baker's departure. "It needed considerable work," said Fleischer, who immediately resigned himself to the Furie method of rewriting as he went along, although vowing to keep a couple of days ahead at all times.

Production resumed on *The Jazz Singer* on Monday, March 17. The first scene shot was the "Robert E. Lee" musical sequence inside Molly's (Lucie Arnaz) Venice apartment. "That whole sequence was so up and lively and bubbly," EMI executive Dennis Brown recalled. "I think some of us had the impression, 'My god, things have changed, it's turned around' . . . [even though] it was the same sequence that Sid was going to shoot."

Meanwhile, the appearance alone of the quiet, soft-spoken yet authoritative Dick Fleischer seemed to have a galvanzing effect. "When he arrives on the set General MacArthur arrives on the set," supervising film editor Frank Urioste said. "He's the commander."

Ironically, "commander" just happened to be the word Fleischer used to describe Diamond as he watched him drill his band members for the first time: "He knew exactly what notes each should play and how to play them. 'No, do it this way,' and bang, they'd do it that way . . . Each one is an artist, but it's a little army, and he's the commander. He's more in command, or appears to be more in command, than even I am with my own crew. I don't talk to my crew in quite that kind of almost military manner as he does with his band."

That observation led Fleischer to wonder if the *Jazz Singer* set would be big enough for two commanders. Neil's negative reaction to one of Fleischer's first decrees—that his actors not attend the running of dailies, a long-held policy of his—didn't exactly assuage his fear. To avert a clash right off the bat, the director offered a compromise: "OK, I'll run them with you, but I'll have to run them separate from my regular running with the editor, the producer, and whatever staff should see the film." "Fine," Neil responded.

So the director screened the dailies from the "Robert E. Lee" scene for Neil. As he rolled the film, it became obvious to him that Neil had more than his own performance in mind. "I was watching the screen but I was also watching him," Fleischer recalled. "He was looking at me most of the time; he was not looking at the screen very much. And he was probing . . . He asked me questions all the way through—why did I do that, why did this happen, 'Is it right that I should pick up that thing at that time?'

"I had my answers. They were very clear and very precise." Fleischer noted that Neil seemed pleased.

The next night the director dutifully knocked on Neil's dressing room door and announced, "Neil, time to see the dailies." This time, Diamond replied, "Oh, forget it."

"He never asked to see another day's work," Fleischer said, chuckling.

With one "devilish" exception—Diamond's refusal to produce a song lineup as Fleischer had requested for his concert segments at the Pantages Theater in Hollywood, and, at intermission, his decision to change the order of tunes that the director had set his thirteen cameras up for in the second segment (Fleischer: "I said, 'Will you send word back to Mr. Diamond that he is doing the numbers exactly as we had planned'")—Neil was a perfect angel for the rest of the production. "He was so cooperative and enthusiastic," Fleischer marveled. "He would be there to say good morning to me. And this is quite the opposite, I understand, from the way it was before I got on the picture, [when] he would not show up for several hours, [and] he was quite a bad boy all the way through.

"He even showed up at the scenes he wasn't called. He would just come around to watch the shooting . . . We just had a great time."

Helping make the experience a positive one for the director was what he felt was Neil's rock-steady performance in front of the camera. "I was always surprised by the quality of the readings, and the performances he was giving," he said. "I never felt any awkwardness or amateur quality. I thought it was an excellent performance for a nonactor. I think it was a good performance for an actor."

Under the now thoroughly upbeat circumstances it seemed understandable that the one scene Neil had a great deal of trouble with was the "Jerusalem" studio sequence in which he was supposed to become a raving maniac, chewing out his band and then, in the control booth, blasting Lucie Arnaz. "I couldn't get him up to steel in that scene," Dick

Fleischer said. "I did everything to get him to blow up. He would come in and he wasn't convincing. He really wasn't angry. I said, 'You've got to really be furious. I don't care if you forget your lines because of your anger. That's what I want.' So he said, 'All right, I'll try it again.' He was trying to work himself up by showing some impatience.

"I was waiting for him to start [again] in the other room. I'm in a soundproof room, I couldn't hear what was going on. And suddenly I saw Neil go berserk. He knocked down all the microphones, kicked over the music stands. I saw all the guys scatter . . . while he was throwing music all over the place, and chairs. And I grabbed the microphone and said, 'Action, action, action! Roll the cameras!'

"He stormed out, and he came back in and, boy, was he steaming. He did the scene [with the band] beautifully, [and] he just ripped her all to pieces, and then slammed out of the studio. I said, 'Cut.'"

By then, Fleischer continued, Neil's band was in hysterics. The director walked into the studio and, surveying the thousands of dollars of damage Neil had done to the expensive microphones, asked him what had happened.

"Well, I went to my boys and I said, 'Play me something that will make me very angry,'" Neil replied. "They played me a Barry Manilow song."

Toward the end of the filming Dick Fleischer finally put a question to Neil that had been on his mind ever since Neil quietly took his first order from him. "I said, 'You are a person who is in complete control of his own career and his own organization. I've watched you with your band, and you're a tough tyrant. And nobody can talk to you about anything. So how is it that you let me tell you what to do? Does it ever rub you the wrong way?'

"And he said, 'No, never—it's the easiest thing in the world for me.' And I said, 'Well, why is that?' He said, 'Because you love my music.'"

Those words made Fleischer think back to the first time he had played the songs Diamond had written for *The Jazz Singer*, before filming had resumed. At the time he discovered that two of them, "Jerusalem" and "On the Robert E. Lee," weren't being used. "Is there any reason why?" he had asked Neil, to which Neil had replied, "No, there's just no room for them." "Well, I'll *find* room for them," the director had stated, which is what he proceeded to do. Apparently, it had been another one of his right moves.

Lest it seem that the feelings of peace and love that had seemingly enveloped *The Jazz Singer* set were solely a result of the Diamond-Fleischer rapport, however, the truth was that costars Laurence Olivier and Lucie Arnaz played a supporting role.

Fleischer learned of Neil's reverence for Olivier in their first meeting, when Fleischer asked Neil if he had had any training as an actor. "Yes," Neil replied. "Really?" Fleischer said, surprised. "Who was your teacher?" To which Neil answered, "Laurence Olivier." Fleischer: "He had such admiration for Olivier that he was hanging on every word Olivier said and was trying to mimic him in every way possible . . . And it turned out, too, that Olivier was very, very fond of Neil; they got along beautifully."

Fleischer added that in Arnaz, Diamond had another actor that he liked and was learning from. "She's very much the character that she plays in the picture," he said. "She was supporting him; she would laugh at his jokes. But sincerely; it wasn't any form of flattery . . . And she is a dynamite personality; she enjoys doing everything so much . . . Neil caught the spirit from her."

Their easy rapport was such that they were able to improvise their way through rewrites of several of their scenes in Fleischer's office before facing the cameras, as the director committed the new lines to paper. Then, "when we'd get out on the set they'd just fall into the scene, without any problem at all," Fleischer said. "We'd taken out all of the problems."

The same could be said in conclusion about the entire *Jazz Singer* production under Richard Fleischer. The only problem that arose for the movie during March and April, in fact, occurred off the *Singer* set, when Laurence Olivier, who had finished his role, reportedly badmouthed the production. "It was damned embarrassing enough to do once," he was quoted as saying. "But then they switched directors and asked me to go through the whole silly thing again. That makes it doubly embarrassing. It's trash."

(A few days later, Olivier issued a statement categorically denying he had uttered the reported slams.)

Filming was completed on schedule in Venice, California, on April 25. EMI celebrated by renting a soundstage on the MGM lot and throwing a giant wrap party, attended by a bevy of Hollywood types—agents, film executives, and stars, including Lucie Arnaz' mother, Lucille Ball. For entertainment, several members of the production crew put on a skit, Jerry Leider delivered some one-liners, and several scenes from *Jazz Singer* were screened. Then, to the cheers of the hundreds in attendance, Neil and band took the stage.

It was a performance that almost wasn't. After agreeing to sing, Neil suddenly declared at the last minute that he had decided to sit it out instead. "He was very nervous," recalled EMI's Dennis Brown. Once he stepped on the stage, however, Neil was his usual showman self, performing a full concert. "People still talk to me about that wrap party," said Brown, smiling.

As he had done on *Jonathan Livingston Seagull,* Neil dispensed various gifts. To Jerry Leider, who tenaciously saw *Jazz Singer* through its soap opera fits and starts, he sent a case of Dom Perignon. The producer reciprocated with a set of William Shakespeare's plays that he had turned up.

"Now that you've done *The Jazz Singer,* here's your next challenge," he told Neil.

While Richard Fleischer worked on his first cut of *The Jazz Singer* in May, Leider oversaw the production of a twenty-five-minute clip for presentation to key movie distributors and exhibitors at the Cannes Film Festival that month. "If you saw that twenty-five minutes you'd sell your house to buy some stock in the movie; it was fantastic," said supervising film editor Frank Urioste. Enlivening the clip was the presence of no fewer than five of the eleven songs Diamond had written for the movie.

"And then we went to Cannes," Jerry Leider said. "We had a special screening . . . fabulous response . . . and then we took all the foreign buyers to lunch. They didn't know that Neil and Lucie were there. Took the buyers all to a lovely restaurant on the bus, all sat down, had some jackets for them. 'Ladies and gentlemen, Neil Diamond, Lucie Arnaz, and Richard Fleischer.' Everyone then circulated; it was just fabulous.

"And the guy from the *Hollywood Reporter* wrote a story on it. And that was telexed to us that night, midnight, and I went up and got it. And Neil and Marcia were in their room already, and I said, 'Can I come up, I want to read you something.' I read him that article. It was our first review. It was the first positive thing said about the movie in the trade press."

Actually, the article was an interview with Leider, in which the producer, displaying a conveniently short memory, jauntily hyped the filming as "a piece of cake." Of Diamond, Leider said: "He was always on time, and cooperative, likable to the crew, knew his lines, concerned. Just the opposite of all those stories that were circulated about him at the time. How do those things get started?"

In the afterglow of Cannes, postproduction work on *The Jazz Singer* proceeded smoothly. As in the preproduction and production phases, Neil's hand could be felt everywhere—even where it hadn't touched, such as in the work of scorer Leonard Rosenman.

Rosenman, a two-time Oscar winner, had been hired by Richard Fleischer to compose incidental music for the *Singer* soundtrack. At least one person on the movie, veteran supervising music editor Bill Saracino, was surprised that the material Rosenman turned in was entirely original, containing not a hint of a Diamond melody. "I found that a little disturbing," Saracino confessed. "I would have liked to have heard more of the Neil Diamond sound and more of the Neil Diamond themes." So unusual was Rosenman's musical tack that one was apt to assume that Diamond, to remove any possibility of another scoring controversy, had stipulated that Rosenman could not draw on any of his melodies.

Not so, Rosenman said, however, adding that it was his idea to compose completely fresh material. "I felt that a really dramatic score would contrast with and thus bring out Neil Diamond's musical contribution," he explained.

The high-wire act that Neil's producer Bob Gaudio, music mixer Ron Hitchcock, and remote music recording mixer Andy Bloch had to perform with their tasks, however, had totally been orchestrated by Neil. Months before he even began *Jazz Singer,* he informed Hitchcock he was thinking of doing a musical and asked, "Do you think we can do anything *special* on the screen with the music?" Needless to say, Hitchcock speculated that they could, even though he had never worked on a film before. That something "special" was fated to consist of the live recording of Diamond's *Singer* songs, and, in the postproduction phase, the cutting of the original multitrack tapes to the edited film, a nervy, unheard-of method of working. "We probably saved five generations of transfers of the audio by doing that," Hitchcock explained, "the result being this sparkle in the picture's sound."

The recording team's reward came shortly before the film's premiere, when Neil asked for a private screening of the movie with the finished sound track at the Samuel Goldwyn Theatre. After two reels, Neil, the only one in the audience, got up, said, "We don't have to play the whole film; that's the best sound I have ever heard," and walked out.

Diamond was also pleased with the final edit of *The Jazz Singer.* That was hardly a surprise, since, in Richard Fleischer's words, "I think the film as it stands reflects what Neil's concept of it was."

Neil's concept. For even a script specialist like Joyce Webb, it had been all but impossible to draw a bead on Diamond's script game plan as he reworked individual scenes. With a finished product at last, however, it was a simple matter to gauge his input on the *Jazz Singer* story by charting the script's evolution from the time Jerry Leider produced his original *Jazz Singer* synopsis in October of 1977.

Among the noteworthy changes in the script that had occurred over the years:

- *Shiksa* Molly finds new life as Jess Robin's permanent lady, instead of being killed off in an airplane crash after giving birth to their child.
- First wife Rivka performs a permanent fade in Robin's life, instead of reappearing at the end of the film as an accomplished career woman, and likely recipient of Jess' future affections.

• Jess Robin ends the movie not at his father's deathbed, but in a blaze of concert glory, with his father bopping along in the audience.

Substitute his show-biz savvy second wife, Marcia, for Molly; his *hamish* first wife, Jay, for Rivka, and Neil himself for Jess Robin, and one could hazard a guess that the method to Neil's script madness was in approaching the story as he approached songs like "I Am . . . I Said"— as an exercise in would-be autobiography. (Indeed, screenwriter Stephen Foreman recalled Neil rebelling against a reference in one *JS* draft having to do with an extramarital affair of Robin's: "I was later told it was because he didn't want anybody believing that he would do that sort of thing as a human being.")

There was an obvious psychological benefit to this approach: Neophyte Neil didn't have to burden himself by stepping out of character. He could just play himself . . . rather, the version of "Neil Diamond" he was marketing to his public.

"Love on the Rocks," the first single from *Jazz Singer,* was released in October. The next month, the soundtrack album hit the stores. Both shot onto the charts, helped by a spate of interviews Neil did with the press.

"The movie is today, even though I wear a yarmulke for the first half," he told *Daily Variety.*

"I know I get zingers from this movie, private little chills that harken back to my own life," he told the *Chicago Tribune.*

"For me, this movie was the ultimate bar mitzvah," he told the *Los Angeles Times.*

The only party pooper of the lot of reporters was the *Los Angeles Times'* Lee Grant, who asked Diamond about *Jazz Singer's* various reported troubles during filming. "They weren't really in touch with it," Neil said of the press.

The Jazz Singer received its world premiere December 17 at the annual fund-raiser of the Women's Guild of Cedars-Sinai Medical Center at Plitt's Century City. A tuxedoed Diamond, flanked by three bodyguards in the wake of John Lennon's assassination eight days earlier, was there with Marcia on his arm. So were daughters Marjorie and Elyn, son Jesse, and Neil's parents, who were celebrating their forty-second wedding anniversary a day early. (Rose and Kieve had viewed the film for the first time two weeks earlier, making liberal use of the box of Kleenex that their son had provided. "My father loved the idea that Laurence Olivier was playing his part," Neil said at the time. "He thought it an excellent choice.")

The next day, Neil and producer Leider flew to New York for the local premiere of *Jazz Singer* on December 19. Their spirits were still soaring over the enthusiastic response the movie had received at the Plitt, which duplicated the boffo sneak previews earlier in Seattle, Houston, and Costa Mesa, California.

But by the time the projector rolled at the Ziegfeld Theatre, however, Jerry Leider's feet, at least, were back on the ground. The reason was that he had happened into the lobby of the MGM building on Fifty-fifth Street the night before as the New York press screening let out, and he had overheard two critics talking contemptuously of the film. "Despicable!" he heard one of them exclaim about the scarf Neil had worn across his shoulders for a portion of his concert segment. "Imagine that white scarf as if it were a *talis!*"

"My heart sunk," Leider confessed. "It was the first indication I had that the press was gonna come down heavy on the movie."

·21·
DOWNSHIFT

As Jerry Leider feared, most of the *Jazz Singer* reviews that followed the preview were pans. "A vanity production from the word go," dismissed "Cart." in *Variety.* "*The Jazz Singer* is so shameless, its gall so super-abundant that treating it with the contumely it probably deserves is impossible," wrote Kenneth Turan in *New West.*

As the movie's reason for being, Neil was the target of much of the criticism. Among his detractors were the *Chicago Sun Times'* Roger Ebert and the *Chicago Tribune*'s Gene Siskel, cohosts of TV's "At the Movies." "He never comes alive in this movie," complained Ebert. "He's so closed up in himself he can rarely look the other actors in the eye." Agreed Siskel: "He hasn't done anything here. He's just played Neil Diamond."

(One pan that was never broadcast was uttered by Diamond's former partner, Jack Packer, whose special perspective on *The Jazz Singer* was acknowledged by Diamond himself in 1980 when he told a British interviewer, "I remember knowing a boy who wanted to make it in pop music, just like Jess Robin." Said cantor's son Packer of Neil's performance: "When I heard him singing 'Hava Nagila' out of tempo, and pronouncing the words like he was Yugoslavian . . . I mean really weird . . . and talking just like he talked when he was a kid, I couldn't stand watching it. It was assaulting my eyes and my ears.")

Girded as he was for some bad notices, Jerry Leider admitted, "We were *not* prepared for the devastating, scathing reviews." He said that the critical thumping was "very difficult" for Diamond. "We didn't talk about the bad reviews." (In 1986, however, Neil finally did: "I read all the reviews and laughed. It was either that or shoot myself.")

Yet even as *The Jazz Singer* was being critically torpedoed, Leider performed his best John Paul Jones impersonation: "The second weekend of the show, Saturday, between Christmas and New Year's, my wife and I were walking in Beverly Hills. We stopped in the Konditori restaurant, were sitting by the window and Neil and Marcia and their kids walked by. We knocked on the window and said, 'Come on in.' And so he came in, sat down, and we had lunch together—he hadn't shaved and he was wearing a baseball cap and no one recognized him.

"And we were talking. *'You gotta go out there and do some promotion.'*"

But Neil, who had already appeared on "Good Morning America" with his old *Stretch on a River* screen test costar, David Hartman, never did do the "Today," "Tonight," "Tomorrow," Merv Griffin, Mike Douglas, John Davidson, and Toni Tennille shows, as he had been scheduled to do.

As he stewed in private, Neil the businessman could find consolation in the fact that while *Jazz Singer* the movie was flopping—the $15.3 million production, which needed a gross of $35 million to break even, only pulled in $14 million on its initial domestic run—"Jazz Singer" the soundtrack LP was doing boffo business.

Bruce Wendell, Capitol Records' promotion vice-president, had predicted in an interview with *Radio and Records* months earlier that the album would set new records for soundtracks. "It'll be my number-one priority for Neil to get several hits," he said.

Singles-wise, he delivered. In fact, if it hadn't been for Kenny Rogers' chart-topping "Lady," Neil would have had a number-one *Billboard* hit with "Love on the Rocks," which nested for three weeks at number two. Following "Rocks" onto the Top 10 was the syrupy ballad "Hello Again" and "America."

While the hits didn't translate into the record numbers for the soundtrack LP that the Capitol executive had forecast, they did propel the album to number two on the *Billboard* chart. In the process, the LP totaled a reported 4 million units in sales domestically. Depending on Neil's royalty rate, that meant a payday for Neil of perhaps $2–3 million more than his $3 million guarantee. Add to this his acting fee of $2.5 million (based on *Singer*'s eventual worldwide take of $25 million, including videocassette sales), his income from his hit singles, and his probable performance royalties from ASCAP, sheet music payments and foreign royalties, and Neil stood to become *Jazz Singer*'s $10 million man.

The only thing missing was an Oscar nomination. "It's my dream that Neil will win an Academy Award," Capitol's Wendell had enthused. No doubt it was Neil's dream, too; he had attempted to put the *Jonathan Livingston Seagull* controversy behind him in 1977 by agreeing to present the Best Song Oscar at the Academy Awards that year. (One of the nominees, coincidentally, was Barbra Streisand, cowriter of "Evergreen," from *A Star Is Born*. "Before I mention a winner, about three weeks ago I was talking to Barbra, and I said, 'I love your song so much that no matter who wins I'm gonna read your name,'" Diamond said from the podium. "But I have to cancel out on that, Barbra. So if I call your name out, you actually won. And if I don't call your name out, you wrote a fantastic song first time out." Diamond then opened the envelope and announced that "Evergreen" and Streisand had won.)

But when the 1980 Oscar nominations were announced in February, Diamond once again came up empty. In the scoring category that he had entered and been declared eligible in, Best Original Score, the nominees were *Altered States, The Elephant Man, The Empire Strikes Back, Fame,* and *Tess.* Meanwhile, in the Best Song category, the members of the Academy's music branch overlooked his three eligible tunes—"America," "Hello Again," and "Love on the Rocks"—while voting onto the nominees' list a song that never even made the charts: "People Alone," from *The Competition.* Diamond's shutout fueled speculation that certain members of the music branch had a long memory.

"What keeps me going is the passion—and the fear. And I have plenty of fear. I'm just a scared Jewish boy wondering what will happen next."

—Diamond, 1981

Actually, in dueling with his demons in the wake of *Jazz Singer,* Neil seemed to have suffered a temporary loss of will. No more was heard in 1981 of his plans to musicalize a legitimate play ("I'm in a writing mood—and Broadway is very interesting," he told *Daily Variety*'s Army Archerd in the heady days before the premiere of *The Jazz Singer*). And his late-1980 vow to finally get serious about starring in *Death at an Early Age* didn't lead to the start of filming in 1981, or in 1982 for that matter, despite *Death*'s listing on Columbia Pictures' production agenda for that year.

Neil's planned 1982 TV special for CBS never came off either, even though he had committed himself to the project to the extent of selecting his producers, Dwight Hemion and Gary Smith, and his special guest, John Denver. What did come off for Neil in 1981 and 1982 were biding-time projects: two less-than-ambitious studio albums and four short- to medium-length tours.

On the writing and recording fronts, Neil's world was all the more insulated, thanks to his purchase, several years earlier, of the old sixteen-track United Artists recording studio on Third Street in West Hollywood, which he named Arch Angel. Although the '60s-era control room was an antique by 1981 studio standards and therefore unsuitable for serious recording, the studio itself was a players' dream for its "live" sound. The fact that Diamond could rationalize buying it, moreover, was a revealing indication of his financial clout by the late '70s. (Neil's post-deduction earnings for several years in the '70s were made public the next year when the Internal Revenue Service handed him a bill for $81,422 in additional income taxes, charging that he wasn't entitled to take the deductions he claimed for losses in a real estate partnership. The IRS papers showed that Diamond had taxable earnings of $2,363,585 during 1975, the last year of his "sabbatical"; $6,429,076 in 1976; $4,266,857 in 1977, and $6,275,752 in 1978.)

Neil's white Porsche Carerra with the license plate "NDRRT"—

which stood for Neil Diamond Road Racing Team—could be found parked behind Arch Angel on a regular basis from the start. When Gilbert Becaud journeyed to Los Angeles in 1978 to collaborate with him on some *Jazz Singer* songs, they wound up doing much of their writing at the studio. Some of the *Jazz Singer* soundtrack overdubs were recorded there as well, with a rented remote recording truck.

By 1981, Neil had firmly established Arch Angel as a home base for both himself and his band, whom, as further proof of his multimillionaire status, he kept on salary year round. "When Neil's ready to do whatever, the band members all come to Arch Angel like you'd go to a regular job, and work pretty much every day," noted engineer Rick Ruggieri, one of the "September Morn" and "Jazz Singer" engineers. Much of that "whatever" turned out to be songwriting, with Neil airing his latest song fragments, as he'd done years earlier with the likes of Hal Blaine, Larry Knechtel, and Joe Osborn. "Members . . . all throw in their ideas, and they work up the songs quite extensively," said engineer Ron Hitchcock. Meanwhile, even during the most idle song noodling, Neil would keep a tape recorder rolling, lest he miss a lick he could use in a song someday.

When it came time in the summer of 1981 for Neil to record his latest batch of songs, he decided to maintain the family character of his Arch Angel work by hiring his drummer, Dennis St. John, as coproducer.

It was a plum assignment for St. John, who had twirled the knobs briefly on the "Love at the Greek" album before being replaced by Robbie Robertson, and it was the best proof yet of his tight bond with his boss. TV director-producer Kac Young had seen that bond at work in Australia in 1976: "Dennis had sat on the front of a boat in Brisbane and received third-degree burns. He was blistered and red and unhappy. But he was on the stage, the gauze wrapped around his legs and part of his arms, pounding out the beat, being there for Neil.

"And I think that you could see their relationship on stage. I would always see Neil look at Dennis, key off him, introduce him as 'the heartbeat of my band.'

"And Dennis was always smiling. Dennis was what Neil wanted to be, and that was totally secure and absolutely happy at the moment with what he was doing, in love with being alive."

Flash ahead a few months in 1981, however, and not only was Dennis St. John not singing life's praises, neither was anyone else inside the walls of the Record Plant—including Neil. "Just walking in the door you'd feel electricity," said engineer Ron Hitchcock, who joined the album project two-thirds of the way through. "Everybody was uptight. *Everybody* was uptight . . . Something wasn't right, and I didn't know what."

About a week after he clocked in on the project, Hitchcock arrived for work one day and promptly noted that the seat next to him, the seat that had been occupied by St. John, was empty. It wasn't long before he learned that St. John had been drummed out of Diamond's album, his band . . . and his life.

"Well, it's personal—I don't want to talk about it," Neil said briskly when Hitchcock asked him what had happened. The band members weren't any more helpful. "Nobody knew why Dennis was canned, or they weren't saying," commented another person with ties to Diamond's organization.

Since then, various rumors have circulated along the Neil Diamond alumni grapevine regarding infractions Dennis St. John allegedly committed to warrant his excommunication. However, one knowledgeable source who had seen the same drama acted out before with the likes of axed manager Ken Fritz and executive assistant Totty Ames, didn't buy the gossip: "Dennis lived his life for Neil. They were closer than any two brothers.

"I think Neil has a very strong glass wall around him—that protective thing that we all have. And sometimes when people step inside that, he'll let you in, but on his terms only. Then when he's ready, you better be out."

The source did claim to have knowledge of the way St. John learned that the glass wall had closed him out after a decade's employment: via Diamond's attorney, Jeffrey C. Ingber. "Neil didn't even talk to Dennis."

Following the drummer's dismissal, engineers Ron Hitchcock and Andy Bloch and keyboards player/arranger Alan Lindgren assumed associate producer chores on "On the Way to the Sky." "We all kind of threw our ideas together and helped Neil," Hitchcock clarified. "He really made his own record."

It was a development in Neil's career that the engineer regretted. "I think Neil got more involved in the production of the record than the writing of the songs, so I think the songs suffered," he said. "I think it shows when he's allowed to take that last minute to rewrite a verse."

Hitchcock was given a challenging assignment by Neil one night at the Record Plant: breathing Top 40 life into the blandly romantic "Yesterday's Songs." "He said, 'I think I have a single here—I'm not happy with it. Do your thing on it. Give me a tune.'"

Hitchcock vaguely recalled mixing the song months earlier. He located the tape, put it on, "and it was terrific—'How are we going to better that?' And Neil said, 'Well I think I changed a couple of lyrics; we can't use that.'" After hours of agonizing, Hitchcock finally seized upon the notion of mixing the bass up front, creating a walking-bass effect to carry the tune along.

Neil liked the results. "Wrap it up," he told Hitchcock. "Columbia wants a single on it right now."

"Yesterday's Songs" was released in October, a couple of weeks before the "On the Way to the Sky" album. It made *Billboard*'s Top 20, but it didn't win any praise from *Los Angeles Times* reviewer Paul Grein, who called it "wallpaper music that's easily the least substantial single in Diamond's fifteen-year career."

This was one pan that Neil probably shrugged off. In October, Columbia Records, obviously betting that there would be more than "Yesterday's Songs" in Neil Diamond's song bag for years to come, agreed to a new contract guaranteeing him more than $30 million for ten more albums. For a few weeks it stood as the richest deal in recording history. Even the news that the Rolling Stones had cut a $35 million deal with Atlantic Records, however, couldn't tarnish Neil's achievement. Fifteen years after his first hit, and years after virtually all of his contemporaries had given up the singles scene, Neil Diamond was still regarded as one of the most potent record sellers around.

Around that time, Neil's papers were up at the William Morris Agency. He chose not to re-sign, thereby severing his association with yet another associate, Tony Fantozzi. It was Fantozzi, of course, who had pushed Neil to commit to *The Jazz Singer*.

"There were two people who were so devoted to him, so loyal to him, and so good to him. One was Dennis St. John and one was Tony Fantozzi," said one former employee.

When Diamond returned to the road in December for a brief series of dates, he did so with a new "heartbeat," this one supplied by Ron Tutt, one of the most respected rock drummers in the business.

It seemed fitting that Tutt had been Elvis Presley's drummer—Neil had been emulating *the* King ever since his Bang Records days, when Lillian Roxon wrote in her *Rock Encyclopedia:* "There's still a lot of the Elvis era in him, brushed-back hair, sinister cowboy gear." (In an interesting twist, Diamond bought the Holmby Hills house next door to Presley in 1972. Shortly after moving in, Neil stood chatting with set designer Jim Newton on his front lawn as a tour bus drove by. The driver dutifully pointed out Elvis' home, while motoring right past the other "king" of pop. "It was kind of funny," Newton said.)

Diamond's Elvis bent was more evident than ever in 1981 with his full-blown sound, glitzy clothes, and grandiose shows. Regarding his concert spectacles, lighting director Scott Johnson had been in a perfect position to watch Neil's show grow beyond the confines of Joe Gannon's precise Formula. "After the European tour in 1977, the shows started really expanding," he noted. "It was during a period where we were doing mostly American cities. They were very comfortable things to do. The travel arrangements were very smooth. All the physical and creature comforts were just fine. Nobody was put out over anything. You could bring your wife, bring your kids, whatever you want. And in that way, with such a degree of comfort, I think there was this kind of license to let the shows amble on.

"Some shows ran close to three hours, more than three hours, without intermission. Some of them were fantastically wonderful—they were a demonstration of his commitment and energy. But some of them," he added, "were just, I'm afraid, long-winded . . . And I think there was nobody to say, 'Maybe you ought to tighten this up here, leave 'em wanting more'—which is a tried-and-true axiom of the theater. I think often at the shows the people were sated . . . maybe even before the show got over."

That didn't seem to be the case when Neil began his three-night stand at San Francisco's Cow Palace on December 20, however. *San Francisco Examiner* music critic Philip Elwood: "An observer had no trouble . . . discerning the star's popularity—these 14,000 customers like his songs, like his stagey immodesty, eagerly accept his invitations to sing along and obviously find in Diamond an alternative to rock 'n' roll."

That night, Neil used a performance device that had by then become a midshow staple of his: egging on the crowd to demand he reprise a particular song again, and again, and again. The tactic succeeded in raising the decibel count, while removing what remained of the crowd's inhibitions. The only problem with the cleverly conceived, albeit slick segment was the song choice. For Neil to sing "Forever in Blue Jeans" no fewer than six times while decked out in a spangly shirt and slacks with a spangly stripe seemed about as sincere a statement as a tuxedoed Vegas lounge singer crooning "My Way."

Compared to the *Jazz Singer* soundtrack, "On the Way to the Sky" was only a middling success, peaking at number seventeen on the charts. Still, it sold more than one and a half million units.

As the LP's title song was released as a single in February, Neil sat down with *People* writer Carl Arrington for his second profile in the magazine, whose readers in 1979 and 1980 had voted him one of their five favorite pop singers. "We made the film for fans, not critics," he replied to the inevitable question about *Jazz Singer,* and he gave the impression that he was pursuing his acting career with gusto. He hoped to star in either *Death at an Early Age* or a thriller called *The Unknown Man* in 1983, he said, explaining, "I learned I can act, work comfortably on a collaborative effort and get a great deal of satisfaction."

As for the inevitable personal queries that the *People* writer put to him, Neil sounded the same upbeat tone. On parenting his children, Marjorie, Elyn, Jesse, and Micah, now 16, 14, 11, and 4, respectively, he said, "The best thing I can do . . . is give them a normal life, be supportive, and let them find their own way." (By 1982, Diamond had a long reputation in his camp for being a devoted dad. During his "sabbatical" he hosted his daughters on summer trips west with grandparents Rose and Kieve. "Neil was always marvelous about making terrific arrangements for them . . . the royal treatment at Disneyland, a Universal tour," former executive assistant Totty Ames said. As for Jesse, Neil's doting gestures included making a special instructional music recording with his band and distributing copies to his son's classmates at the private West Hollywood school Jesse attended. He also allowed his son to play on an unmiked conga drum alongside percussionist King Errisson in rehearsals, and, later, onstage. "I try to do the best by [my children] and hope they don't hold me too guilty," he explained in 1980. "I don't want no *Daddy Dearest* written about me.")

In the *People* interview, Neil also tossed a bouquet of praise to Marcia, telling of the time he found himself alone, hungry—and helpless—in the kitchen: "My wife keeps me alive." The tribute was one of a series of verbal valentines that Neil had been delivering via the press since he and Marcia had patched up following an apparent period of estrangement. (Totty Ames: "They separated . . . with all intentions, I think, of divorcing—and then the next I heard, she was pregnant again [with Micah].") Among Neil's earlier comments: "[Marcia keeps] my sanity intact because she is saner than I am. None of my career would have been the same without her . . . She made it possible for me to go on filming *Jazz Singer* when I was emotionally drained. She kept me calm . . . Anyone who puts up with me for that length of time . . . deserves some sort of medal."

The month after the *People* article appeared, Ellie Greenwich had a backstage encounter in New Jersey with Marcia. Ellie saw a woman who looked like she needed some kind attention herself. "She goes 'Ellie?'" Greenwich recalled. "And I . . . said, 'Oh, Marcia, of course—how are you doing?' I didn't even recognize her. She looked tired, she looked forlorn . . .

"When we walked away, my friend said to me, '*That's Neil's wife?*' I said, 'Yeah.' 'Well, forgive me, but she looks like a tired housewife.' I said, 'Well, she probably is . . . What did you expect? The girl has not had it easy, believe me.'"

While Diamond was playing to packed arenas from New Jersey to San Antonio in 1982, a new superstar by the name of E.T. began doing boffo business in movie houses around the country. While he was in

New York, Neil caught *E.T. the Extraterrestrial* with Burt Bacharach and Carole Bayer Sager.

By then, Neil and Marcia had become friends of the couple. The Diamonds were the only guests of the two songwriters, in fact, when they were married at the Beverly Hills home of record executive Neil Bogart in April, a week after they had won the Best Song Oscar for cowriting, with Christopher Cross and Peter Allen, "Theme From *Arthur* (Best That You Can Do)."

Now, collaboration happened to be on Neil, Burt, and Carole's agenda. After years of leaning on studio musicians to help him finish tunes that carried his name only on the credits, Diamond had turned to formal collaboration. "I thought 'Maybe this is a part of my coming out of myself,'" he said of his 1976 collaboration with Robbie Robertson, "Dry Your Eyes," which, he claimed, changed his thinking on cowriting. "Maybe I didn't *have* to lock myself into a room and do it all by myself; maybe I wasn't that 'solitary man' anymore . . ." His 1979 single "Forever in Blue Jeans" had been cowritten with one of his guitar players, Richard Bennett, and the "On the Way to the Sky" LP featured the greatest number of cowriters yet: Gilbert Becaud, Sager, and, most interestingly, four members of his band. (Regarding the bestowal of cowriter credit to various members of his band, Emory Gordy, who had played on the "Jonathan Livingston Seagull" and "Serenade" LPs, commented: "I think it was a little too late for a lot of people; a lot of things Neil had written should have been shared by some other people, and they weren't. Maybe what his definition of what a cowriter was, was different from what everybody else's is.")

After the screening of *E.T.*, Diamond, Bacharach and Sager agreed there was a song in the year's biggest star. The result was "Heartlight."

The tune was one of six Diamond-Bacharach-Sager collaborations that wound up on "Heartlight" the album. Like the previous couple of Diamond albums, the LP was recorded in lavish style. On one night, in fact, engineer Ron Hitchcock counted *six* studios being used simultaneously by Neil in his effort to finish the LP in time for an early fall release: two for overdub recording, two for mixing, one for the recording of his vocals, and one for songwriter-producer-arranger Michael Masser's work on a track he and Neil had collaborated on. It was a method of working that drove another engineer on the project, Rick Ruggieri, up the wall: "I hate to see people waste money . . . And I see a lot of waste in some of Neil's projects. He can afford it, more power to him, but it's not necessary to spend $600,000 to make a record . . .

"You know where all this started from? When they did the movie . . . There's a whole different process of making movies than making records . . . it seems like anybody who's making a movie can't make a decision if their life depended on it, and would rather do it all in postproduction. The movie people also use an abundance of people in an abundance of different places, all at the same time . . . Well, some of this rubbed off on Neil . . . [and he realized] that, yeah, you could be in eight places at once."

The album project turned out to be crazy-making for engineer Hitchcock as well, for the place Diamond instructed Hitchcock to be in: squarely between him and Bacharach. The assignment was to mix "Front Page Story," one of the tunes Neil, Burt, and Carole had written and produced together, and Bacharach had arranged. "I was doing the mix," recalled Hitchcock, "and Burt and Carole walked in the door. 'Oh, hi! That's not what I had in mind at all!' . . . The chemistry was wrong . . .

"And it turns out that Burt Bacharach had his engineers, his people, and his trip," Hitchcock continued. "He's a very strong producer, a very strong writer, and he knows what he wants, how and when he wants it. And I got in the middle of these two . . . And I was like thrown to the lions, quite frankly."

Before "Front Page Story" was finished, Hitchcock added, no fewer than four engineers—two assigned by Diamond, two by Bacharach—had taken a crack at the tune.

The engineer got a firsthand look at the lions of "Heartlight" together on several occasions. "There are two very serious egos involved there," he said, referring to Diamond and Bacharach. "They got pretty intense." As for Sager: "She's real intense. *Real* intense . . . She made their life difficult at times in the studio. She's not pleasant to work with . . . Once Neil and Burt seemed to decide they liked something, she would always dislike it and throw a real kink into it."

Yet when the sessions were over, he noted, the trio would sit around and joke.

It was at the end of one of the album's last late-night mixing sessions at Bill Schnee's studio that Schnee, another of the LP's engineers, retired for a few minutes to the studio's maintenance room, where he had a radio. As he cleared his head to the sounds of current Top 40 fare, he heard the first strains of a new but very familiar tune. "Guys, come here!" he called out, and Neil, Burt, and Carole hurried over. "We all just sort of froze," Schnee recalled. "Time just sort of stood still while 'Heartlight' played."

The warm pop ballad became a smash for Neil, soaring to number five on *Billboard*'s Hot 100. "The Neil Diamond *E.T.* hit that lit up the charts," headlined a one-page *People* magazine piece that featured a photo of a grinning Diamond and an E.T. doll, each flashing a number-one sign.

It was also the hit that lit up the phone lines in MCA's legal department. Universal, the studio that had made *E.T.*, happened to be the exclusive licensing agent for *E.T.*, and it regarded "Heartlight," with its obvious *E. T.*-inspired lyrics, as an infringement on its copyright. Rather than risk a lawsuit from the parent company of his former record label, a put-out Diamond and Bacharach and Sager paid MCA a $25,000 fee for the right to cash in, song-wise, on the *E. T.* phenomenon.

Meanwhile, the album "Heartlight," a collection of generally tame middle-of-the-road tunes, cashed in on the success of the single, lodging in *Billboard*'s Top 10.

The album cover photo, however, was striking: Standing in black T-shirt in a forest setting, Neil appeared fresher and younger looking than he had in years, giving the impression that post–*Jazz Singer* life, indeed, was agreeing with him.

It wasn't his close encounter with E.T., however, that had reversed his aging process. Instead, Neil, ever image-conscious at forty-one, had elected to use a photo that had been shot five years earlier.

·22·
FACE=OFF

"I still have the same insecurities and doubts about myself. So you begin to wonder if you really have changed."

—Diamond, 1982

Using a years-younger photograph to sell his album seemed the mark of an insecure artist. It also seemed symbolic of Neil's attempt in 1982 to turn back the pages in his career to a more artistically inspired time. Over dinner with Tom Catalano in 1976, Neil had displayed his concern about living up to past glories when he dismissed his well-received "Beautiful Noise" LP with the words, "Well, it's not 'Moods.'" Songwriter Al Kasha, who had watched Neil's career ever since producing his earliest Columbia tracks, talked in 1983 of the struggle he felt Neil was going through: "Deep down he's in Malibu and he wants to be with those folks. And yet part of him—and this is the craziness of it—wants to be back in those Brooklyn days, to get that insight pouring out of him." There was evidence that Kasha was right: A *Jazz Singer* official recalled being told by a Diamond employee of the night Neil jetted to New York for the sole purpose of driving around his old haunts. The next morning, however, he was on a jet back to Los Angeles.

In 1983, Neil tapped into his past once again, this time by agreeing to write some tunes with none other than Jeff Barry. The coproducer of Diamond's Bang Records hits had complained to *Rolling Stone* in 1976 that Diamond's songs "haven't changed, really; they just get harder to understand." In his 1983 talks with Neil, Barry made it clear where he stood on his artistic direction.

"I told Neil, 'Come on, let's lighten up—whatever happened to *cheeka-cheeka-cheeka?*'" Barry recounted. "I think he kept dipping into this well . . . trying to be heavier, more emotional, deeper and bigger . . . [and] had finally gotten down to a point where . . . there's nothing there anymore. 'You're manufacturing "deep" at this point. Let's take some of the clear, clean water off the top, and get out of the silt' . . . I would like to believe that a lighter, happier side is there and can be encouraged to come out. A Neil Diamond who can say, 'You know what? I've really been getting away with it. I don't mean I don't deserve what I have, but I've had a good life. I'm a very lucky man . . . I've got a house at the beach, I've got a house over here, I've got a lot of nice stuff, great kids . . . I have millions of people out there who come to see me, and love me, and buy my records.' And I think they would *love* it if he would say to them musically, 'Hey, I'm having a good time now—at least I think I can allow myself to. And I'm gonna give you some *cheeka-cheeka-cheeka*—"Hey, baby, you're the greatest" and "Come on, let's walk on the beach, and I want to hold your hand, come on and kiss me."'' Because it's *got* to be there. I mean, I make him laugh. To me he's Neil. He probably goes to the bathroom and everything."

In March of 1983 Diamond and Barry had their first writing session together, in Diamond's office.

"It was interesting when we started—I had never really written with him," Barry said. "And there we were . . . and it was amazing the different [styles]. He was the one who brought it up. He said, 'I never *dreamed* that you write like that!' 'What do you mean, "like that"?' He said, 'Well, you're like a *professional writer.* You walk around the room, and you try to get the line, and you think about it—"maybe it should be this way; let's make that the second verse."'' And I think Neil writes more stream-of-consciousness, feeling what he feels . . .

"And I was trying to create with him songs he feels, but songs that were a little *lighter.* I was taking a lead in a direction. I was heading into the caves and I said, 'Come on, Neil, get your lantern and let's go this way' . . . [And] he was allowing me to lead him down that tunnel. He was Becky to my Tom Sawyer."

The tunesmithing adventures of Neil and Jeff did not end in a pay-off, however. Barry: "Between his busy life . . . and the things I was doing, we never finished any of the songs."

It wasn't the only pending project of Neil's that didn't reach fruition in 1983. The Columbia Pictures/Ray Stark production of *Death at an Early Age* moved no closer to the cameras; a new project, a CBS TV movie based on "Brother Love" and starring Neil, didn't pan out; and no more was heard of his 1982 musing about possibly starring in a thriller called *The Unknown Man.*

In fact, as the kindling of unconsummated projects piled up in Neil's career, his only notable undertaking in 1983 was a June performance stand at Los Angeles' Forum, his first hometown appearance since his "Love at the Greek" dates six years earlier.

The four concerts were announced March 20 with a two-page, full-truck, four-color ad in the *Los Angeles Times Calendar* magazine, featuring "DIAMOND" in two-inch-tall red letters and the photo of Neil that had graced the cover of "On the Way to the Sky."

The next morning at eight, the 72,000 tickets went on sale. By noon, they were gone, and a fifth show was added.

Then Tuesday morning, a sixth, tying British rocker Rod Stewart's 1979 Forum record.

And then on Wednesday, a seventh—after which the Forum's and Ticketron's ticket sellers rested, after dispensing a total of 130,000 tickets priced from $10.50 to $15.50.

The sales feat warranted a Robert Hilburn interview in the *Los Angeles Times* the next month. Asked by Hilburn if he were surprised that he just set the Forum's all-time attendance and gross records, Neil responded: "Surprised? *Stunned* was more like it . . . I don't even feel like I'm particularly warm."

Having apparently taken Jeff Barry's lighten-up counsel to heart, Neil went on to say, "It's not like I'm without the doubts and fears. But I do feel much more at ease these days."

During the interview, a *Times* photographer quickly snapped a couple of candids of Diamond. As if to demonstrate his new ease, the man who once said "I find it difficult to smile on cue" remarked, "Hey, how about getting one of me smiling? I always look so serious in pictures."

Having made Forum history, Neil began to seriously consider having the dates recorded for the *fourth* live album of his career. "Can we do something special?" he asked recording engineer Ron Hitchcock. "Let me go digital," Hitchcock replied, referring to the new high-fidelity recording method that the engineer had briefly considered for *Jazz Singer* but abandoned because not enough was known about it at the time.

Hitchcock didn't hear any more about the would-be project until Neil gave him the go-ahead a week before the engagement. The engineer then rented two Sony digital machines and two remote recording trucks from the Record Plant—one for him to record Diamond and the band, one for his associate, Rick Ruggieri, to record the hall.

In miking the Forum, Ruggieri wound up hanging two of his small mikes—which he'd attempted to camouflage by wrapping in black tape—some sixty feet above the floor in front of the stage. "You're going to get the best reaction out of those people because they're the closest, they're paying the most for the seats," he reasoned.

The microphones were spotted by Diamond during his first sound check. "Take those down," he said. "I don't want people to know we're recording. I want them to feel at ease."

"All right," Ruggieri replied, disheartened. "But you're not going to get the audience reaction you're looking for. I want you to know that ahead of time. So if you get a couple of good things the first night—"

"I don't care," Diamond interrupted. "It's the first night, there's gonna be a lot of important people out in the audience. I just want everybody to feel good, have a good time."

Ruggieri yanked the mikes. "It was probably the most nervous I'd ever seen Neil," he said.

By 1983, however, Diamond could boast of a proven ability to channel his nervousness before a big show into a dynamic performance. And that's what he did in his two-and-a-half-hour opening night concert.

Somewhere in the glitz and bombast of his opening number, "America"—accompanied by crisscrossing laser lights forming a diamond pattern, the unfurling of a giant American flag, and flash-pot explosions—the last vestiges of Neil's Solitary Man persona were blown to smithereens.

His concert conduct, moreover, proved to be a textbook for arena performers. There he was prowling the stage during "America" with his cordless microphone, establishing immediate contact with all sections of the house, including the poor souls in the $10.50 seats behind the stage . . . using those fans as his midshow foil during his multiencore number, "Dancing in the Streets" ("This is definitely my group back here. You're cooking. You're happening") . . . delivering his songs with exaggerated expressions and gestures . . . using his guitar as a prop on "I Am . . . I Said," pantomiming the part that Richie Bennett actually played in the shadows . . . and finishing up with a blast, literally, reprising "America," flash-pot explosions and all.

And yet, the truly moving moments from the Forum shows were the ones that hadn't been manufactured: the spontaneous flicking on of hundreds of lighters in the darkened arena as he began "Heartlight"; the unprompted singing along, swaying, and arm waving of 18,000 people as he performed "Song Sung Blue."

A traveling spot illuminated pocket after pocket of the crowd during that tune. It revealed an overwhelmingly white, middle-class group, more women than men, the majority pushing or entrenched in middle age—not exactly the makeup of the usual crowd to inhabit the Forum on concert night.

One could appreciate their musical lot in life in 1983. Although many of them no doubt considered themselves to be in the prime of life, and still game to let their hair down, they had precious little music to call their own.

For years Neil had catered to these people, churning out his grandly uplifting, sentimental, or poignant lyrics, set to sweeping melodies, frequently irresistible rhythms and a toe-tapping beat; singing them in his husky, sexy baritone for all seasons. And at the Forum, he seemed just as tuned in to the over-thirty crowd's wants in his performance, putting on the kind of high-energy, committed show that spelled R-E-L-E-A-S-E. As the crowd responded with cheers, foot stomping, and standing ovations, one sensed they weren't demonstrating only for Diamond. They also seemed to be declaring a collective "I'm Alive," to quote the title of his unabashedly positive 1982 anthem.

All of which may explain why Neil Diamond could succeed in selling 130,000 tickets in a soft concert market when he didn't even consider himself "particularly warm."

After the first two shows, cassette tapes of which Diamond was handed as his limo pulled out of the Forum each night, he buttonholed engineer Rick Ruggieri.

"Not a lot of audience happening, is there?" he said.

"No," Ruggieri replied.

"Want to put the mikes back?"

"Yeah."

"Do it—you were right."

The mikes were in place for his Wednesday show. After he heard the tape, he cracked: "Audience sounds great, Rick; we're happening."

Ironically, engineer Ron Hitchcock was wringing his hands at the time. He'd heard the hard-singing Diamond's voice get rougher and rougher through the first three performances, and by the end of Wednesday night, "I thought he was finished for the week."

Neil's gruff vocals had sparked reviewers' comments for years; the *San Francisco Examiner*'s Phil Elwood, for example, wrote in 1981 that his voice during his opening-night Oakland Coliseum concert "had all the quality and timbre of a coyote gargling splinters of glass." Neil had never been forced to cancel a concert because of throat problems, however, and he showed up Thursday night at the Forum with as clear and resonant a voice as he had at the beginning of his opening night show. "He amazes me in that respect," Hitchcock remarked.

Still, it wasn't until the sixth show that the engineer felt that he had gotten the extra-special performance he was hoping for.

"So the last night the band cut loose," he said. "They figured, and even Neil figured, they had something under their belt. I knew that night was special when I heard the roar of the crowd coming down the hall, coming through the door of the truck, not just coming out of the monitors . . .

"Neil felt it that night. In fact, as he drove out in the limo, he said, 'Think that's the one?' And I threw him a cassette of the night. It was just like in the movies."

However, work on "Live at the Forum" wasn't on Neil's agenda in the six months that followed, as he decided, instead, to focus his energies on the recording of another studio album.

He had reason to put the live LP on his already-crowded career back burner. In May, Columbia Records released "Classics: The Early Years," a collection of his Bang recordings, which Neil now owned lock, stock, and copyright. The album, which followed by a year the release of a package of Columbia-era Diamond recordings, "12 Greatest Hits, Vol. II"—which followed the release, in 1978, of a Columbia Record Club version of the "Classics" album on Diamond's own Frog King Records label, which followed MCA's 1974 "Greatest Hits, Vol. I" release—barely dented *Billboard*'s Top 200 chart. The dismal showing seemed a clear indication that Neil had gone to the oldies well once too often, that his fans didn't need, and didn't want to buy, yet another version of "Cherry, Cherry."

At the end of 1983, however, Neil switched courses yet again, ordering Ron Hitchcock to get to work on "Live at the Forum." "So," the engineer recalled, "I went in the studio with a cassette of every night's performance, meticulously went through every song, and got what I thought was the best performance, technically, of the band, him . . . [and also] considering the crowd. And I pieced together a cassette for him of what I thought was the best opening song, best second song . . . following his show order.

"He sent it back to me and said, 'Nah, doesn't feel good. It's not a performance—it's just some songs pieced together.' I said, 'Yeah, but it's the best.' He said, 'It just doesn't feel good.' . . . So I went to that seventh night tape, to see what needed replacing in that . . . and replaced two or three of the tunes where he missed the song or didn't connect with the crowd like he did one of the nights before."

Hitchcock turned in the tape. This time, Neil was pleased with the mix: "It's the finest live album I've ever heard," he told the engineer. However, that was the last Hitchcock heard from Diamond at the time, Diamond deciding once again to table the LP.

Neil continued working on his new studio album, "Primitive," through early 1984. For the first time since 1975, when he was still on his "sabbatical," a year had gone by without the release of an album.

When in early February Columbia's top brass—in the person of CBS Records Chairman Walter Yetnikoff and CBS Records President Al Teller, who had succeeded Bruce Lundvall in 1981—finally did get their hands on the tapes, they heard an album that had been written and produced largely by Diamond himself. The only new hand involved in the project was producer Richard Perry (the Pointer Sisters), who had twirled the knobs on the couple of tunes Neil had co-written with Burt Bacharach and Carole Bayer Sager.

It was not the album that Yetnikoff and Teller, obviously concerned about Diamond's recent lack of blockbuster sales, were hoping for. "The heads of the company in New York did not feel [it] was a complete album, or the best album that Neil could deliver," said Denny Diante, CBS Records' vice president/executive producer. "I think the objection was to three or four of the songs not being quite up to what we all felt was Neil's capability . . . And they asked if Neil could go back in and do some more songs, new songs."

Neil made his reaction to CBS' entreaty public on March 1, when he filed suit against CBS in Superior Court in Santa Monica seeking an order forcing its Columbia label to release the album in "timely" fashion . . . just as he had submitted it.

That Neil's clash with the titans of CBS Records would reach the lawsuit stage was an indication of just how poorly the two parties were communicating by 1984.

Relations had been deteriorating ever since Neil had decided to record his "Jazz Singer" soundtrack LP for Capitol instead of Columbia. "Yeah, there was a lot of bitterness [at CBS] about it," Bruce Lundvall, then CBS Records president, acknowledged. "What happens is it takes an artist off the roster for a period of time . . . so you lose communication." While he didn't harbor a grudge against Neil at the time for making the Capitol deal, he allowed that others in the organization might have: "There's always that feeling in the company, 'Well, I hope the movie is a stiff.' Which is really kind of dumb, because the more successful the movie and album, the better it would actually be for CBS in the future."

That seemed to be CBS Records' thinking in 1981 when the company made its $30 million deal with Diamond, warding off competition for Neil's signature from Warner Brothers Records and Polygram Records, the latter headed by David Braun, Diamond's former attorney.

By then, Lundvall had taken a top executive post at Elektra-Asylum Records. His departure seemed another factor in the distancing between Neil and CBS. Lundvall: "I think Neil viewed Walter [Yetnikoff] as the guy making the basic business and contractual decisions; but the guy he wanted to play the music for, or show the album package to was basically myself . . . I think he respected my marketing background; he also respected the fact that I love music, and I happen to love his music . . .

"He was fairly closed, except with people who he did feel a sense of companionship and trust for . . . He did not like to deal with the company as a whole."

According to Denny Diante, Neil did have conversations during the "On the Way to the Sky" project with Al Teller, who as a marketing executive had distinguished himself on the "Jonathan Livingston Seagull" sales campaign years earlier. On "Heartlight," however, contact between the two appeared to wane. "I don't think there was a good line of communication between Neil and the company at a given point in time," Diante said.

Certainly by 1984 that given point in time had arrived. The first time Yetnikoff and Teller heard any of the "Primitive" songs was after Neil turned in the completed album on February 6.

In choosing to take on CBS Records' Walt Yetnikoff, Neil wound up squaring off with one of the industry's best-known hardball players. Yetnikoff had demonstrated his grit several years earlier when he extracted $1.5 million from longtime Columbia artist Paul Simon and Warner Brothers after Simon had announced he would be joining the roster of the archrival label one album short of fulfilling his CBS obligations.

Journalist Maureen Orth was in Yetnikoff's office when he received a call from one of CBS' attorneys regarding the Simon–Warner Brothers negotiations. "Make him wait," she quoted Yetnikoff as saying about Simon's lawyers in a *New York* magazine article. "I don't feel like settling with the little bastard today."

Yetnikoff didn't feel like settling with Diamond immediately, either.

Eight days after Neil filed suit, John F. Daum and Steven J. Roman, attorneys for CBS, filed a "Notice of Taking Depositions" in Superior Court; among the forty-seven individuals CBS announced it would be taking statements from between March 29 and September 4 were employees of the eight studios Neil had utilized since 1981; the members of his band; Burt Bacharach and Carole Bayer Sager; Richard Perry; his manager, Jerry Weintraub; his attorney, Jeffrey Ingber; and, on April 10, Neil himself. The same day, CBS also asked for the right to subpoena from the various studios "all contracts, correspondence or other documents relating to any recording of any song or any music by or on behalf of Neil Diamond" since January 1, 1981.

Just as his suit had gotten CBS' attention, so, apparently, did CBS' response get Neil's attention. Negotiations between attorneys for both sides began before the end of the month, before discovery could begin.

By April 14, it was evident publicly that a settlement was imminent. That night, Yetnikoff chaired a benefit dinner at the New York Hilton for the T.J. Martell Foundation for Leukemia and Cancer Research. One CBS executive commented that Yetnikoff's presence at the head table amounted to the benefit being an "offer you couldn't refuse."

Among the attendees was Neil, in town for his appearance the next night at a National Academy of Popular Music soirée, at which he was inducted into the group's Songwriters Hall of Fame. Two weeks later, it was official: Neil's request that his suit be dismissed was filed in Superior Court.

It was a victory for Yetnikoff and CBS Records. Neil capitulated to the company's demand that he replace several tunes on "Primitive" with new songs. He agreed, further, that a new producer be called in to handle the job. That producer turned out to be Denny Diante.

Diante's first order of business was to listen to the album. "I personally did not feel that the majority of the songs were perhaps up to the standard that he had done before," he said. "I loved 'Sleep With Me Tonight,' but I wasn't crazy about the title; I thought it had been said before . . . I remember I liked 'Primitive,' I liked 'Fire on the Tracks,' I liked 'Crazy'—I thought it had a lot of potential." Among the several tunes he didn't like was the midtempo "Marlene," which, like another midtempo song and a ballad, was subsequently dropped.

"And after I chose my one-two-three-four-five favorite songs," Diante continued, "I started listening to the production." What he heard, he added, was an album that, by and large, sounded "dated."

"Sounds change," he explained. "Funky basses aren't in anymore, it's synthesized bass. Certain guitar riffs are out, certain ones are in . . . I felt that all the latest technical production values were not fully taken advantage of." It was a situation he intended to correct on the tunes he would be producing.

At their first meeting, in Neil's Melrose Place office, Neil got right to the point: "What do you want to do with me?"

"Put a ribbon around you and send you to my wife for Christmas; she loves you," replied Diante, flashing the wit that would help win Diamond to his side. He then explained his desire to find several good songs, and then bring in a new arranger, Michel Colombier, to work them over.

"OK, I'm yours," Diamond said.

"So I heard a work tape that he and Burt and Carole had done of 'Turn Around,' a verse and a chorus," Diante recalled. "I asked him to finish it, and I met with Burt and Carole and Neil five, six times in Burt's house.

"Watching them work was a treat. Burt would keep playing it over and over, and Carole and Neil would throw words back at each other. I took the end part and put it in as the chorus; Burt loved it . . . It was a relatively simple process."

The next song added to "Primitive" was "My Time With You," a collaboration between Neil's keyboard players, Alan Lindgren and Tom Hensley. "He played me a demo of the song that they did. And Neil really liked it. I remember him telling me, 'If you like Neil Diamond and you like hopelessly romantic songs, you'll like this.' I said, 'How can I say no?'"

The third tune was another nonoriginal, the energetic "Love's Own Song," cowritten by guitarist Doug Rhone and Diamond's "album production coordinator" and all-around man Friday, Sam Cole.

Diante would have liked a fourth song, this one a Diamond original. He confessed that he waited until the last moment, hoping for Neil to pen another "You Don't Bring Me Flowers," but to no avail. "Well, you know, I'm tapped right now," Neil admitted to him.

So Diamond and Diante went in the studio—The Complex, owned by Maurice White of Earth, Wind & Fire—to record what they had. Of the tunes, "Turn Around" was the hardest one to get on tape, because of Burt Bacharach's presence. "I remember Neil inverted a note," Diante recalled. "We were on the third chorus on the way out, and Neil, instead of going 'da DA' went 'DA da.' And, of course, Burt had a fit: *'That's not right!'* . . . I tell you, I have so many punch-ins on 'Turn Around,' on words, inverted melodies." He added that Neil was the model of accommodation through it all.

For the most part, Neil was that way with Denny Diante as well: "He came in every day that we had the studio, that we were working—he'd show up at two in the morning and listen to a mix . . . And he was totally supportive; he never broke my chops about anything. One night he was in kind of a bad mood . . . [but] he mellowed out real quick. In fact that night was the night he and I started talking . . .

"And I remember being impressed that he and I could sit down and talk about his kids and my kids . . . families and problems. I was going through a marital problem and he said, 'Ohhhhh, a pain in the ass.' I mean, stuff that the guys would sit down and talk about.

"He's the kinda guy you could go bowling with, you know? The kind of guy who won't shave for a week."

Yet even though Diante noted that Neil would enter the studio looking like he had just gotten off a Mack truck, with his three-day growth and Frog King Records jacket and hat, he added that there was no mistaking Neil's star quality: "You definitely feel his presence . . . Even when he's real mellow, you know he's there. I guess that's why he's a star."

After finishing a nightmare of an album project like "Primitive," many artists would have opted for a vacation. But not Neil. "The trouble is I'm restless," he told a British interviewer in June. "Normal people will go away on holiday for two weeks, which would drive me totally up the wall . . . There's a lot of tension in resting."

So Neil unwound by hitting the road. The ultimate destination: Europe. Among the notable concerts was a planned July 5 benefit for the Prince's Trust in Birmingham, England, that industrialist Armand Hammer had helped arrange after learning from Princess Diana over lunch that she was a Diamond fan. What's more, Di and Prince Charles were planning on lending their royal presence to the event.

·23·
STALLED

Diamond warmed up for Princess Di and Europe with a three-day engagement beginning June 16 at Atlantic City's 15,000-seat Convention Hall. The stand was his second produced under the banner of a casino-hotel, in this case the just-opened Harrah's at Trump Plaza.

Making a return to Vegas or playing the new East Coast gambling mecca had been another one of Neil's long-simmering notions; in 1981 he reportedly mulled over a $500,000 per week offer from the Riviera.

The Harrah's deal was much sweeter: $500,000 per *show*.

With the casino holding back thousands of tickets to bestow on its favored customers, the concerts were an immediate sellout. By opening night, the choicest of the twenty-dollar seats were being hawked for ten times their face value.

Diamond put on his usual generous show, despite the fact that he was suffering from a cold. Among the new numbers he sang were "Fire on the Tracks" and "Primitive" off his upcoming LP.

Five days after taking his last bow at the Convention Hall, Neil took his first bow at London's 15,000-seat Earl's Court. For the sold-out six-show stand he not only had to overcome his health problems—he now had a case of bronchitis—but also a touch of British reserve-itis. "The audience is not a Neil audience," one eyewitness commented on the second-night performance. "He cannot win them over." The show was a short one by his standards, a bare two hours.

The next night, however, both Neil and audience were in fine fettle. Among the tunes he sang was "Jingle Bells," complete with confetti shower. He explained to the crowd in the warm hall that he had decided everyone needed cooling down.

From London, Neil and party traveled to Dublin, where on June 30 he performed his first-ever concert on Irish soil, before 35,000 wildly enthusiastic fans at creaky Croke Park, a rugby stadium. Getting into the spirit of the occasion, he took the stage wielding a hurling stick, with which he flung a ball into the crowd. "He dominated the centre of the field from the start, finding his rhythm easily, and scoring repeatedly with splendid deliveries of all his hits," the *Sunday Independent*'s Michael Denieffe wrote.

From Ireland, Diamond returned to England, where on July 2 he commenced his engagement at Birmingham's National Exhibition Center, and where on July 5 he got to meet and then perform for the Prince and Princess of Wales.

Diamond had waxed effusive on the royal couple in an interview shortly after their 1981 marriage: "I'm a hopeless romantic and they are such perfect romantic symbols." For his meeting with them, he was briefed that he could invite a dozen people to be presented. In addition to Marcia and Micah, now six (fourteen-year-old Jesse was not present), he asked the members of his band to share the moment with him. He also brought along a giant stuffed Garfield doll, a gift from Micah to two-year-old Prince William.

Neil had the doll by his side when the seven-months-pregnant Di, in an emerald green dress that matched his own plum-colored shirt for sparkles, approached him with Charles.

"You must be terribly uncomfortable with that [doll], let me take it from you," she told him. Then the princess, who had turned twenty-three only four days earlier, added: "I wanted to see you in 1977, but my father wouldn't let me. But now he can't tell me what to do."

"She was very sweet and giggly," Neil later said, adding, "All of our hearts were beating fast."

The royal couple took their seats in a box on the left side of the hall, but they didn't remain in them for the entire show. During his "Forever in Blue Jeans" workout, Neil announced, "I want to see everyone up shaking their fannies," and Di quickly complied, followed by Charles and the other forty members of the royal party. She swayed and clapped to the beat, as did Charles, although the prince seemed to be listening to another song in his head, clapping on the off-beat and not as often.

On a well-publicized roll now, Neil moved on to Germany. Diamond is "Frank Sinatra, Elvis Presley and Johnny Cash in one evening," marveled the *Abendpost/Nachtausgabe*'s Hartmut Scherzer on his first German show, at Frankfurt's Festhalle. Neil went on to perform in Stuttgart, Berlin, Munich and, finally, Bad Segeberg, where he exclaimed to the 14,000 in attendance at a lime-rock outdoor amphitheater, "This was the greatest, most beautiful and most wonderful concert of my life."

Neil then returned to the United States . . . and the problems.

Even Diamond's most casual fans must have sensed that something was strangely wrong when a two-song clip of him performing in front of Princess Diana and Prince Charles was broadcast as part of ABC's pre-Olympic gala July 27. In the poorly engineered clip, Neil looked and sounded terrible as he warbled "America," to the unfurling of the Union Jack side by side with the Stars and Stripes, and "Forever in Blue Jeans."

Recording engineer Ron Hitchcock cringed when he watched the segment on television. He had been asked by Diamond, via a call from Sam Cole in London, to do what he could to make the recording presentable to an international TV audience. But after listening to the tape, which had been made by a British engineer, he had thrown up his hands: "It was beyond fixing . . . It was like Amateur Hour . . . the worst tape I ever heard."

Hitchcock said that another engineer took his crack at mixing the recording, and in the process dubbed the videotape several times, which accounted for Neil's sallow complexion and the clip's otherwise ghostly, washed-out quality. "It just went over the edge of being acceptable," he commented. The fact that it ran nevertheless surprised the engineer. Noting that Neil's manager, Jerry Weintraub, produced the gala, he added in puzzlement: "It was Neil's hour; all he had to do was make a phone call."

The broadcast of the clip came at a time when Neil was confronted by other, more disturbing news: the mediocre performance of his latest releases.

The polished but uninspired "Turn Around" failed to turn around singles buyers, failing to crack *Billboard*'s Top 40. The LP, "Primitive," did, but only barely, cresting at number thirty-five; it was the poorest showing of a new Diamond studio album in fifteen years. In fact, the only hit that Neil enjoyed that summer was a reggae version of his 1967 chestnut, "Red Red Wine," which the group UB40 sang to the top of the British charts.

Promotion conscious as Neil was (Bruce Lundvall: "Sometimes he would pop a call in to . . . whoever was running promotion, cause he wanted to know what was going on"), he must have been keenly aware that CBS Records wasn't hyping "Turn Around" and "Primitive" with its usual fervor. There was no Sunset Strip billboard this time; no print ads, other than in *Billboard*; no in-store posters and/or displays. As for the national television campaign that the label promised in its July 14 memo to record stores, a weekend blitz of spots touting "Turn Around" and the album did occur—several weeks *after* the records were released.

All the more galling to Neil, no doubt, was the fact that while his records were dying on the vine, the first American single from middle-aged Spanish crooner Julio Iglesias—a duet with Willie Nelson called "To All the Girls I've Loved Before"—managed to make *Billboard*'s Top 10, as did his LP, "1100 Bel Air Place."

By 1984 it was well known among Diamond insiders that he did not view the successes of certain fellow middle-of-the-road superstars with charity. His contempt for his would-be *Jazz Singer* successor, Barry Manilow, had been documented on the set of *Singer,* and in regard to Kenny Rogers, Neil was said to have furiously demanded one day that his then-executive assistant Marge Johnson remove Rogers' recording of "Sweet Music Man" from the office turntable. "He hated that song so badly," confided one source. "He was furious that Kenny Rogers would have the kind of success he's had."

As for Iglesias, making his lightning-fast rise all the harder for Neil to take, no doubt, was the fact that Iglesias was a Columbia label-mate, and had benefited from the label's all-out promotional push.

There seemed to be a message in that to Neil from Chairman Yetnikoff.

When the going had gotten tough before, the road had always seemed to be a welcome refuge for Neil, and he just happened to have a month's worth of Midwest, East Coast, and Southern dates in August. As it turned out this time, there were moments, both on stage and off, where he appeared to be at loose ends.

Certainly, he wasn't his gregarious supershowman self at Chicago's Poplar Creek on August 25. "It was a defeated man who walked out on stage that night, and he didn't even try," commented one longtime observer who had witnessed dozens of his shows. "I've never seen a show like this one . . . He glared at the audience like he hated them at times . . . Even his occasional smile was not genuine, but pasted on . . .

"The audiences usually give back what they get and there was no giving that night . . . Neil came back out for 'Brother Love' to a still-seated audience. I've never seen an audience sit during 'Brother Love' before, but that's what they did . . . Neil didn't do his usual screaming, and afterwards literally ran offstage, visibly relieved that it was over."

It was in Chicago, too, that Neil caused dismay in his fan camp by taking steps to distance himself from his most intensely dedicated admirers, dozens of whom, mainly women, were known to fly to his concerts around the country. Hairdresser/personal assistant Jerry Kerns was the one who dropped the ax. "Jerry was telling fans not to stay at the same hotels as Neil anymore and that they were going to get rude," one source reported. "He told one woman that Neil was tired of seeing the same old faces and wanted to see some new ones. He told another that Neil could not understand the intensity of the fans' feelings and it spooked him. He told another that the same old faces sent up the same old pile of shit to the room to be signed and that Neil was getting sick of it. He said a huge pile of stuff came up and it was all being returned, unsigned, with a warning that anything else would not be returned and would be left unsigned."

Neil seemed to be building up to his fan decree at his previous tour stop, Detroit, where he was said to have blown up at his ever-present security for allowing a female to grab his arm and kiss him as he attempted to board the band bus. That reaction, in turn, may have been sparked by an unsettling experience in London, where he was tailed constantly by two female fans.

Actually, Diamond's ambivalence toward his most intensely devoted fans probably dated back to the '70s—when he and his family began receiving death threats. He had no choice, of course, but to take the threats seriously, investing heavily in security—up to fifteen guards at a time. "My private detective bill is phenomenal," he said in 1982. "There are a lot of crazies out there." (Because of a spate of threats just prior to his 1983 Forum engagement, for example, he hired extra plain-clothes personnel to patrol the arena. Demonstrating that they were primed for action, several went for their guns when the first flash pot exploded during his opening-night performance of "America.")

But buying security wasn't the only expense Neil had to incur as a response to obsessive fans. In 1983 he was forced to hire a truck equipped with a paper shredder to make daily pickups at his Melrose Place office, this after discovering that a woman had been making nightly pickups of his trash.

In view of these headaches, it seemed understandable that he would elect to finally make himself less accessible to any and all fans. But one fan had a point, too, when she commented on behalf of all the good apples in his fan basket: "Neil works at wrenching every last ounce of emotion out of his fans, yet he can't understand it when they respond in a positive way? There are too many mixed signals."

As difficult as this tour seemed for him, Neil was undoubtedly relieved to return to Los Angeles and his and Marcia's two homes—a five-bedroom pad in the Malibu Colony, purchased in 1977 for more than $1 million (and which was registered under Marcia's name only), and their eight-bedroom, 8,000-square-foot home on Mapleton Drive in Holmby Hills, purchased for approximately $2 million in 1978. Until he returned to the road for a few dates in December, his public appearances were limited to the Los Angeles social scene. In September he attended the special invitational screening of *Amadeus* at the UA Coronet Theatre in West Los Angeles. In October, he sang the national anthem at a Walter Mondale–Geraldine Ferraro fund-raiser at the Beverly Hilton. In November, he attended the "Night at the Races" benefit tribute to late record executive Neil Bogart at Hollywood Park. In December, he attended the American Friends of Hebrew University's benefit gala at the Beverly Hilton, where Barbra Streisand was given the group's annual Scopus Award.

Photos of a grinning Diamond at the latter two events made the "Click" page of the *Los Angeles Herald Examiner*. A shot from "Night at the Races"—this one of Neil and Marcia in a laughing embrace—also was published in *People*. The message for public consumption was clear: Diamond the dichotomy was having a ball in 1984, despite reports or intimations to the contrary.

Amid Neil's social sightings was the publication of a page-one *Daily*

Variety piece on his manager's film-producing plans for 1985–1986. Jerry Weintraub had struck it rich with *The Karate Kid,* and, according to the *Variety* piece, had nine more pictures scheduled for filming. Among them was not only the endlessly discussed Diamond-starring vehicle, *Death at an Early Age,* a coproduction with Ray Stark for Columbia, but also *Beautiful Noise,* which Weintraub reportedly was set to coproduce with Neil for Paramount.

The formal news that *Noise* had been returned to Neil Diamond's front burner along with *Death* came six months after Paramount took out a double-truck ad in *Variety* announcing the project, and three months after columnist Marilyn Beck reported that Neil had met in London with Stevie Wonder about Wonder making his acting debut in the film.

Suddenly, 1985 loomed as a potential big year for Neil, stalled at the proverbial career crossroads.

Diamond started 1985 as if he truly did mean business, film-wise. In January, he met with Gil Cates, whom he had chosen to direct *Death.* In February, syndicated columnist Shirley Eder reported that he had penned four songs for the drama, as well as six additional tunes for *Beautiful Noise.*

It seemed an interesting time for Neil to be interviewed by Barbara Walters on her ABC special March 25. The interview, which had actually been taped the previous summer in the Diamonds' Malibu home, had been advertised as his first in-depth TV interview in twelve years. That wasn't correct—Neil had granted an extensive television interview to Robert Hilburn in 1980 for "Midnight Special"—but it *was* the most important interview he had given since *Jazz Singer.*

Walters thus had a golden opportunity to get Neil on record on such newsworthy career topics as his widely publicized battle with CBS Records and the state of his recording career; his false starts on the film and TV fronts in the wake of *Jazz Singer,* and the reasons why; his current involvement with *Death at an Early Age* and *Beautiful Noise;* and his amazing popularity as a performer at a time when he was selling fewer records than in the past.

But if Walters tackled any of the above subjects, the segments were left on the cutting room floor. In the excerpts that were broadcast, she trod on safe turf, mostly Neil's early career. Her questions were easy lobs, and Neil, appearing personable even though his conversational voice sounded oddly tearful, handled them with aplomb.

Walters did ask one intriguing question. Alluding to the line in "I Am . . . I Said" in which, fourteen years earlier, he likened himself to a frog who became a king, she asked, "What are you today, the frog or the king?" Neil replied: "Um, I'm neither. I realized a long time ago that I was not about to be a king. And, uh, I'm not a frog either. I'm, uh, I'm a human being."

He then lapsed into the same kind of onstage patter he had used in the early 1970s to introduce "I Am . . . I Said": "I hurt. I *lovvvve*. I feel guilt. I love to laugh."

The airing of "The Barbara Walters Special" came at a poignant time in Neil's life. Two days earlier, March 23 at 9:05 P.M., his father died of a heart attack at University Hospital in Tamarac, Florida, where he had been a patient. Kieve Diamond was sixty-seven years old.

Although death had come at a relatively young age, one couldn't say that life had cheated Kieve. Thanks to Neil's generosity, he had been able to retire in the early '70s. Having already mastered the art of enjoying life, he and Rose had then made a smooth transition to an active retirement.

Some of their favorite times, no doubt, had come watching Neil perform on stages around the world. On tour with their son, Kieve and Rose were celebrities in their own right, often being approached by fans for autographs and conversation.

They kept on the move at other times, too, shuttling between their homes in Brooklyn, Tamarac, and Woodland Hills, California, where they were within easy visiting distance of both Neil and family, and brother Harvey, who lived in Studio City with his wife, Alice, and their two children.

Rose and Kieve never ceased to be outgoing. One of the first things Rose would do when she and Kieve arrived in Florida was to phone all of their Brooklyn friends who had moved south to arrange dinners and dances. Back home in Brooklyn, meanwhile, they stayed in close touch with granddaughters Marjorie and Elyn, who lived with their remarried mother in New Jersey. "As proud as they were as parents, that's how proud they were as grandparents," said Neil's Lincoln High pal Bobby Feldman, who saw Rose and Kieve with Marjorie and Elyn from time to time.

It was in Brooklyn one night in the summer of 1984 that Kieve dusted off his old costumes and took the stage at the Brighton Beach Tennis and Racquet Club one last time to perform his hilarious pantomimes of female singers.

During that summer, Kieve had his first conversation in more than two decades with Neil's former singing partner, Jack Packer. Recalled Packer, still a Brooklyn resident and by then a successful society singer and bandleader performing under the stage name of Jan Harris: "He was telling me how proud they were of Neil, how he achieved this success *beyond their wildest expectations* . . . that they could not believe his drive and motivation themselves. And that Neil is wealthy beyond belief.

And that Harvey is doing unbelievably fantastic in numerous business ventures. And that they're living a good life . . . "

It was precisely Kieve's ability to live the good life that had earned the envy of his elder son. "I wish I had that basic nature to relax and go with it," Neil confessed once. But, of course, he didn't, which may explain why he was said to have run his family—Rose and Kieve included—the same way he ran his career. "Neil does what Neil wants to do," commented a reliable source in 1984. "He's the king of his family. You can imagine what his mother and father feel about him, but he treats them the same way. If he wants the family around him, fine. But if he doesn't . . . He's always in control."

Neil had his father's body removed from Siegel Memorial Chapel in Tamarac and flown, via private jet, to Los Angeles. On Tuesday, March 26, funeral services were held for Akeeba Diamond at the Eternal Light Chapel in Eden Memorial Park in Mission Hills, after which Kieve was laid to rest.

Three days later, Neil, who had been in the midst of a Northwest Canada concert swing, performed in the first of five sold-out shows at Seattle's 14,000-seat Coliseum. "We are alive tonight," he stated at the beginning of his subdued performance. "We're here, you're here and we are all alive. God bless us."

After making up in early April the two Calgary concerts he had postponed because of his father's death, Diamond returned to Los Angeles. Not long after that, there was word that he intended to make an appearance in public at sometime-collaborator Gilbert Becaud's opening night performance at the Beverly Theater in Beverly Hills on April 20.

A half hour before Becaud took the stage that night, Marcia Diamond entered the Beverly and took a place at the bar in the center of the cozy lobby, a sure sign that Neil was indeed about to make an appearance. A few minutes later, Neil, puffing on a cigarette, was spotted handing his ticket to an usher.

More than one head turned. Dressed in a black turtleneck sweater and a gray jacket, he walked into the lobby not like someone prepped to do another smiling star turn, but like a heavy from Central Casting. Although he was not "made up" for the occasion—his thinning hair, for example, teased and styled by Jerry Kerns for his photos and performances, was in serious need of a "do"—his appearance wasn't as surprising as the vibes he sent shuddering through the lobby. The apparent message: "I am *not* to be approached."

As he sided up to Marcia at the Beverly's bar, Neil got his space. There he and Marcia made quiet conversation for a few minutes. Several times during their talk his lips formed a fleeting smile, but the rest of his face remained cold.

And then he was gone, entering the theater alone as Marcia remained at the bar with her drink and cigarette.

Although one was tempted to chalk up his curious public behavior to moodiness in the wake of his father's death, the fact remained that, when Gilbert Becaud introduced "my best friend" from the stage a half hour later, the spotlight located an entirely different man in his sixth-row aisle seat. This Diamond warmed the hall with a 100-watt grin.

As the audience erupted into applause, Neil sprang to his feet, genially acknowledged the greeting, and flung a long-stalked lily to Becaud.

The summer of 1985 passed with nary a public word from Neil's camp on the progress of his movie projects. As for Neil himself, he was sequestered in the studio for a portion of the time working on a new album, giving the impression that serious work on *Death at an Early Age* or *Beautiful Noise* was still months, or more, away.

Neil had been so impressed by CBS Records' and Denny Diante's criticisms about the "dated" sound of the tracks he had produced on "Primitive," that this time, for the first time ever, he produced the *entire* LP himself. He did, however, apparently take to heart one of Diante's comments during their search for additional "Primitive" songs: "Why are we doing this? You should really write. You're your own best song-writer." Of the nine songs he planned for the new album, the only one that he didn't write by himself was "Falling," a collaboration with Becaud. Underscoring the in-house nature of the project was the fact that all of the tunes were arranged by his keyboardists, Alan Lindgren and Tom Hensley.

In September, Neil turned in the album, tentatively titled "The Story of My Life." A sentence at the bottom of the liner notes provided a clue as to why he had decided to make the LP his most self-contained one yet: "This album is dedicated to my father."

As touching as the gesture was, one didn't have to listen long to the uneven LP to realize that he had made a mistake by going the solitary record-maker route. Among the LP's low points: "Midnight Rider," with its Lawrence Welk brand of ersatz country bop; the typewriter sound effects on the insipid "I'm Saying I'm Sorry (and Then I'm Saying Goodnight)," Neil's lyric to "Dancing to the Party Next Door," in which he reveals his desire to be "grooving" with the rock 'n' rolling "kids." Even his Big Song, "Angel Above My Head," an interesting meditation on growing older that seemed inspired by Kieve's passing, was marred by his muddled lyric and the plodding arrangement.

In short, there was little doubt that the story of "The Story of My

Life" would be a short one. In fact, soon after Neil submitted the album to Columbia, word leaked out that CBS Records Chairman Walter Yetnikoff had turned it down, ruling that it was not "commercial" enough.

This time, Neil did not file suit in an attempt to get the label to see matters his way. He simply returned to the studio in November.

His second LP rejection in a row apparently doomed the release of another album Diamond had tentatively planned to release at the end of 1985: the all-but-forgotten "Live at the Forum" double LP from 1983. At Neil's request, engineer Ron Hitchcock had recently remastered the album, but once again he did not hear back from Neil after delivering the tapes.

In November, meanwhile, Diamond's manager, Jerry Weintraub, was named chairman and chief executive officer of United Artists Corporation. To take the position, he not only had to resign control of his management company, Management III, but also his film production company. That left Neil's pending film career in limbo, along with his recording career.

Appearing relaxed and congenial, however, Diamond in the early fall posed for *People* with his brother, Harvey, inside one of the $10,000 stereo-equipped "Bath Womb" Jacuzzis that the younger Diamond, owner of a thriving hot tub business in Canoga Park, had designed. Then in November, he and Marcia traveled to the White House, where they attended President and Mrs. Reagans' dinner in honor of Princess Diana and Prince Charles, and where Neil gave his impromptu performance. (Speaking of Diamond's periodic hobnobbing with royalty over the years, one former employee said: "There was always that feeling that he enjoyed being in that presence . . . And yet he would resent hearing that so much because he feels he's one of the guys. He likes to get down with the fellahs. But he never really does.")

In December, it was back to business as usual, a tour of the Midwest. But even on the concert trail, he could find some cause for concern. His two shows at Cincinnati's 16,336-seat Riverfront Coliseum, for example, took weeks to sell out, while his previous six shows at the venue had sold out in a matter of hours each time. "This had his handlers quaking in their Gucci loafers," wrote *The Cincinnati Enquirer's* Cliff Radel. "In calls to *The Enquirer* . . . they acted as if the concerts were bombing." Neil's mood couldn't have been brightened, meanwhile, by news from back home: the publication of a Robert Hilburn–authored piece in the *Los Angeles Times* headlined "The Big Deal" that was angled on record executives' hypothetical listings of their dream artist rosters. Neil's name not only did not appear among the top twenty scorers, he was dismissed by the two executives whom Hilburn quoted. "Why bother to even discuss him at this point?" remarked one. "Not what he used to be," said the other.

And yet, as Neil held the stage at the eventually sold-out Riverfront Coliseum, sold-out Kemper Arena in Kansas City, and the sold-out Civic Center in St. Paul, he had the cheers of his fans to assure and comfort him. They accepted him for just who he was today, and their beautiful noise, no doubt, made it all too easy for him to jam the striving inner voices of Neil Diamond past. One wondered if he heard those goading voices much anymore, anyway.

Oh, in 1982, he had renounced his "I dream of being Beethoven" quote of a decade earlier, declaring, "After years of therapy, I have finally forgiven myself for not being Beethoven."

But lately there had been nothing but silence from him on many of the other goals he had set for himself since he'd become a superstar—some of them not outlandish at all, but necessary ones for a serious artist to undertake.

The screenplay he was going to write.

The lessons in composing and arranging he was going to take, so he could compose that ballet and that string quartet piece, and lead the New York Philharmonic.

The early legit Broadway play that he was going to musicalize.

The TV movie of "Brother Love" he was going to make.

The feature film career he was going to carve out for himself with such properties as *You Don't Bring Me Flowers, Beautiful Noise,* and *Death at an Early Age.*

The fact was, in the dozen years since he had talked of the necessity of "broadening" his career, Neil had but two TV specials and a predictable movie vehicle to show for all his goal talk, and his tortured ambivalence about committing to *Jazz Singer* was already legend. Moreover, his shrinking rather than expanding career horizons had seemed to have had a negative effect on the activity he claimed was the bedrock of his talent: his songwriting.

So what had happened to make Neil Diamond something less than a "Big Deal" by the end of 1985?

Did the ferocious insecurity that had fueled his drive to stardom, and then compelled him to tout himself publicly—while treating the Lee Holdridges in his life less than magnanimously—now hold him hostage as a superstar? Did it prevent him from daring any longer, lest he fail once too often and be exposed as something less than an infallible "king" of pop?

For those fans looking for a sign, any sign, that Diamond hadn't stopped striving, they could find a laser ray of hope in a new song he was using to open his December shows. The tune featured a *Star Wars* synthesizer line, unusual sound effects, and a determinedly upbeat lyric.

Its title: "Headed for the Future."

·24·
STIRRINGS

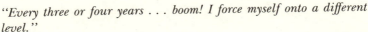

"Every three or four years . . . boom! I force myself onto a different level."

—Diamond

The first public hint that Neil had resolved to get aggressive again in 1986 came in January, when he performed for only the second time since the early '70s on a U.S. television program. The show was a January 20 NBC extravaganza celebrating the first official Martin Luther King, Jr. national holiday. Diamond flew his band to New York, where, along with the likes of Bill Cosby, Harry Belafonte, and Bette Midler, he participated in the Radio City Music Hall portion of the telecast. He took the stage in a new Bill Whitten creation, a short black jacket with the requisite number of sparkles, and gave his familiar growling rendition of "America."

He didn't tarry in New York. Four days later he was back in Los Angeles performing a couple of nonpublicized "mini-concerts" for a select group of fans and friends. The occasion was the taping of a portion of his first network TV special in nine years.

For the CBS special, Neil had retained the services of Dwight Hemion and Gary Smith, the Emmy Award–winning team who had produced his "Love at the Greek" hour. They, head writer/producer Kenny Solms and Diamond had decided on a day-in-the-life formula featuring guest stars Carol Burnett and Stevie Wonder, who had served as host and executive producer of the King TV special. Much had already been shot, including, a few days earlier, Diamond's fantasy segments with Burnett. In one, they had duetted, semiseriously, on a medley of his hits, the comedian going momentarily limp-limbed in Neil's arms. And in the other, she reprised her "Eunice" and "Stella Toddler" characters in a studio question-and-answer segment that Neil conducted.

The skits, amazingly, were the first ones that Neil had ever performed on TV. Between takes, he revealed his usual nervousness, calling out to director Dwight Hemion at one point, "Can I sing now?" (What the audience didn't know was that Neil was so uptight about doing the scenes with Burnett that he had Kenny Solms, who had served as head writer on Burnett's show, take his place in the first reading.)

On January 24, his forty-fifth birthday, Neil finally did get to sing, for more than three hours in two audience tapings. "I thought it was going to be my lucky day," he announced after taking the stage, "but then I got a ticket." Later, he spotted Rose Diamond, now sixty-seven, in a less-than-great seat: "Is that my mom back there? You shouldn't be behind that camera—you can't see very well, mom." He directed her to a new seat. "Say hi to everybody, mom." After she did, and the audience applauded, he asked her, "How am I doing? She's the worst person to ask because whatever I do—since I was sixteen—'It's great, just keep doing it.'"

Diamond also had something to say about the Aquarius Theater, site of the taping; in a past life, the room had been known as the Hullabaloo. "I still have the newspaper review on my wall," he said, alluding to his performance there back in 1966. "It was my first newspaper review ever. They said that, uh, 'Diamond beat a strategic retreat from the stage.' And they were absolutely correct. But we've been practicing a lot since then." Then Neil launched into "Cherry, Cherry," a tune he'd performed at the onetime teen dance club. "Well, we may have beat a 'strategic retreat from the stage' twenty years ago, but we got 'em by the balls tonight!" he declared afterward.

Neil didn't display quite the same bravado when asked by a fan during one of the TV special tapings if he planned to make another movie soon. He responded that his new manager, Sandy Gallin—his sixth since Bang Records days—was in charge of those matters. "You'll have to ask him," he said.

Diamond had a good reason to be coy. There was nary a hint that his plans for the year included a film. Regarding the CBS-TV movie he was going to fashion from "Brother Love," for example, one network source chuckled at the time, "It's not dead here, [but] it's dying." The truth was, however, that "Brother Love" was probably never in robust health. Pete Hamill, whom Diamond's then-manager, Jerry Weintraub, had signed in 1983 to write the "Brother Love" screenplay, described Diamond as being "vague and blurry" about the project the one time they discussed it. Hamill wrote a fifteen-page outline anyway, casting Brother Love as "essentially cynical, a modern version of Elmer Gantry." He turned the outline in and, he added with a laugh, "I never heard from anybody!"

As for the Paramount production of *Beautiful Noise*, trumpeted in a 1984 double-truck ad in the trades, one well-placed studio source insisted, "It's not dead yet." He was contradicted, however, by another Paramount contact, who reported: "The project was dropped—it's been taken out of development. It's no longer on our books."

Meanwhile at Columbia Pictures, *Death at an Early Age*, the property that Neil claimed "I'd work my ass off to get" fifteen years earlier, seemed near death at an elderly age. "The project fell into the abyss of just three dots," stated Gil Cates, the man who had been hired to direct it in 1985. "I have no idea what happened to it . . . The screenplay [writer] Bobby Huston and I came to was first class. I thought Neil would have been wonderful in the script."

By deciding not to play the film card in 1986, it was clear that Neil had opted for a safer road back to a high profile—through his music. That meant turning in a new album in time to set up his TV special that would not only please the powers-that-be at CBS Records, but also the public.

Not long after Columbia had rejected his LP in 1985, Diamond served notice that he was serious about reworking it. He recorded "Headed for the Future," which he'd cowritten with Alan Lindgren and Tom Hensley, and he invited Maurice White, of Earth, Wind & Fire fame, to lend a producing hand.

The selection of the hip rhythm-and-blues-oriented rocker wasn't as surprising as it might have appeared; White, a Columbia artist as well, had produced several tracks on Barbra Streisand's 1984 album, "Emotion." Micah Diamond and White's son, Kahbran, also happened to be classmates at the same private school in West Hollywood, and one day in 1985 Maurice attended a party Neil and Marcia hosted for the school in their home. "Neil and I were just sitting, talking about music, while the kids were playing," he explained. "I think he called me mainly because of that conversation. So I must say that our kids brought us together."

Diamond gave White a tape of the album he'd submitted to Columbia, asking for his opinion ("I felt the sound wasn't innovative as of today," White noted). Then Neil turned White loose on a song search, White eventually running about ten tunes by him. In November, they stepped into Bill Schnee's studio to record four of them: the hooky, high-energy "Stand Up for Love," which White had cowritten with his coproducer, Greg Phillinganes, and Martin Page; "We're Doing It," which White described as a "Bruce Springsteen thing, with funk"; the driving, midtempo "Angel"; and, for a change of pace, the ballady "Love Doesn't Live Here Anymore."

"There were sparks flying once in a while; I would want to work a little later, he'd want to go home," White said, recalling the sessions. "But with him being a perfectionist also we didn't really have a problem . . . So we were pretty cool . . . very compatible."

White added that he found Neil "sometimes a little distant. Has his days. But we all have our days. As a whole . . . very warm. Very concerned. I find him very serious—concentrated in life."

The producer did recall one moment when Neil cut up in the studio, to his own momentary chagrin: "I was trying to show him a line in 'Angel.' I'm a singer, so I'm out there singing this song for him. And he looks at me after me doing all these fantastic runs, and started laughing. And I'm wondering, What is the guy laughing about—this is not funny. So, he told me, 'Well, look, let me let you in on one thing—I'll never be able to do those acrobatics like you're doing.'" White added that from then on he watched Diamond "react to the songs as a poet. He does a *reading* on the song. That's the thing that impressed me . . . You don't need to do acrobatics on songs, you can just do a reading . . . It's easier, and it probably gets through to the other side."

White finished mixing the tunes in February. By then, Neil had finished work on his May special, including the taping of a "rehearsal" segment with Stevie Wonder in which they teamed up on "Sir Duke," Wonder's musical tribute to Duke Ellington and contemporaries (Neil had recorded the tune in 1978 but had never released it). It wasn't long afterward that word leaked out that he had decided to extend the overhaul of his album, tapping the songwriting, producing, and arranging services of David Foster, who, since playing piano on "Heartlight" and coproducing "I'm Alive," had become one of the hottest names in the business, working with Chicago, Lionel Richie, Kenny Rogers, and Barbra Streisand. Then, there was the news that Diamond was giving birth to even more new tunes in the studio with Burt Bacharach and Carole Bayer Sager—and Stevie Wonder. "I guess once his juices got going . . . he probably decided, 'Hey, I might as well just go for it, and be done with it,'" speculated Columbia Records vice president Denny Diante, who acted as the label's liaison with the producers.

The album, renamed "Headed for the Future," was finally at the finishing-touches stage in April, when Neil and band embarked on a two-week tour of the East Coast. In his review of Diamond's sold-out opening night concert at Philadelphia's Spectrum, the *Daily News'* Jonathan Takiff joined the ranks of critic nonbelievers who felt obliged nonetheless to tip their hat to Neil: "I commend his ability at crossing over age and cultural boundaries with his work, touching even staid and proper people where they live and encouraging them to let it all hang out—to loosen their ties, flick their Bics, shout out requests, clap along and hug their spouses when the mood hits 'em."

On April 26, two days after his final Philadelphia appearance, Diamond and his fans put on an even more impressive display of their enduring bond at a benefit UCLA tribute to Carol Burnett, his first public appearance in Los Angeles in almost three years. Even though he was only one guest on a bill that included Elizabeth Taylor, Beverly Sills, and Julie Andrews, it was he who the majority of fans in Pauley Pavilion had paid twenty-five dollars and up to see. The cheering and screaming began the instant a clip of his upcoming TV duet with Burnett filled the screens on either side of the stage, and it built to a thunderous arena-wide ovation as he walked onstage a few moments later.

It was the biggest response of the night, even bigger than that accorded the subject of the tribute when Neil introduced Burnett at the conclusion of his four-song set.

"I don't know why I still have people screaming in the audience, but I love it," Neil told *USA Today* in an interview published the day before the benefit. He continued: "I know my audience and they know me . . . I didn't suddenly get hot, disappear and then come back with an entire new sound."

Several days after the benefit, "Headed for the Future" was released as Neil's twenty-fifth Columbia single. A week later, "Headed for the Future" the LP hit the stores on schedule, a full three weeks before his May 25 special.

The album was immediately noteworthy in one respect: On the cover was an up-to-date—albeit with wrinkles airbrushed out—photograph of a pensive Neil in a black corduroy jacket, the first time in five years that he had gone with a current shot on an album cover. (At one of his tapings for the special, the audience had cheered his promise that this LP would come with a "brand-new" photo; they would not have been happy with the nine-year-old photograph that had appeared on a mockup of the rejected album he had submitted to Columbia.)

As for the songs, one listen to the LP revealed that Diamond had tried to contemporize his sound, too. Of the ten tunes he'd turned in on his original album, only one remained, his ballady paean to Marcia, "The Story of My Life." ("Make believe I'm just a little boat in an ocean very big," he told *USA Today*. "She's my harbor.") In their place, he'd substituted a largely impressive batch of adult contemporary tunes.

"Headed for the Future" the album and "Headed for the Future" the single debuted on the May 24 *Billboard* charts. By then, Diamond had already beat the drums for both the LP and the TV special in a handful of additional interviews.

Architect of his press campaign was his new public relations firm, Solters, Roskin & Friedman. (As for Paul Wasserman, new manager Sandy Gallin was said to have informed the veteran PR man of the account change, Diamond choosing not to talk to Wasserman himself, despite the fact that Wasserman had been in his employ for more than a dozen years.) The firm came up with a list of interviews that promised maximum exposure for minimum investment of time and/or risk of journalistic ambush: among them, *TV Guide,* "Entertainment Tonight," *People,* the *Los Angeles Times,* UPI, and Knight-Ridder News Service.

Solters, Roskin & Friedman official Beverly Magid served notice as to the upbeat approach her firm's new client intended to take in his interviews when she told one of the publications, "There's so much that's positive happening in Neil's career right now." UPI's Vernon

Scott, one of the first to get a crack at Diamond, came away believing: "Diamond looked the picture of a successful man, at ease with himself and his visitor." But the most striking statement of Neil's positive bent came from Neil himself when he literally jumped for joy in front of a *People* photographer. The full-page photo introduced his *People* profile.

However, no spate of Diamond interviews, no matter how glowing, was without some weighty personal confessions. To Leeza Gibbons of "Entertainment Tonight," Neil allowed that "I constantly fight the battle of my own self . . . I want to be a better person. And I have a feeling that it's a lifetime job." And to the *Times'* Robert Hilburn, he admitted that 1985 was a "hell of a [bad] year" for the death not only of his father in March but also of Marcia's mother, Evelyn Murphey, in December. Yet in each of the interviews, his bottom-line words were affirmative ones. "I've loosened up quite a bit," he told "E.T." "[After my dad's death] I began to feel that I couldn't hold back any more. I have to go out there and enjoy myself, enjoy my life, try to live it to the fullest," he told the *Times*.

Standing in stark contrast to these neatly wrapped journalistic packages was Elaine Warren's questioning *TV Guide* profile. The headline to the piece made it clear that she was one journalist who did not hew to the everything-is-coming-up-roses-for-Diamond-at-forty-five theory: IF BOY GEORGE IS PASSÉ, WHERE DOES THAT LEAVE NEIL DIAMOND? But beyond the "mid-life *predicament*" she sensed Diamond was going through as a recording artist, she observed a vexing, dichotomous personality. In one breath Diamond talked of wanting "excitement and challenges" in his life; in the next breath he portrayed himself as a confirmed homebody, adding "I live just the most mundane kind of life you could possibly imagine . . ." Wrote Warren: "What *is* this nagging contradiction about Diamond?"

Warren hinted at a possible answer earlier in her article when she made note of Diamond's "repressed . . . powers of introspection" in doubting, years earlier, that "Solitary Man" was partly autobiographical. She put her suspicion in the form of a question to Diamond, asking him if he felt that he really knew himself.

It was a question that *Jazz Singer* screenwriter Jerry Kass might have asked Neil after failing to get him to open up in any substantive way during their several days together on tour. It was a question that Ellie Greenwich might have asked him after he told her that his ultimate high in life was walking out on a stage to cheers. It was a question anyone might have asked him after studying his ultimately resentful attitude toward his Brooklyn roots, or observing his "king" and *mensch* personas vie with one another. But it was Elaine Warren of *TV Guide* who was the first to ask Neil Diamond on record if he really knew what he was about as a person.

The query seemed to take Neil by surprise. "I don't know. Let me know when you find out," he said finally.

Diamond's special was aired as scheduled on Sunday, May 25, the middle of the three-day Memorial Day weekend. To ensure that it would get the lion's share of viewers on a down evening for TV watching, CBS moved the show up an hour from its original 9 P.M. slot, when it would have gone up against a "Perry Mason" TV movie on NBC. At eight, its only network competition was "Amazing Stories" and the second half of a two-segment "Disney Sunday Movie."

The airing of the special revealed that the same kind of play-it-safe thinking that the network had employed in its scheduling had been used by Neil and producers Dwight Hemion, Gary Smith, and Kenny Solms in the conception of the show itself. Titled "Hello Again," after Neil's 1980 *Jazz Singer* hit, the program proved to be a visual greeting card to his fans; no more, no less. The determinedly lighthearted day-in-the-life formula was a trite one, and the comedy segments were tame prime-time fodder (for example, Diamond being pitched on godawful lyrics by the mailman, the gas station attendant, and the parking lot attendant). And the thirty-minute concert segment that ended the hour wasn't the least bit daring either, Neil having dispensed with "Headed for the Future," the one new song, in the opening minutes of the show. (The special did only OK in the Nielsens, finishing twenty-first.)

But striking familiar chords, literally and figuratively, was the way Neil Diamond and manager Sandy Gallin had obviously plotted his comeback in 1986. His campaign to regain the pop spotlight, in fact, had taken another familiar turn the week before the special with the shrewdly timed announcement, via a two-page ad in the *Los Angeles Times,* of his first concert stand at the Greek Theatre in a decade that August.

It didn't take any special powers of insight to figure out why Neil might want to tap into that old Greek magic in 1986. The Greek had made him a superstar and it had yielded him two double albums, the first of which, "Hot August Night," still ranked as his all-time best seller. Moreover, with the expected immediate sellout of all his shows in the amphitheater, which had been enlarged to a seating capacity of 6,100 in 1984 but which still was tiny compared to the cavernous arenas he had been filling for years, he was destined to appear more in demand than ever.

In fact, that is how Diamond's Greek saga began to unfold. On Monday, May 19, the day seats to the ten announced dates went on sale, 4,000 people showed up at the theater's box office, and thousands more lined up at Ticketron outlets around the Southland. By late afternoon, all 61,000 tickets had been sold. On May 27, two days after the special, tickets to an additional four shows went on sale. In just over an hour they, too, were gone.

By then, Los Angeles' scalpers—including one who had driven in a busload of laborers to the Greek to stand in line for tickets—were touting Diamond's name en masse in their Sunday *Los Angeles Times* ads. One scalper's opening prices: $350 and *up* for a Section A ducat.

As it turned out, Neil's Greek engagement would serve as the capper to one of his busiest summers in years. He could be seen making the party rounds in Los Angeles, appearing on a prestigious TV special, and entertaining 160,000 New Yorkers in a record-setting eight-night engagement at Madison Square Garden.

Ironically, one of the few pans he received was for his "performance" at the June 25 Century Plaza soirée celebrating the opening of the Disney comedy *Ruthless People*. "It was an all-industry party at which you move around," explained one of the attendees, a regular on the Los Angeles social circuit. "But Neil stayed put at his table, smoking constantly. He puts up a wall, and he just doesn't talk. Maybe it's shyness. He looks as though he should be there, but he's not sure why. Meanwhile, Marcia is social and chats it up. She's the one with social aspirations."

There was no doubt that Neil felt more in his element on New York's Governor's Island on July 2 as he rehearsed for his moment in the glow of the newly relit Statue of Liberty. Of all the pop stars scheduled to appear the next day on the prime-time entertainment extravaganza inaugurating Liberty Weekend, Diamond impressed observers by rehearsing the longest and hardest. He also raised eyebrows by forbidding photographers from shooting him and having a bodyguard accompany him everywhere he went, despite the already airtight security. When it came time to eat, however, Diamond was plain old *hamish* Neil, munching on burgers Marcia had sent out for. (Keeping Neil company part of the time was Marjorie Diamond, now twenty, who was serving as a production assistant on the David Wolper–produced special.)

The next night, one could better appreciate why Neil would want to be well prepared: His song, the appropriately patriotic "America," both opened and closed a twenty-minute segment of the show chronicling the flood of immigrants to the United States in the late nineteenth and early twentieth centuries. Neil braved the bitter, windy cold with a vigorous, upbeat performance. Afterward, he retreated to the warmth of the downstairs performers' area, electing not to use any of the six seats in the audience he had requested.

While he was in New York, Neil guested on Scott Shannon's morning radio show on Z100. He had much to plug while he wasn't fielding calls from adoring fans: his new releases (by then, however, only his album was showing any "legs" sales-wise, the single "Headed for the Future" already having become passé on the charts); an upcoming autograph signing at Tower Records; and especially his concerts at Madison Square Garden later in the month. The Garden dates were to be his first ever, and his first in New York in a decade.

However, while Diamond agreeably elaborated on his activities, he was not at all like the hyped-up thirty-one-year-old who met—and occasionally confronted—the press in the days preceding his Broadway engagement fourteen years earlier. Speaking in a soft, nearly monotone voice, he sounded determinedly low-key, a curious contrast to deejay Shannon's own antic delivery.

Beginning July 24, Neil let his performance do the talking. He had much to overcome singing in the giant Garden, and his show suffered in some respects. Because of the Garden's horrible acoustics, for example, it sounded as if he were speaking in the Holland Tunnel between songs, instead of on a concert stage. Still, he sang well, his lighting, laser displays, and staging were typically top notch, and the crowds—with the exception of an unusually undemonstrative Saturday turnout—were with him all the way.

Bad acoustics or not, Neil couldn't resist addressing the hometown folks with autobiographical tidbits. On the second night he took a few moments to chronicle his New York performance history, beginning with the Bitter End in 1966. (When more than a few members of the audience indicated by their applause that they had seen him there, he cracked, "I doubt it.") There were also references to the moving around he'd done in Brooklyn as a youth, and the Saturday night "rumbles" in Flatbush's Prospect Park he'd witnessed as a twelve-year-old. The sharing of those personal notes with the audience helped to shrink the size of the vast arena. So, too, did the screens on each side of the stage that carried Neil's giant image.

Neil had packed in the engagements in the several weeks before Madison Square Garden—three nights in Chicago, five nights in Detroit, two nights in Cleveland. The New York homecoming concerts, however, were his last ones until he began his Greek Theatre engagement two weeks later.

The breather he'd scheduled was yet another indication of the importance he attached to the Greek. As he said a couple of months earlier, "It's probably the biggest challenge of the year for me."

It was a Diamond tradition, of course, that a Greek show contain some special touches, and Neil spent part of the time supervising work on them. Among the flourishes were a new stage, another Stan Miller–designed quadraphonic sound system, the hiring of a string section to augment the synthesizer players in his band, and a more elaborate laser display from Laser Media.

Finally, August 14, opening night, rolled around. The unseasonably cool weather that day was a big surprise. If it was going to be "Another Hot August Night," as the souvenir T-shirts predicted, it was up to Diamond to supply the warmth. And he did.

Stupendous as his "Headed for the Future" opening was—the smoke, rotating searchlights, crisscrossing laser beams, and blaring quad sound made it seem for a moment that the Greek was going to blast off into the night—it was the human touches that once again carried the show. Never one to reduce his past hits to medley fodder, for example, Neil sang songs like "Brooklyn Roads," "Red Red Wine," "If You Know What I Mean," and "Love on the Rocks" with intensity. Meanwhile, the sight of nine very familiar faces playing and singing behind him—all save drummer Ron Tutt and percussionist Vince Charles were veterans of the 1976 Greek stand—spoke warmly of Neil in other ways . . . namely as a generous, loyal—if demanding—boss.

However, the relationship that was the main focus of opening night was that of Diamond and his fans. Over the years, Neil had warred with associates, a movie producer, record companies and, most of all, himself. But for the most part, he and his fans had carried on a lovefest for years, egging each other on in concert after concert. As Diamond confessed in 1982: "It's much more difficult for me to deal with real life than being that guy on stage."

During his rendition of "Sweet Caroline," Neil Leslie Diamond said all he needed to say about why he continued to court his fans as a forty-five-year-old Solitary Star. The moment came when he yelled out, rather than sang, the slightly revised line, "How can I hurt when I'm here with you!"

The audience, many of whom were already standing and clapping along, let out a cheer.

ACKNOWLEDGMENTS

This book is the result of three years of research, including interviews with more than 100 people.

Neil Diamond was not one of them. He was informed of my project at its outset in the spring of 1983; through his attorney, Jeffrey C. Ingber, he declined to grant me an interview or otherwise cooperate with me. I wrote to him in late 1984 and in March of 1986, asking him to reconsider. Each time Ingber responded on Neil's behalf, informing me that Diamond's original decision stood.

My thanks to those who did grant me interviews: Rachel Ames, Totty Ames, Brooks Arthur, Bill Backer, Jeff Barry, Hal Blaine, Neil Brody, Artie Butler, Joe Cal Cagno, Charles Calello, Hugo Castello, Gil Cates, Randy Ceirley, Tom Cerone, Gene Chrisman, Herb Cohen, Mike Deasy, Carl D'Errico, Bill DeSeta, Saul David, Denny Diante, Bobby Emmons, Wes Farrell, Bobby Feldman, Hal Fine, Richard Fleischer, Stephen B. Foreman, Dick Frank, Joe Gannon, James Galloway, Jim Gitter, Eugene Glazer, Ben Goldman, Emory Gordy, Jr., Al Gorgoni, Ellie Greenwich, E. Darrell Hallenbeck, John Hammell, Pete Hamill, Ron Hitchcock, Don Hockett, Lee Holdridge, Jake Holmes, Carol Hunter, Nat Jeffries, Scott Johnson, Stanley Kahan, Artie Kaplan, Al Kasha, Don Kerr, Jefferson Kewley, Larry Knechtel, John Kosh, Ron Larson, Mike Leech, Jerry Leiber, Jerry Leider, Bruce Lundvall, Abby Mann, George Memmoli, Reid Miles, Frank Military, Jay Morgenstern, the late Jim Newton, Burt Nodella, Michael Ochs, Tom O'Horgan, Joe Osborn, Jack Packer, Pat Pipolo, Stephen Prince, Don Randi, Jim Randle, Joe Renzetti, Artie Richards, Julie Rifkind, Gail Roberts, Tim Rose, Herb Rosen, Leonard Rosenman, Rick Ruggieri, Bill Saracino, Bill Schnee, Eric Sears, Sidney Sharp, Vincent "Bud" Shelton, Roy Silver, Shelby Singleton, Rick Sklar, Bud Smith, Fred Smoot, Jack Spector, Tom Steele, Armin Steiner, Mike Stoller, Joe Sutton, Frank Urioste, Marty Walsh, Joyce Webb, Robert M. Webb, Larry Weiss, Bill Wexler, Jerry Wexler, Maurice White, Bobby Wood, Marvin Worth, Kac Young, and Burt Zell.

Others talked to me on the condition that they not be identified. I appreciate their help, too.

One of the pleasures of this project was getting to know Nan Cretens, Marie Kelly, Scott Kelly, and Linda Perry. Neil Diamond superfan collectors all, they furnished me with an array of materials as well as the occasional hot tip. Thanks, also, to the others who aided me in my research: my East Coast liaisons Joey McGowan and Julie Malnig; Michele Kort, Ric Ross, and Janet Tomey.

One way or another, each of the following helped get me a step or two closer to the finish line: Ronald D. Coleman at Coca-Cola, Tom Duggan at McCann-Erickson, Pauline Epstein at the Lincoln High School Alumni Association, Ben Fong-Torres, Eleanor Funk, New York University Sports Information Director Robert Goldsholl, Mary Lyn Maiscott, Jim Mallesch, Mike McGrady, Cheryl Preston and Judy Pearlman on the *Los Angeles Times* permissions desk, Cinde Rubaloff, Joan Shulman of EMI Music, Lou Stevens, Donna Vazquez, Josh White, and Kathy Wilson.

In closing, thanks . . .

To Elissa Rabellino, for reading my manuscript at precisely the time my perspective vanished, and getting me back on the track with her wise suggestions . . .

To Peter Skolnik, for selling the book . . .

To Cynthia Vartan at Dodd, Mead for buying it—and for being a pleasure to work with . . .

To my friends at the *Los Angeles Times* for their encouragement . . .

And to Ginny, for clearing the decks at home so that I could undertake this book in the first place, and then for living all the ups and downs with me. Honestly, I couldn't have done it without you.

DISCOGRAPHY

Singles

"You Are My Love at Last"/"What Will I Do." Neil and Jack. 1960. (Duel 508)

"I'm Afraid"/"Till You've Tried Love." Neil and Jack. 1961. (Duel 517)

"Clown Town"/"At Night." July 1963. (Columbia 42809)

"Solitary Man"/"Do It." April 1966. (Bang 519)

"Cherry, Cherry"/"I'll Come Running." July 1966. (Bang 528)

"I Got the Feeling (Oh No No)"/"The Boat That I Row." October 1966. (Bang 536)

"You Got to Me"/"Someday Baby." December 1966. (Bang 540)

"Girl, You'll Be a Woman Soon"/"You'll Forget." March 1967. (Bang 542)

"Thank the Lord for the Night Time"/"The Long Way Home." June 1967. (Bang 547)

"Kentucky Woman"/"The Time Is Now." September 1967. (Bang 551)

"New Orleans"/"Hanky Panky." December 1967. (Bang 554)

"Red Red Wine"/"Red Rubber Ball." March 1968. (Bang 556)

"Brooklyn Roads"/"Holiday Inn Blues." April 1968. (Uni 55065)

"Two-Bit Manchild"/"Broad Old Woman." June 1968. (Uni 55075)

"Sunday Sun"/"Honey Drippin' Times." September 1968. (Uni 55084)

"Shilo"/"La Bamba." September 1968. (Bang 561)

"Brother Love's Travelling Salvation Show"/"A Modern Day Version of Love." January 1969. (Uni 55109)

"Sweet Caroline"/"Dig In." May 1969. (Uni 55136)

"Holly Holy"/"Hurtin' You Don't Come Easy." October 1969. (Uni 55175)

"Shilo"/"La Bamba." January 1970. (Bang 575)

"Until It's Time for You to Go"/"And the Singer Sings His Songs." February 1970. (Uni 55204)

"Soolaimon"/"And the Grass Won't Pay No Mind." April 1970. (Uni 55224)

"Solitary Man"/"The Time Is Now." June 1970. (Bang 578)

"Cracklin' Rosie"/"Lordy." July 1970. (Uni 55250)

"He Ain't Heavy . . . He's My Brother"/"Free Life." October 1970. (Uni 55264)

"Do It"/"Hanky Panky." October 1970. (Bang 580)

"I Am . . . I Said"/"Done Too Soon." March 1971. (Uni 55278)

"I'm a Believer"/"Crooked Street." May 1971. (Bang 586)

"Stones"/"Crunchy Granola Suite." October 1971. (Uni 55310)

"Song Sung Blue"/"Gitchy Goomy." April 1972. (Uni 55326)

"Play Me"/"Porcupine Pie." July 1972. (Uni 55346)

"Walk on Water"/"High Rolling Man." October 1972. (Uni 55352)

"Cherry, Cherry" (From "Hot August Night")/"Morningside." February 1973. (MCA 40017)

"The Last Thing on My Mind"/"Canta Libre." July 1973. (MCA 40092)

"The Long Way Home"/"Monday, Monday." July 1973. (Bang 703)

"Be"/"Flight of the Gull." October 1973. (Columbia 45942)

"Skybird"/"Lonely Looking Sky." February 1974. (Columbia 45998)

"Longfellow Serenade"/"Rosemary's Wine." September 1974. (Columbia 10043)

"I've Been This Way Before"/"Reggae Strut." January 1975. (Columbia 10084)

"The Last Picasso"/"The Gift of Song." April 1975. (Columbia 10138)

"If You Know What I Mean"/"Street Life." June 1976. (Columbia 10366)

"Don't Think . . . Feel"/"Home Is a Wounded Heart." August 1976. (Columbia 10405)

"Beautiful Noise"/"Signs." November 1976. (Columbia 10452)

"Desiree"/"Once in a While." December 1977. (Columbia 10657)

"You Don't Bring Me Flowers" (duet with Barbra Streisand)/"You Don't Bring Me Flowers" (instrumental). October 1978. (Columbia 10840)

"Forever in Blue Jeans"/"Remember Me." February 1979. (Columbia 10897)

"Say Maybe"/"Diamond Girls." April 1979. (Columbia 10945)

"September Morn"/"I'm a Believer." January 1980. (Columbia 11175)

"The Good Lord Loves You"/"Jazz Time." March 1980. (Columbia 11232)

"Love on the Rocks"/"Acapulco." September 1980. (Capitol 4939)

"Hello Again"/"Amazed and Confused." February 1981. (Capitol 4960)

"America"/"Songs of Life." April 1981. (Capitol 4994)

"Yesterday's Songs"/"Guitar Heaven." October 1981. (Columbia 02604)

"On the Way to the Sky"/"Save Me." February 1982. (Columbia 02712)

"Be Mine Tonight"/"Right By You." May 1982. (Columbia 02928)

"Heartlight"/"You Don't Know Me." August 1982. (Columbia 03219)

"I'm Alive"/"Lost Among the Stars." November 1982. (Columbia 03503)

"Front Page Story"/"I'm Guilty." April 1983. (Columbia 03801)

"Turn Around"/"Brooklyn on a Saturday Night." July 1984. (Columbia 04541)

"Sleep With Me Tonight"/"One By One." September 1984. (Columbia 04646)

"You Make It Feel Like Christmas"/"Crazy." December 1984. (Columbia 04719

"Headed for the Future"/"Angel." May 1986. (Columbia 05889)

"The Story of My Life"/"Love Doesn't Live Here Anymore." July 1986. (Columbia 06136)

Albums

"The Feel of Neil Diamond." August 1966. (Bang 214)

"Just for You." August 1967. (Bang 217)

"Greatest Hits." June 1968. (Bang 219)

"Velvet Gloves and Spit." November 1968. (Uni 73030)

"Brother Love's Travelling Salvation Show." April 1969. (Uni 73047)

"Touching You, Touching Me." November 1969. (Uni 73071)

"Gold." July 1970. (Uni 73084)

"Shilo." July 1970. (Bang 221)

"Tap Root Manuscript." November 1970. (Uni 73092)

"Do It!" December 1970. (Bang 224)

"Stones." November 1971. (Uni 93106)

"Moods." June 1972. (Uni 93136)

"Hot August Night." November 1972. (MCA 28000)

"Double Gold." December 1972. (Bang 227)

"Rainbow." August 1973. (MCA 2103)

"Jonathan Livingston Seagull." November 1973. (Columbia 32550)

"His 12 Greatest Hits." May 1974. (MCA 2106)

"Serenade." October 1974. (Columbia 32919)

"Beautiful Noise." June 1976. (Columbia 33965)

"And the Singer Sings His Songs." September 1976. (MCA 2227)

"Love at the Greek." February 1977. (Columbia 34404)

"I'm Glad You're Here With Me Tonight." November 1977. (Columbia 34990)

"You Don't Bring Me Flowers." November 1978. (Columbia 35625)

"September Morn." December 1979. (Columbia 36121)

"The Jazz Singer." October 1980. (Capitol 12120)

"Love Songs." July 1981. (MCA 5239)

"On the Way to the Sky." November 1981. (Columbia 37628)

"12 Greatest Hits Vol. II." May 1982. (Columbia 38068)

"Heartlight." September 1982. (Columbia 38359)

"Classics: The Early Years." May 1983. (Columbia 38792)

"Primitive." July 1984. (Columbia 39199)

"Headed for the Future." May 1986. (Columbia 40368)

INDEX